ACCELERATE!

ACCELERATE!

A History of the 1990s

James Brooke-Smith

The History Press

First published 2022

The History Press
97 St George's Place, Cheltenham,
Gloucestershire, GL50 3QB
www.thehistorypress.co.uk

British Library Cataloguing in Publication Data.
A catalogue record for this book is available from the British Library.

ISBN 978 0 7509 9683 9

Typesetting and origination by The History Press
Printed and bound in Great Britain by TJ Books Limited, Padstow, Cornwall.

MIX
Paper from responsible sources
FSC® C013056
www.fsc.org

Trees for Life

Contents

Acknowledgements

Thank you to everyone who helped over the course of this book's writing. Thanks to my research assistants, Jason Liboiron, Anthony Matarazzo, Kirsten Bussière, Alan Orr and Ryan Pepper. Thank you to Ryan, in particular, for help with last-minute fact-finding missions and copy-editing conundrums. A big thank you to Sally Holloway, my agent, and to Simon Wright and Mark Beynon, my editors at The History Press, for believing in the project and helping to whittle the manuscript into shape. But, most of all, a huge thank you to my family, Sara, Leo and Freya, for love and support and high jinks through the long days of lockdown. I love you.

1

Pre-Post-Everything

WRITING HISTORY by the decade is like trying to put a hairnet on an octopus. The more you try to squeeze the recalcitrant stuff of history into a neat ten-year slice, the more it oozes through the gaps. The forces that shape our lives run deeper and longer than any ten-year perspective can grasp. Dig deep enough into the causes of any historical event, and you find yourself slipping backwards through time in search of stable ground.

The decade is an arbitrary product of calendrical time, which stems from the accident of our having ten fingers and ten toes, the source of our decimal number system. Had our bodies evolved differently, bookshops might be stocked with volumes that divide the chaos of history into neat seven-, twelve- or fifteen-year chunks – all essentially arbitrary units.

Our penchant for histories of single decades is a relatively recent phenomenon, a product of the historical short-sightedness of the modern age and our desire to chop reality into bite-sized pieces. If you cast your mind back and try to remember the great decades of history, the further you go, the harder it becomes. The twentieth century is full of good, chunky decades. The 'greed is good' eighties, the anxious seventies, the swinging sixties, even the 'low, dishonest' thirties and the 'roaring' twenties. But once you get beyond, say, the 1890s – the era of the Oscar Wilde trial and the crumbling of the not-so-timeless Victorian verities – easily recognisable decades are hard to find. No one outside the academic conference circuit talks about the 1870s, let alone the 1470s.

And yet there's no getting past the fact that we have ten fingers and ten toes. As a historical unit, the decade has a pleasing weight to it. It fits nicely in the palm of your hand. A single decade usually contains at least one or two changes of government, one or two transformative technological breakthroughs, some major new social trends, a few significant cultural movements and a handful of deaths of major historical figures. The decade may be an arbitrary construct, but it is, as the anthropologists say, good to think with.

This is particularly true of the 1990s, the subject of this book. The 1990s come ready packaged as a decade – not quite a ten-year slice, but near enough. The 1990s began in the autumn of 1989 with the fall of the Berlin Wall and the rapid, almost entirely bloodless collapse of the Soviet Union. And they ended on 11 September 2001 with the attacks on the World Trade Center in New York, a spectacular assault launched by a millenarian Islamic sect seeking to end the hegemony of America and the Christian West and replace it with a global caliphate. On the one hand, a tumbling wall and the end of the Cold War; on the other, collapsing towers and the beginning of the 'global war on terror'.

My aim is to explore what happened in between these two epoch-making events. For many in the affluent West, the 1990s were a time of relative political stability and cultural optimism, perhaps the last such epoch in recent memory. This was the decade in which the American political scientist Francis Fukuyama declared that history had ended with the fall of communism and that liberal democracy would inevitably spread throughout the world. The election victories of Bill Clinton in the US and Tony Blair in the UK signalled the triumph of 'third-way' politics, which sought to replace the ideological divisions of the past with an inclusive vision of modernisation and progress. Political parties of both the left and right sought to occupy the political centre ground. This was a much-touted 'post-ideological' age, in which politics fused ever more intimately with the public relations and media industries. Class consciousness was passé; turnout at elections declined across much of the Western world.

And yet Harold Macmillan's famous statement about the role of the unexpected in history still held true. In 1963, when the British prime minister was asked by a journalist what could possibly knock his reforming government's plans off course, he replied, 'Events, dear boy, events.' Over the course of the 1990s, the events piled up as usual. Presidents Bush and Clinton deployed US forces overseas on no fewer than seven separate occasions, from the First Gulf War in 1991 via Somalia, Haiti, Bosnia, Iraq again in 1998, Sudan, Kosovo, and then the invasion of Afghanistan after 9/11. The 1990s saw the fall of dictators, from Pinochet in Chile to Suharto in Indonesia; the release of Nelson Mandela from prison and the end of apartheid in South Africa; the 1998 Good Friday agreement and end of the Troubles in Northern Ireland. Genocides in Rwanda and Kosovo signalled a grim return of the systematic mass slaughter that had characterised mid-twentieth-century European history. While Europe and North America enjoyed the dubious pleasures of consumerist anomie and postmodern weightlessness, history still raged elsewhere.

After an early period of recession, the 1990s witnessed one of the longest cycles of economic growth in modern times, roughly from 1992 until the collapse of the dot-com bubble in 2000 and the shock of the World Trade Center attacks in 2001. The long boom was fuelled by technological change and productivity increases, but in many countries, especially the US and the UK, the Anglo-Saxon centres of free-market economics, it was also driven by the deregulation of vast swathes of the economy, in particular banking, telecommunications and energy. In many ways, the 1990s were a slicker, more tasteful version of the 1980s, a period of full-throated free-market economics, but this time overseen by centrist politicians who wanted to channel some of the proceeds of growth into social programmes such as education and health.

The 1990s were also the great decade of globalisation, both as a geopolitical and as a cultural process. The European Union (EU) came into being in 1993, the North American Free Trade Agreement (NAFTA) in 1994 and the World Trade Organization (WTO) in 1995. The International Monetary Fund and the World Bank advised governments in the developing world on how to reform their economies along neoliberal lines, often threatening to punish those who did not by withholding credit. At WTO meetings in Seattle, Prague and Genoa there were large demonstrations in opposition to the free-market model of globalisation. Loose coalitions of trade unionists, religious groups, anarchists and environmentalists protested the lack of democratic oversight, the erosion of workers' rights and the heavy environmental cost of global capitalism. Nativist politicians in Europe and America started to make space in the public sphere for virulently anti-immigrant views, the likes of which had not been heard for decades. Islamic extremists used hyper-modern communication technologies to form decentralised networks and spread an anti-modern ideology of religious purity and violent jihad.

In the 1990s the future seemed to arrive on an almost daily basis with the rise of the internet, the spread of mobile phones, the first cloned mammal, Dolly the Sheep, and the mapping of the human genome, a pioneering feat of human ingenuity that was achieved ahead of schedule due to the exponential growth of micro-processor speeds. Pundits and theorists thrilled to the progressive possibilities of the new digital age: Manuel Castells analysed the emerging forms of the 'network society', Nicholas Negroponte extolled the human potentials of 'being digital', and cyber-theorists took up Donna Harraway's techno-feminist vision of 'A Cyborg Manifesto'. Before the Big Five tech corporations (Apple, Amazon, Google, Microsoft and Meta (Facebook)) monopolised the internet, cyberspace represented a new frontier of human possibility. *Wired* magazine, *Mondo 2000* and online communities like The WELL (The Whole Earth 'Lectronic Link) espoused a libertarian hacker ethos that cast personal identity as a malleable construct and human societies as problems to be fixed with smart technology.

Many of the decade's most exciting cultural forms emerged from the creative use of new digital technologies, from hip hop's culture of sampling to the futuristic sounds of rave and techno music to Hollywood movies such as *Jurassic Park*, *Toy Story* and *The Matrix*. Videogames became both a mass-market industry, which rivalled movies and recorded music for market dominance, and, in some quarters at least, a critically recognised art form with its own canons of value and taste. This was also the era in which the underground went mainstream. Grunge, hip hop, Brit Pop, the indie cinema of David Lynch, Danny Boyle and Jane Campion, the edgy conceptualism of the Young British Artists, extreme sports: what in previous decades were the preserves of alternative scenes and hipster elites rushed into the overground cultural spaces of MTV, broadsheet newspapers, multiplex cinemas and publicly funded art galleries. On the one hand, this produced a sense of cultural insurgency as avant-garde forms seeped into public consciousness and disrupted the status quo; on the other, it spurred debates about 'selling out' and the dangers of co-option by the corporate media.

↖↑↗

The question that faces the historian of the recent past is this: does a pattern emerge? Is there a figure in the carpet, a discernible order to this otherwise chaotic selection of events and trends? Or, to use a more historically apt metaphor, does a clear image emerge from the Magic Eye picture that is the 1990s? These optical illusions could be found everywhere from high street malls to popular kids' magazines for a brief moment in the early 1990s. If you stared for long enough at the dense, staticky mess of dots and scribbles that comprised the image, a second, three-dimensional image would reveal itself. What looked like an error message from an industrial printer became a shimmering hologram of a spaceship or a fantasy landscape. The craze was short lived and yet the Magic Eye poster serves as a neat metaphor for the era, not only because it mixed a vaguely hippy-ish, Op Art visual style with the technophilia of the early internet age – a characteristically 1990s combination – but also because it was so difficult to see clearly. Often it took hours of cross-eyed staring before the holographic elves or sports car revealed themselves. And sometimes, nothing happened at all. Sometimes, in spite of the promise that a hidden vision lurked within, the surface remained stubbornly flat and meaningless.

At the beginning of the nineteenth century, Romantic historians sought to encapsulate the vast, churning forces of history in the form of single resonant images or heroic individuals. William Hazlitt wrote a series of biographical sketches of luminaries such as Jeremy Bentham and William Wilberforce, who he thought embodied the 'spirit of the age'. Today, we are rightly sceptical of such 'great man' theories of history; we are more attuned to the impersonal forces that shape historical experience – the social structures and environmental conditions that affect our behaviour and configure our identities. Not even the greatest of statesmen, nor the most famous of historical personages, are present at all of the key moments of their era. We might call this the Zelig paradox, after the Woody Allen character who is miraculously present at all the major events of early twentieth-century history, but only at the cost of having no personality himself, of always blending in with the time and place in which he finds himself.

But distinct periods, even distinct decades, still have their own moods and atmospheres, their own local historical weather patterns. Whether or not they add up to a unitary 'spirit of the age', there are always shared points of reference, common experiences that anchor us in the stream of time. The fall of the Berlin Wall; the last days of British rule in Hong Kong; the end of apartheid in South Africa; the experience of logging onto the internet for the first time; the first mobile phone in your pocket; the thrill of being swept up in the insurgency of youth cultures like hip hop, grunge and rave – these are just the some of the things that shaped what it was like to be alive in the 1990s.

The best way to capture this sense of history as both impersonal force and subjective experience is via culture. We can learn as much, if not more, about the 1990s from the history of the first-person shooter videogame or the beginnings of online pornography, as from yet another study of Bill Clinton's presidency or the signing of the Maastricht Treaty. Or, better still, it is via the juxtaposition of these two kinds of things – world events and popular culture, CNN and MTV – that we can get a real feel for the age. Because this is how most of us live in the modern world, constantly jumping back and forth between news and entertainment, the serious and the silly, the high and the low.

If the 1990s can be defined at all, then they are surely the 'pre-post-everything decade', the cusp between the analogue twentieth century and the fully digital twenty-first. This was an era in which we still read physical newspapers, called our friends on a landline and travelled to bricks-and-mortar stores to buy the latest CDs, books and videotapes. But it was also a time in which there was a growing awareness of the vast new technological system that was powering into life, the radically transformative effects of which we could barely fathom at the time. This was the last era before all that was solid melted into the digital air. Before online trolls and flame wars. Before the great siloisation of politics and culture into algorithmic filter bubbles. Before file sharing and streaming services turned music, film and television into an endless torrent of cheap content. And before the fragmentation of mass media eroded the very idea of a shared popular culture with a productive tension between mainstream and avant-garde, centre and margins.

No doubt every modern era is fated to think it is undergoing a unique period of acceleration. As new technologies emerge and the forces of economic production advance, we feel as though everyday life itself is gathering pace. Nevertheless, in the 1990s the confluence of technological change, a prolonged economic boom, the rapid expansion and interconnection of the global economy and post-ideological 'third-way' politics sparked a sense that a new world was coming into being. Looking back from the present, it is impossible not to be struck by the sense of social and cultural effervescence that defined so much of the era. It was as though history's source codes had been scrambled, the grand narratives of the twentieth century cast aside, but nothing of appropriate gravity put in their place. Into this vacuum rushed all manner of utopian dreams, millenarian fantasies, liberal triumphalisms and retro nostalgias.

Today, we are older if not necessarily wiser. We live in a post-9/11 world. We have watched as the blithe statements of American politicians about clean and quick military interventions have turned into decades-long conflicts in Afghanistan and Iraq. We have lived through the greatest financial crisis since the 1920s and the subsequent years of economic austerity. We have witnessed the return of authoritarian populism and the emergence of China as a superpower to rival the US. We have seen the digital utopianism of the early days of the internet give way to fears about surveillance capitalism, social-media-driven anxiety and attention obliteration. We have heard the warnings about global climate catastrophe go unheeded again and again.

One of the central historical debates about the 1990s hinges on whether we should regard the decade as a lost silver age (certainly not gold but better than the tin one we have now) of liberal tolerance and political consensus or as a seedbed for the civilisational discontents we face today. After much consideration and several years of diligent research, I can now finally reveal the answer: yes and no, both and neither. Yes, given the state of the world today, many of us would welcome a return to the rather bland political landscape of the 1990s. And yes again, it is possible to detect in that decade the emerging forms of some of our current discontents. But both of these positions are limited by their insistence on judging the 1990s solely in relation to where we are today. Perhaps it would be better to try to return to the 1990s some of their historical quiddity, to try to see the decade on its own terms. Even the very recent past is like a foreign country ... and yet it only seems like yesterday.

2

Surfing at the End of History

WHEN SOMEONE asks what my favourite book was when I was young, I'm usually able to come up with an appropriate-sounding answer on the spot. 'Ooh,' I respond, 'that's a great question,' while I perform a quick mental search for something that has just the right combination of intellectual credibility and juvenile plausibility. 'It's hard to choose just one example,' I simper, 'but it would probably have to be Albert Camus's *The Plague* or Iris Murdoch's *The Bell*.' I know I'm on stable ground with a response like this, not only because these really were among my formative teenage reading experiences, but also because they sound so exactly like the kind of existentialist fiction that would capture an adolescent's emerging moral imagination.

But while my answer has the ring of authenticity, it's only a half-truth, an artful selection from the available facts, designed to showcase the precocious side of my teenage self. The truth is that I spent vastly more time as a kid watching television than reading books. I came of age as a morally self-aware human being in an atmosphere of ubiquitous television. There were moments when I got lost in books, but for the most part I spent the time when I wasn't at school or hanging out with friends slumped in front of the TV. I was a binge watcher in the era before digital super-abundance. With only four channels available on analogue TV throughout most of my teens, I simply watched what was on, at great length. I watched American sitcoms, Australian soap operas, gritty crime dramas, sumptuous costume dramas, the lunchtime news, the Six O'Clock News, the Nine O'Clock News, investigative reporting, docudramas, classic movies, lawn bowls, horse racing, American football, those weird five-minute experimental slots that came on after *Channel 4 News*, rural affairs programming, game shows, more American sitcoms and, because it was the 1990s, I watched *Baywatch*.

Baywatch was *the* show of the 1990s, a high-gloss encapsulation of the Californian ideology – personal freedom, hedonistic lifestyles, softcore humanitarianism – which at its height reached a billion weekly viewers around the world. You'd struggle to find a better emblem of the age of globalisation than an 'action drama' shot on location in Will Rogers State Park in Southern California that was broadcast in all of the world's regional television markets and watched by 18 per cent of the earth's population. There may have been a few slippages when the show's American English was translated for foreign audiences – *Alerte à Malibu*! *Mishmar Ha-Mifratz*! – but the theme song was pure Esperanto, a joyous surge of energy and desire that was instantly comprehensible from Quito to Tehran. It was paired with what was reliably the best part of the show, the opening credit sequence, a delirious montage of pounding breakers, infinite beaches, chiselled torsos, spinning life floats, cleavage of almost geological proportions and repeated shots of lifeguards launching themselves into the surf from a variety of fast-moving watercraft. For at least a couple of minutes each week it really did seem, as the theme song assured us, that 'it's gonna be alright'.

Once you'd come down off the high of the credit sequence, though, it didn't take long to realise that the actual content of the average *Baywatch* episode was pretty forgettable. The show was dropped by the US network TV giant NBC after its first series in 1990 due to lacklustre ratings, but continued until 2001 as a low-cost, high-volume title for the syndication market. As with so many commercial TV shows, *Baywatch* was designed as a kind of live-action wallpaper that would capture viewers' attention for just long enough to guide them between what were, financially speaking, the main events: the frequent commercial breaks.

The narrative formula was simple. Each episode intertwined two main plots. Plot A usually involved some sort of action-adventure scenario. Hobie's delinquent cousin surfs too close to the condemned San Dimas pier and has to be rescued. Partygoers on an illegal offshore casino come to blows, fall overboard and have to be rescued. An underwater photographer is attacked by what seems to be a sea monster and the crew investigate. As with many an exotically located American crime drama – *Magnum, P.I.*, *Hawaii Five-O* and *Miami Vice* spring to mind – it's hard to grasp why the frequency of natural disasters and criminal conspiracies hadn't seriously undermined Malibu's property values and driven the neighbourhood into disrepute. Plot B tended to be more personal, often revolving around an emotional issue in one or more of the crew's private lives. Romance, parenthood, adolescence, divorce, body image, unexpected pregnancy, drug abuse, eating disorders, animal welfare – that kind of thing. This was part of the *Baywatch* formula: action adventure combined with a social conscience, all wrapped up in a glossy package that fatally undercut any serious intentions the show's writers might have had.

In Britain, the show aired on Saturday afternoons around 5 p.m., in the sweet spot between whatever afternoon activity had taken place and the evening meal. I know this can't actually have been the case, but in my memory I'm always watching *Baywatch* in the autumn or winter. The nights have drawn in, it's cold outside and I've recently got back from some kind of bracing outdoor pursuit – school sports, perhaps, or a family hike, something that heightens the sense of warmth and comfort when you finally get back indoors. Instead of a log fire, I warm myself in front of the glowing TV screen, which transmits a diluted but still powerful simulacrum of the Southern Californian sunshine.

The novelist David Foster Wallace once compared the television set to an 'overlit bathroom mirror before which the teenager monitors his biceps and determines his better profile'. The problem with TV, according to Foster Wallace, is that it produces false representations. It is a cracked mirror, which reflects not the world as it is, but our desires about how we'd like the world to be. If we stare into this distorted mirror for too long, we start to base our own sense of identity on the phantom projections that stare back at us. Soon, we're in the fun house of late twentieth-century postmodern culture, where the boundary between simulation and reality is meaningless and our desires are no longer our own. 'Who am I?' and 'What do I want?' become irresolvable philosophical conundrums.

So, what exactly did I learn from watching *Baywatch* as a kid? How did it shape my emerging moral imagination and burgeoning sense of self? Albert Camus and Iris Murdoch's insistence that man's ultimate fate is to be free, that we are all faced with the stark reality of our own moral agency, has stayed with me for the long term. But what have I retained of Mitch, Hobie, Stephanie and CJ's weekly struggles? Not a lot, if truth be told. And yet that probably misses the point of *Baywatch*, which was always more of an ambient than a narrative experience. Plot details unfolded, but nothing ever really happened. As you tuned in each week, it quickly became clear that whatever catastrophe befell the *Baywatch* community, its way of life would continue unimpeded, possibly forever. SoCal beach life seemed like one of the few steady states in the history of human civilisation, an enduring form of social organisation that could easily outlive the slings and arrows of weekly catastrophe. The viewer simply went with the flow of experience, like a surfer launching himself into the ocean's current.

⇖↑⇗

If *Baywatch* represents the ultimate form of self-enclosed televisual spectacle, then its polar opposite would surely be the images that were broadcast from the fall of the Berlin Wall in November 1989. This was history happening in real time, an epoch-making event fuelled by the collective bravery of ordinary people that was broadcast to billions of viewers around the world. *Baywatch* abounded with pseudo-events that unfolded with the unreal logic of serial television. The images from Berlin, by contrast, were palpably, authentically real. Crowds of people pouring through checkpoints. Strangers hugging each other and crying in the streets. Stony-faced border guards looking on in resignation. And the most memorable images of all: crowds of people atop the graffiti-covered wall, chipping away with hammers and chisels at a piece of infrastructure that not only marked the border between two halves of a divided country, but was also a psychic fault-line within twentieth-century history, the symbolic frontier between East and West, communism and capitalism, Them and Us. We watched the live broadcast at school as a kind of immersive history lesson, assured by our teacher that this event would shape all of our lives for years to come. A new era was being born before our eyes. Its final form was still unknown, but the old oppositions that had shaped politics for half a century were finished. The implication, of course, was that it was us in the West who were triumphant. Our side had won. We'd been right all along.

Contrary to Gil Scott-Heron's famous line, the revolutions of 1989 *were* televised. The presence of TV crews on the streets of Berlin, Prague, Warsaw and Bucharest acted both as a shield against repressive police actions and as an accelerant that fanned the flames of resistance. In June of that year, the violent suppression of pro-democracy campaigners in Tiananmen Square in Beijing had played out in front of the world's media. In East Germany a few months later, Erich Honecker's deputies used the example of Tiananmen to dissuade their leader from using force against his own unruly citizens. The world was watching. And, more importantly, the citizens themselves were watching. After years of propaganda and surveillance, TV images of crowds massing in the streets offered glimpses of an alternate reality that had been hidden from view. They helped to break the spell of resignation and passivity that had held together a crumbling political system. In this case, television was not the distorting mirror that Foster Wallace warned against, but a powerful tool for revealing the truth about the world.

In Berlin, the trigger that finally caused the Wall to fall was a gaffe made at a televised press conference by Günter Schabowski, a prominent member of the East German Politburo. Schabowski had been wheeled out to announce a hastily drafted law that relaxed travel restrictions to the West, a move designed to end weeks of demonstrations and allow dissident troublemakers to leave the country. When he was asked by an Italian journalist when the decree would come into effect, Schabowski stumbled and said that, as far as he knew, it took effect immediately. Within the hour West German TV announced that the border was open and masses of East Germans were heading for the exits.

One of the defining moments of the Romanian Revolution, which unfolded the following month, December 1989, was the capture of the National Television Tower, a giant hulk of Brutalist concrete from which the Ceauşescu regime broadcast its propaganda. The first revolutionaries on air were Ion Caramitru and Mircea Dinescu, an actor and a poet, who declared the end of the regime and appealed for calm. Even if you don't speak Romanian, you should watch the speech on YouTube. It is a wonderful slice of history in the making. But what is it that gives this footage such a clear stamp of authenticity? Is it the drab clothes that the revolutionaries wear – the rough shepherds' jackets, the patterned sweaters, the pleated jeans? Is it the quality of the filmstock itself, the flat, grainy texture of poor-quality videotape that paradoxically marks these images as real? Or is it the timbre and rhythm of their voices as they deliver their hastily prepared speeches? It is possible to make out some of the key phrases in a garbled kind of way – *populisce, momente, dictutora fugit, victorios*! – but what comes across most clearly is the mixture of moral urgency and existential doubt with which they deliver those words, as though they can hardly believe this is really happening, can hardly believe that they are, at least for now, in the driving seat of history.

The historian Timothy Garton Ash has called the year 1989 'one of the best in European history'. Across Eastern Europe, popular movements deposed repressive governments and set in train the domino effect that would see the collapse of the Soviet Empire within a couple of years. But change came from above as well as below, from the party nomenklatura as well as the streets. The last days of communism were a multilateral tug-of-war between the communist old guard, enlightened elements within the party who sought to speed up the process of reform and pro-democracy dissidents who had been throwing stones from outside the party machine for decades.

There were also powerful global actors, who exerted influence from afar: the Catholic Church and its beloved Polish pope, Karol Wojtyła (John Paul II); Ronald Reagan and George H.W. Bush, successive 'leaders of the free world', who, after years of mounting tension, chose in the late 1980s to engage diplomatically with the USSR and move toward nuclear disarmament; and, perhaps most important of all, Mikhail Gorbachev, a new kind of affable and humane Soviet leader, who began the processes of *perestroika*, or the reform of the Communist Party, and *glasnost*, a new openness and transparency to be achieved via the relaxation of constraints on the media. Gorbachev also formulated Russia's new 'Sinatra doctrine' for the Eastern Bloc: 'Go your own way.' In 1991, a group of ageing Russian generals mounted a putsch while

Gorbachev was away at his dacha on the Crimean peninsula, but the coup quickly fizzled out when the troops whose tanks encircled the Duma sided with the large crowds of protestors that gathered in the streets. This was, in the words of an American State Department official, 'the last hurrah of the apparatchiks'. Before too long, Boris Yeltsin arrived to break up the siege and stake his own claim as the guardian of Russian democracy. By the end of the year the Soviet Empire was no more. On 31 December, the hammer and sickle of the Soviet flag was replaced atop the Kremlin by the horizontal white, blue and red flag of the Russian Federation.

The unprecedented speed and ease with which Soviet communism was dismantled lends the events of 1989–91 an almost magical aura. What had seemed for decades to be one of the great immovable forces in world politics exited the stage without the mass mobilisation of troops or significant bloodshed (there was fighting in the streets and numerous deaths in Romania, but the violence was relatively small scale and did not spread to neighbouring states). Unlike the events in Paris in 1789 and Moscow in 1917, the velvet revolutions of 1989 eschewed revolutionary ideology in favour of a more peaceable, humane demand for freedom from oppression. Many of the dissident leaders were drawn from the ranks of the intelligentsia, a class that had resisted Soviet rule by writing samizdat literature and embracing the 'internal exile' of reading and friendship. In Prague, the uprising began when students at the National School for the Dramatic Arts went on strike. In the following weeks, the Magic Lantern Theatre became the centre of operations for Václav Havel's Charter 77 movement, a dissident pressure group which improvised press releases and policy statements as though they were workshopping a forthcoming play. For a brief moment, as with the National Television Tower in Bucharest, poets and artists were in charge of the signal, broadcasting their message of hope and freedom around the world.

↖↑↗

It was in this heady atmosphere that the American political scientist Francis Fukuyama made his notorious argument about the 'end of history'. Fukuyama originally made this bold – some might say foolhardy – claim in a specialist political science journal in the summer of 1989, a fact that only added to his intellectual glamour, as though he had somehow foreseen the events that were to unfold in Berlin later in the year. The full version of the argument was published in book form as *The End of History and the Last Man* in 1992, by which time his claims about the historical inevitability of the triumph of liberal democracy over all other political systems seemed even more plausible. Because that is, ultimately, what Fukuyama was proposing. As a matter of historical necessity, communism had to fail and liberal democracy had to win. The timing was up for grabs, but the outcome was inevitable. With the collapse of the Soviet Union, history was coming to a close.

Flat-footed critics mocked Fukuyama's theory for its patent absurdity. They took him to task for projecting a future without historical events, a future in which there would be no more palace coups, popular uprisings, religious revivals or scientific discoveries. How can history end, they laughed, if time keeps rolling ever onwards? Surely something is bound to happen? But Fukuyama didn't predict the end of historical events, the complete cessation of stuff happening. Instead, he argued that future events would unfold against a settled background of political theory. Fukuyama pointed out that over the course of history the number of different types of political organisation had been dwindling. Over the long term, humankind had been engaged in a giant collective experiment, testing out different forms of political organisation to see which most fully met its needs and desires. Hunter-gatherer bands, tribal councils, early tax-raising agrarian states, aristocracy, monarchy, theocracy: these governmental forms had all been tried on for size and rejected due to their inescapable deficiencies. After November 1989, it looked like there was only one game left in town. Fascism had been discredited by the middle of the twentieth century, and now communism was on its way to historical irrelevance. Free-market capitalism allied to liberal democracy was the framework within which history would unfold from here on. Fukuyama acknowledged that wars and politics and social movements – all of the strife and clash of billions of humans occupying the same small planet – would continue; but he insisted that the fundamental questions about political institutions had been settled, once and for all.

As it turned out, Fukuyama was an even stranger creature than most of his critics recognised. He was no run-of-the-mill Washington policy wonk, one of the standard-issue blazer-and-chino realists who could often be seen on cable news proclaiming American-style democracy to be the best available means of minimising inter-state conflict and maximising aggregate global happiness. Fukuyama was a singular being, an anti-bourgeois neoliberal who furnished a whole-cloth theory of human nature and civilisational history for the North Atlantic alliance. In the media hype that followed the publication of his theory, most commentators focused on the first part of his title, *The End of*

History …, and debated the validity of his claim that liberal democracy would continue inexorably to spread throughout the world. Significantly less attention was paid to the second half, … *and the Last Man*, no doubt because it was an allusion to Hegel's notoriously obscure philosophy of history.

In fact, Fukuyama was intervening in a long-standing debate between two of the heavyweights of nineteenth-century German political philosophy, Marx and Hegel. Of these two greats, claimed Fukuyama, it was Hegel who had got things right. The arc of history bent not towards a Marxist utopia, as the revolutionaries of 1917 had claimed; the final destination of man's historical journey was not the triumph of the global proletariat and tractors for all. Instead, it was the bourgeois liberal nation state, a kind of permanent EU of the soul. Hegel claimed to have seen this historical destiny embodied in the all-conquering figure of Napoleon at the battle of Jena in 1806, whom he famously dubbed 'the world spirit on horseback'. With the collapse of the USSR, the horses were back in the stable and the campaign was all but complete.

All of which makes *The End of History and the Last Man* not simply an expression of American triumphalism in the wake of communism's demise, but also a rebuttal of postmodern relativism. Contrary to the post-1968 generation of continental philosophers, such as Michel Foucault and Jacques Derrida, who sought to undercut the great edifice of Western philosophy by stressing the relativity of truth and the illusion of selfhood, Fukuyama made a case for universal values. There is a single human nature, he claims. This human nature is the same across all historical periods, all geographical regions and all ethnic and cultural systems. Ethnicity and culture matter, but they are underpinned by a fundamental sameness that is rooted in our nature as human beings. And it just so happens that this universal human nature conforms almost exactly to the socio-political outlook of the United States of America. Liberal democracy and free-market economics are the rational end point of history because this is the only form of government that can satisfy the unchanging requirements of human nature. Stick that in your pipe and smoke it, Mister Fancy French Theorist.

Today, with the rise of political Islam, the success of authoritarian capitalism in China and Singapore, the spread of far-right nationalisms throughout Europe and North America and the apocalyptic threat of climate change, Fukuyama's dream of the end of history seems like a curio from another age, an expression of liberal optimism that is almost unthinkable now. At the beginning of the 1990s, however, his theory echoed a new political orthodoxy that had been most succinctly articulated by Margaret Thatcher: 'There is no alternative.' In the politicised 1980s, this mantra had been not so much a descriptive statement as a performative one, which sought to create a new reality through the sheer power of naming it. Thatcher had used it as a rhetorical cudgel with which to undermine her enemies – the Labour Party, trade unions, left-wing local councils. By the early 1990s, however, TINA – the acronym lent a jovial, feminised air to the doctrine – had teeth. With the collapse of the Soviet Empire there was no actually existing alternative to capitalism. In the years immediately following the velvet revolutions, all of the former Soviet states converted to some form of market economy and representative democracy. The free-market 'shock therapy' that was administered to the sclerotic, centrally planned economies of former Soviet states was turbulent in the extreme, but at the time few commentators foresaw the rise of Putin and the klepto-oligarchic nationalist petro-state that Russia would later become.

On the other side of the world, China observed the events of 1989 and accelerated its own transition towards consumer capitalism. China's market reforms had been launched as early as 1978 by Deng Xiao Ping with the formation of 'special economic zones' that permitted foreign investment, but it wasn't until its 1992 national conference that the Chinese Communist Party officially announced its commitment to what it called a 'socialist market economy'. The great Chinese experiment in capitalism without democracy was underway. At the time, many Western observers assumed that eventually the Chinese state would be forced to introduce democratic elections to accompany its market reforms. They tend to be less sanguine today. But back in the heady days of the early 1990s it was still possible, if you squinted hard enough at the Rorschach blot of global affairs, to see a trend towards a steady state of democratic harmony.

In *The End of History and the Last Man*, Fukuyama eschewed partisan judgements and analysed liberal democracy in the abstract; on first principles, as it were. Beyond the confines of the printed page, though, Fukuyama placed himself firmly on the neoconservative wing of the post-1989 liberal consensus. He was associated with the influential right-wing think tank Project for the New American Century, under whose auspices he co-signed letters in 1998 and 2001 urging Presidents Clinton and Bush to invade Iraq in order to spread democracy in the Middle East. In this sense, Fukuyama was at the cutting edge of both theory and practice in the post-historical age. It was but a small step from his elegantly argued thesis to the high-minded belligerence of the Neocons: history as a rational process guided from above by targeted air strikes from American fighter planes. After the debacle of the Second Gulf War, Fukuyama retracted his support for the Neocon project, casting its acolytes as a self-appointed Leninist vanguard who thought themselves justified in using violence to do the necessary work of history. This is one of the great ironies of the late twentieth century: after the collapse of the Soviet Union, it was the free-market fundamentalists who kept alive the ancient dream of a universal historical destiny for mankind.

↖↑↗

Fukuyama may have claimed that history ended in 1989, but he looked all the way back to Plato for his definition of human nature. There are three essential components in the Platonic soul: logos, eros and thymos. Most of us are familiar with the first two of these terms. The opposition between reason and passion is wired deep into Western culture, present everywhere from introductory philosophy lectures to popular psychology books to guiding metaphors in literature and film. Eros and logos are the Captain Kirk and Lieutenant Spock of Western culture: diametrically opposed yet inextricably linked characters in the human story. Somewhat ironically, however, Plato's third human component, thymos, is relatively under-represented in the general culture. Rarely outside of academic debate do we hear of the 'thymotic drive', let alone the excessive states of megalothymia (too much) and isothymia (too little). It's ironic because thymos relates to the human need for recognition, our inherent desire to be acknowledged and respected by others.

In Plato's *Republic*, thymos is usually translated as 'spiritedness'. It encompasses the emotions of pride, shame, honour and resentment that underpin ethical judgements and are the cornerstones of social life. Within Plato's ideal republic the thymotic aspect of human nature is aligned with the military class, just as logos is associated with the political class and eros with the productive class of merchants, craftsmen and farmers. The concept echoes throughout the history of Western philosophy. Machiavelli speaks of man's desire for 'glory', Hobbes of our 'vainglory', and Rousseau of our 'amour-propre'. Hegel describes the spark of perversity that causes a man to fight to the death simply in order to win prestige. Thymos denotes, then, the choleric, gingerish, spritely, up-and-at-'em part of the human soul that is at one moment so charming and the next such a pain in the ass.

As with all three of the component parts of human nature, thymos must be properly channelled and controlled in order to ensure social harmony.

Unchecked it leads to domination and exploitation. The tyrant does not simply demand more power and wealth than his subjects, but also a grotesquely excessive tribute of recognition. Hence the giant palaces and bad public art erected by the likes of Joseph Stalin and Nicolae Ceauşescu to monopolise their subjects' attention. But Fukuyama also recognises the presence of thymos in the plight of social minorities who seek recognition in the eyes of the state. The campaigns for Black, Indigenous, LGBTQ+, disabled, or women's rights all emanate from the thymotic desire for recognition by our peers. This is why, according to Fukuyama, liberal democracy constitutes the rational end point of human history, as it is the only form of government that grants equal recognition to all citizens. Perhaps that is also why the TV images from the velvet revolutions of 1989 are so affecting, even at a distance of thousands of miles and over thirty years. When they poured into the streets and showed themselves before the TV cameras, the citizens of Berlin and Bucharest were acting in recognition of one another's inherent dignity.

The challenge for liberal democracy, warned Fukuyama, lay in satisfying the public's thymotic urges over the long term. After all, the forms of recognition on offer in your average democratic society tend to be of a fairly milquetoast variety. Basic human rights and the opportunity to cast a vote every four or five years constitute a decidedly minimalist conception of civic life. If this were a gym membership, it would be the silver package. The gold and platinum packages, which offer attractive perks such as mass-name recognition and boosted self-importance, are reserved for the likes of statesmen, oligarchs, artists and celebrities. This is one of the reasons why Fukuyama welcomed economic inequality as essential to the smooth functioning of liberal societies, as those individuals who exhibit megalothymic tendencies are able to win their peers' recognition by becoming entrepreneurs and CEOs.

But what about the rest of us? How can the great mass of people in bourgeois liberal democracies express their thymotic urges? The opportunities for genuine, widescreen thymotic glory have been steadily diminishing over time. This is due to the inexorable triumph of what the sociologist Max Weber called the 'iron cage' of bureaucratic rationality. The history of the modern world is the history of the gradual bureaucratisation and professionalisation of what were once irregular and spontaneous activities. In ancient Rome, thymotic man might join an army to fight against the barbarian hordes. In Victorian Britain, he might help to annex a distant colony. In the golden age of aviation, he might don goggles and scarf and take to the skies in a balsa wood contraption. And in the post-historical 1990s? He went surfing. Or bungee jumping, sky diving, base jumping, zorbing, tombstoning, free climbing, deep-water soloing, hang gliding, kite surfing or any number of other extreme sports that surged in popularity during the decade. In many ways, extreme sports are the ideal outlet for humankind's inherent need for acts of vainglory, as they combine public spectacle with the potential for death, or at least serious injury. In their most glorious moments, extreme sports stars exist outside historical time, suspended, as they fall, twirl, plunge and soar, in another mode of existence, another dimension of time that is attuned to the primal truth of man's capacity for perverse acts of self-annihilating glory.

It was in the 1990s that extreme sports crossed over from the margins to the mainstream and became mass media spectacles. The first sign of the public appetite for extreme sports was the founding of the X Games in 1995 by the American broadcaster ESPN. Heavily sponsored by Mountain Dew, a carbonated soft drink brand owned by the mighty Pepsico, the X Games showcased sports such as skateboarding, bungee jumping, roller blading, sky surfing and other feats of hyper-cool daredevilry. The 'X' in the title was meant to refer to the extreme nature of the sports, but it was also pointed out that it could just as easily refer to the highly desirable 'Generation X' youth market, a demographic with money to burn but also a deep distrust of traditional advertising, that ESPN and Pepsico sought to reach. The second was the sudden ubiquity around 1997 of Red Bull, a caffeine- and taurine-based energy drink, which was marketed via a series of air races, snowboarding competitions and water-skiing challenges. At a certain point, it became impossible to determine whether Red Bull was an energy drink with dubious health benefits or an international extreme sports competition, the Champions League of cunning stunts.

The extreme sports lifestyle came with its own sartorial style: combat trousers, retro-branded sportswear, wrap-around shades, bleached hair, ubiquitous tattoos, multiple piercings. The look was part Special Forces commando, part New York break dancer, part tribal initiate. This was the sartorial embodiment of a philosophical ideal of how to live: intensely. Extreme sports were about dialling experience up to eleven. They were about reaching ever new heights of 'peak experience', a series of jumps, waves, climbs and plunges that wrung the very last drops of consciousness from the otherwise jaded human sensorium. This was the only way to feel genuinely alive in the era of godless, post-ideological, high-tech, bureaucratised, late-stage consumer capitalism.

Of course, many of these sports were invented long before the 1990s. The Polynesians were surfing the South Pacific waves for centuries before Captain James Cook arrived in the 1770s on HMS *Resolution* and recorded the practice in his diaries. The modern European taste for mountaineering was born around the same time and evinced the same fascination with the primal and authentic in nature. Shortly after Cook watched the surfers of the Sandwich Islands, Wordsworth, Shelley and the rest of the 'visionary crew' were scrambling up Mount Snowdon and Mont Blanc to enjoy the sublime vistas – both outside and inside the mind – that were visible from the summit. But the version of extreme sports that was popularised in the 1990s was a much more pumped-up, adrenal, madcap affair than the contemplative nature worship of the Romantic poets.

For the origins of this intensified version of extreme sports, we need only look back to the late 1970s and the formation of the Dangerous Sports Club, a group of posh daredevils who wanted to inject some aristocratic glamour into the otherwise drab undergraduate life of Oxford University. The group's main activity was an annual downhill ski race in St Moritz, during which club members would wear black tie, drink copious amounts of champagne and race a variety of improbable contraptions down the slopes, including a grand piano and a four-poster bed. On 1 April 1979, three club members invented bungee jumping when they leapt off the Clifton Suspension Bridge in Bristol with only a length of elasticated ship's rope attached to their waists. David Kirke, the club's charismatic leader, claimed that their aim was to invent a sport 'so beautiful, so absolutely beyond bureaucracy and so totally dependent on using one's own faculties, that it was a work of art within an infinite frame'.

But maybe in the long run this kind of ersatz glory won't be enough to satisfy the human soul. When asked in 1924 by a *New York Times* reporter why he wanted to climb Mount Everest, George Mallory famously answered, 'Because it's there.' He wanted to do it for the sheer, unnecessary, existential grandeur of the thing. And yet, as Wade Davis makes clear in *Into the Silence*, his magnificent account of Mallory's fatal expedition, he also did it to redeem the catastrophic failures of Western civilisation that had precipitated the First World War, which he had experienced first hand as a British army officer at the Battle of the Somme. The attempt on Everest was born out of the ruins of nineteenth-century imperialism and its high-flown civilisational ideals. The aim was both individual heroism and civilisational redemption.

So why do today's extreme sports stars do it? Is there a wider civilisational goal, a broader moral purpose, in the name of which they perform their feats of death-defying glory? Or do they do it simply because it is there, as proof of man's radical freedom in the face of inevitable death? Maybe for some, but there is another, infinitely more depressing possibility – which is that they do it because it's their job. What was once an *acte gratuit*, performed for the simple delight of being alive and free, has become part of the global extreme sports leisure economy. Don't get me wrong. I'm not advocating a return to empire as a way to redeem the emptiness of post-historical experience. But the tricks and stunts of the X Games crowd, while undoubtedly 'radical' in the extreme, can start to appear somewhat lacking in purpose. After you've watched the fifth round of the BMX half pipe at the X Games, the whole thing can seem kind of routine.

This is precisely one of the possible post-historical futures Fukuyama foresaw for liberal democracy: that it would become unbearably dull. Eventually, society would enter a terminal state of stability and affluence, in which the thymotic part of man's soul would dwindle almost to nothing. Many centuries after history's first culmination, human civilisation would slide into a further dystopian end state, the last suburb of the human soul, populated by what C. S. Lewis called 'men without chests'. The X Games will continue, but only as a purely formalist spectacle. While the crowds will still adore the heroic performers as they somersault through the air, the magic will be gone.

But Fukuyama also imagines another, diametrically opposite future for bourgeois liberal man. There exists the possibility, he claims, that one day, far into the post-historical future, the engine of history will be kick-started back into life, not because some more advanced alternative to liberal democracy has been discovered, but because the terminally bored Last Man is simply fed up and wants some action. It is possible that, over the course of time, some small constituency of the post-historical citizenry will grow tired of having their identities weakly recognised by the liberal state and will elect instead to pursue their own perverse glory at someone else's expense. A few of the last men will seek to become first men once more and re-enter the stream of history.

↖↑↗

This is the existential choice that faces Patrick Swayze's demon-eyed surf god, Bodhi, in the 1991 movie *Point Break*. Directed by Kathryn Bigelow and developed with her then husband, James Cameron, *Point Break* updated the high-concept 1980s action movie for the extreme sports and alternative rock-loving 1990s youth market. Think *Top Gun* with surf boards, or *Days of Thunder* with bleached-blond hair. The film depicts the scuzzier, more intense side of Californian surf culture than the family friendly *Baywatch*, a world in which meth-dealing 'surf Nazis' share the waves with koan-spouting hippies. It centres on the short but intense bromance between Swayze's Bodhi and Keanu Reeves's Special Agent Johnny Utah, a former college football star and now hotshot FBI agent, who goes undercover in Malibu's surfing sub-culture in order to track a daring band of bank robbers, the Ex-Presidents (so named for their highly cinematic use of US president-themed face masks during bank raids).

Like *Top Gun* before it, *Point Break* positively brims with homoerotic significance. Kathryn Bigelow, a female director in the men's worlds of movie-making and surfing, is wise to the unspoken subtexts of hyper-macho cultures. In the movie, Swayze and Reeves cement their friendship by sharing a woman. 'What's mine is yours,' drawls Swayze when his protégé gets together with his old girlfriend. They also spend a large portion of the film locked in various kinds of violent embrace, as they tussle on the beach, in the city streets, or while free-falling from the sky. The crowning moment of homoerotic self-awareness comes when the identity of the bank robbers is discovered as one man, Reeves's FBI agent, recognises the naked buttocks of another man, James le Gros's bank robber surf dude, on a CCTV tape. What could be clearer than that?

If *Baywatch* is set at the end of history, a terminal beachscape where nothing ever really happens and the surf's always up, then *Point Break* depicts the moment when the Last Man finally tires of his gilded cage and reaches out for something new. In *Point Break*, bank robbery is a logical extension of extreme sports, an intensification of the radical, anti-establishment ethos and a refinement of the qualities of courage, guile and agility that are required both for catching a gnarly tube and pulling off a daring heist. Bodhi and his gang are existential daredevils, Nietzschean super-men for the extreme sports generation, who live by their own moral law. As they barrel along the LA freeway on their way to a final heist, Bodhi schools Johnny in his system of ethics: 'See, we exist on a higher plane, you and I. We make our own rules. Why be a servant of the law, Johnny ... when you can be its master?' With his loyal entourage of adrenaline junkies, biker outlaws and surf Nazis, Bodhi could be the leader of a paramilitary group. He's another in a long line of dangerous white males in 1990s Hollywood cinema, which includes Michael Douglas's angry commuter in *Falling Down*, Edward Norton's angry white nationalist in *American History X* and Brad Pitt's underground cult leader in *Fight Club*. These men are frustrated by consumerism, multiculturalism and feminism – all of the post-historical liberal virtues – and yearn instead for a bloodier, more thrilling version of history to break out all over again. In twenty years' time, they'll be hanging out on alt-right web platforms and voting for Trump.

The atmosphere of thymotic glory reaches its highest pitch of intensity in the film's final scene, which takes place a year after Bodhi evaded capture during one last corpse-strewn heist. Instead of the eternal Californian sun, the scene unfolds in lashing rain as the legendary 'fifty-year storm' surges into Australia's Bells Beach. As a bedraggled line of surfers make their way back up from the beach, Johnny Utah heads into the teeth of the storm. At the water's edge, a lone figure stares into the horizon, like Ahab aboard the *Pequod* scanning the waters for the white whale. After a few lines of mournful dialogue – 'I found a passport of yours in Sumatra, missed you by about a week in Fiji' – the two elemental figures wrestle in the surf, until Special Agent Utah finally has his man in cuffs. Now we hear a helicopter overhead and police officers start pouring on to the storm-tossed beach. Bodhi's number is up. A man can only live outside the law for so long. But at the last moment, a spark of recognition flashes across Johnny's face as he sees the look of animal terror in Bodhi's eyes. Bodhi begs to be granted one last wave before he is taken, one last rush before he spends the rest of his life in a cage. Johnny relents. He undoes the cuffs. Bodhi paddles out to meet his destiny in the sublime depths of the ocean. Johnny turns and walks, huddled against the lashing rain, back up towards the cliffs. As he passes, a late-arriving policeman says hopefully, 'We'll get him when he comes back in.' Then the film concludes with a final line that is just as resonant, in its own way, as Humphrey Bogart's at the end of *Casablanca*: 'He's not coming back.'

↖↑↗

Universal human nature, the necessary arc of history, the quest for glory in the face of death – we've travelled a long way from events on the ground in Central Europe in 1989. It's funny how things can get abstract so quickly, when all you set out to do is capture the mood of a particular moment in time.

Let's change the channel. Come back down to earth. Zoom in on a specific time and place. Let's go back to Berlin on the last night of the 1980s, as the curtain falls on one of the greatest years in European history. And let's situate ourselves on the steps of the Brandenburg Gate, one small section of the recently breached boundary between East and West Berlin, and a stone's throw from where JFK declared 'I am a Berliner' and Ronald Reagan urged Mr Gorbachev to 'tear down this wall'. How are the citizens of this suddenly re-unified city celebrating the first New Year's Eve after the fall of the Wall? Are they listening to Beethoven's 'Ode to Joy', the passage of the Ninth Symphony that will soon become the unofficial anthem of the EU? Or maybe the tunes of Old Berlin? Kurt Weill's 'Mack the Knife', or another song from the great cultural explosion of the Weimar Republic? No, to celebrate this special occasion, the citizens of new Berlin are being treated to a free public performance by none other than David Hasselhoff, star of the soon-to-be global hit TV series *Baywatch* and (in Germany at least) a pop music superstar.

It's quite a scene. As he starts to sing his hit single, 'Looking for Freedom', the Hoff is raised above the crowd on a giant crane, and a string of light bulbs on his black leather jacket flashes in time to the music. As he belts out the lyrics – 'I've been looking for freedom, and the search goes on' – he punches the air, rouses the crowd and grins directly at the camera. There is a weird echo of Ion Caramitru and Maria Dinescu in the Romanian National Television Tower earlier that year. The Hoff exhibits a similarly halting air of self-consciousness, as though he is aware that something important is happening, but he's not quite sure how to react. It's almost impossible not to view the performance as some kind of historical allegory, a postmodern mystery play that casts the Hoff as the embodiment of the triumph of Western pop culture and its values of consumerist individualism. The allegory is made all the more eloquent by the fact that he seems just slightly ill at ease, as though he's trapped inside the spectacle, a hapless puppet whose strings are being pulled by the vast, implacable forces of history itself. The Cold War is over. The West has won. A bright future of democracy, free enterprise and endless reruns of *Baywatch* looms deliciously on the horizon.

But what did the people on the streets of Berlin, Warsaw, Prague and Bucharest – and later Kiev, Minsk, Tbilisi and Moscow – really want when they took to the streets in opposition to their communist governments? Did they want an immediate transition to American-style capitalism? Levis and Coca-Cola for all? Or was it some other version of free-market economics, civil society and democratic government that they yearned for? Did they even know what they wanted, other than to be free from the repression and indignity of state socialism – the unfree press, the banned books, the travel restrictions, the empty shelves, the bogus ideology, the spying and surveillance? Triumphalist commentators in the West cast the events of

1989 as a single, unified movement in favour of Capitalism with a capital 'C' and Democracy with a capital 'D', but they were more ambiguous and contradictory than that.

The sense of historical vertigo induced by the collapse of communism is best captured in Svetlana Alexievich's magnificent oral history of the fall of the Soviet Union, *Secondhand Time*. Alexievich weaves together a polyphony of voices from the former Soviet Union, all of whom are old enough to have imbibed at least some of the ideals and much of the psychology of communist rule and then to have lived through its collapse. Again and again, these voices complain of the maddening difficulty of freedom. Of course, everyone wants to be free, but freedom itself is a slippery customer. It sounds great in the abstract, but it's difficult to achieve in everyday life. Many express their dissatisfaction with the new range of choices available in the consumer economy, and how these choices – ten kinds of salami, bananas as well as apples, frozen pizza – fail to compensate for the austere sense of grandeur that accompanied the Soviet imperial project. Alexievich's interviewees are refugees from history, ejected from one of the grandest narratives of the twentieth century and stranded in the dull supermarket of consumer capitalism; a version of capitalism, moreover, which lacks the civic institutions and legal frameworks that enable the system to function more smoothly in the developed West. It is in this wasteland that the conspiracy theories grow, along with the nostalgic dreams of restored greatness, the demagoguery, the religiosity, the flag waving, the demonisation of others. As one of the interviewees observes, 'In the nineties ... yes, we were ecstatic; there's no way back to that naiveté. We thought that the choice had been made and that communism had been defeated forever. But it was only the beginning.'

3

Desert Spectacular

THICK BLACK plumes reach into the desert sky. The towers of smoke billow with an uncanny motion, each new bulb of flame emerging from the molten core of another, a churning fractal of fire and dust that resembles now a nest of vipers, now an undersea vent, now a psychedelic light show. Swirls of oily slime pool in trenches on the ground, their slick surfaces mirroring the jets of flame. The mouth of hell has opened. The sky is dark at noon. The desert is burning.

For hundreds of square miles, the burning oil falls as black rain. It coats roads, vehicles, buildings, pipelines, bodies. The advancing soldiers breathe it in. It clumps in their nostrils, clogs theirs ears, collects in the folds of skin on their necks, combines with the desert sand and rubs their thighs and buttocks to bloody rawness. The oil is invading their very persons, infiltrating the bodies of the US Marine Corps.

The oil fires were set by the Iraqi Army as it retreated from Kuwait in January 1991, pursued by 450,000 US and coalition troops. Burning the oil fields was a frustrated despot's act of spite. It was Saddam Hussein's way of lashing out at the Kuwaitis, whose land he coveted; the Americans, whose power he resented; and even the desert itself, the implacable face of nature that refused to yield to his every whim and stratagem. The fires were also a smokescreen, intended to shield the retreating Iraqi Army from the laser-guided missiles and computerised navigation software of American planes. This was an elemental battle that pitted tiny particles of hydrocarbon against the precision technologies of the most powerful war machine in history. After the war was over, it took emergency crews from Texas, Hungary and the Netherlands months to cap the wells and clean the spills.

In reality, the oil fires revealed more than they concealed. They did little to stop the might of the US Air Force, which bombed the retreating Iraqis to smithereens on what came to be known as the 'highway of death' between Kuwait City and Basra. But in the act of darkening the skies of Kuwait and southern Iraq, Saddam Hussein made visible a fact of modern life that we usually do our best to ignore: our deep and seemingly unquenchable thirst for oil.

Oil is the lifeblood of modern civilisation, but when do we ever actually see the stuff? Certainly not when we go to the petrol station. Filling up at the pump is a carefully stage-managed act of forgetting. We see the price, the hose, the nozzle, the offers on chocolate and newspapers at the kiosk, but rarely the gasoline itself, the liquid energy refined from the decomposed residue of millions-of-years-old organic matter. This is what drives our modern appetite for speed and efficiency. It's not just in our car engines but secreted deep into the fabric of the artificial paradise we call the modern world. It is in fertilisers, lipstick, Sellotape, insect repellent, denture adhesive, contact lenses, celluloid film, surf boards, anaesthetics, toothpaste, solvents, car dashboard casings and countless other products of industrial chemistry. As they sweated their way through the desert wastes of southern Iraq, American marines sardonically renamed themselves the 'Petrol Corps'.

↖↑↗

Operation Desert Storm was America's largest overseas engagement since the Vietnam War and the first major conflict of the post-Cold War era. The sense of waging war in a new geopolitical age was evident in the divergent historical reference points invoked by the combatants. US President George Herbert Walker Bush was a golden boy of the 'greatest generation' that had defeated Hitler and helped build the world's most prosperous nation in the aftermath of the Second World War. A Maine-raised blueblood, his storied career included stints as a teenage navy pilot, a millionaire Texas oilman, a Cold War CIA director and the head of the Republican National Committee. Bush had taken Hosni Mubarak, the president of Egypt, to baseball games and banqueted with King Fahd of Saudi Arabia long before he dispatched State Department officials to enlist their co-operation in Operation Desert Storm. In the run-up to the war, he compared Saddam's invasion of Kuwait to Hitler's invasion of Poland in 1939. In order to drum up international support for the war, he uttered the dread word 'appeasement' and framed the conflict as a defence of liberty against tyranny in the grand tradition of Allied forces in the Second World War.

Several US generals saw the conflict as an opportunity to restore America's military pride after Vietnam. The brief US invasion of Panama to depose its military leader Manuel Noriega in late December 1989 hardly counted as a cathartic reckoning with history. In a post-Gulf War victory speech, Bush boasted that 'the spectre of Vietnam has been buried forever in the desert sands of the Arabian Peninsula'. He also referred to the coalition of nations who sent troops to the Gulf as a sign of the 'new world order' that was coming into being in the wake of the Cold War. For a brief moment it looked like America would dominate this new unipolar world with serene ease. Little did Bush Senior know that his own son, George Junior, at that time a manager of the Texas Rangers baseball team and advisor to his father's re-election campaign, would re-awaken the spectre of Vietnam, with its sense of imperial overreach and logistical 'quagmire', from beneath the desert sands at the start of the next millennium.

For his part, Saddam Hussein was caught between strategic calculations rooted in the 'spheres of influence' model of Cold War geopolitics and the populist brew of Babylonian, Islamicist and post-colonial national liberation rhetoric he had adopted to bolster his waning domestic support. Saddam assumed that his invasion of Kuwait would be shielded, at least temporarily, by support from Russia and China, America's Cold War enemies. But as the Iraqi Army mustered along the Kuwaiti border, the Soviet Empire was in the process of unravelling. George Bush secured Mikhail Gorbachev's support for Operation Desert Shield at a summit in Helsinki. When push came to shove, Saddam's only international allies were Libya and the Palestine Liberation Organization, a not-very-formidable threat to America's global hegemony. For a domestic audience, Saddam invoked Iraq's ancient Babylonian heritage and cast himself as a latterday Nebuchadnezzar, who ruled over a great and heroic civilisation. He ordered faux-folk art murals depicting him with his trademark trilby hat and Ruger M77 bolt action rifle.

Saddam Hussein was a 'son of the alleys' from the poorest echelons of Iraq's Sunni minority who cut a violent swathe through Iraqi society from anti-British demonstrations in the 1950s to Ba'athist political agitation in the early 1960s against Western patsy General Qasim, Iraq's first post-colonial president. After a blood-soaked stint as the head of the Ba'athist security apparatus after the party had taken power in 1968, he became president of the Republic in 1980. In the early years of his reign, Saddam was heralded as the chief architect of Iraq's rapid modernisation. Under the aegis of a Friendship and Co-operation Treaty with the Soviet Union, Iraq embarked on a transformative process of land reform, social welfare investment and infrastructure development that was funded by state oil wealth and bolstered by secret military assistance from the CIA, which courted the Ba'ath Party in the hope of drawing it away from Russian influence.

But then, of course, came the excess, the delirium, the violence. Saddam was an obsessive reader of biographies of Joseph Stalin; he saw the Russian leader both as an echo of his own rise from the provincial streets to the commanding heights of dictatorship and as a sourcebook of political strategy. Like Stalin, Saddam invented specious plots against his authority as a pretext for ceaseless purges of party ranks, prosecuted via surveillance, torture and show trials. Also like Stalin – but this time with added petrodollar pizzaz – he fostered a cult of personality via jutting monuments and dictatorial grandeur: the cod-Babylonian palaces, the chauffeur-driven Rolls Royces, the elegant suits and the massive collection of expensive shoes.

On the reverse side of the grandeur was the gnawing, murderous paranoia – the assassination attempts by foreign spy agencies, the feuds, the killings, the need for multiple body doubles. His sons, Uday and Qusay, were allowed to become the Laurel and Hardy of nepotistic dictatorial torture-porn. Uday graduated with a 98.5 per cent average from Baghdad University but still had his dad murder the professors who didn't give him full marks. He left a trail of casually discarded college 'girlfriends', whose families would be ruined if their daughters didn't sleep with him.

The original spark for the Gulf War was a dispute between Iraq and Kuwait over access to the Rumaila oil field, a vast reservoir of pure and easily extractable oil that lies across the border between the two countries. In the lead-up to the war, Iraq complained that Kuwait was exceeding its OPEC production quota and engaging in 'slant drilling', or angling its drilling equipment in order to filch oil from the Iraqi side of the border. By the late 1980s, Saddam's domestic status as a hero of post-colonial national liberation was long forgotten. After the bitter and fruitless Iran–Iraq War that had lasted for most of the decade, the Iraqi economy was severely depleted and struggled to support its oversized military – at nearly a million men strong it was the largest army in the Middle East and one of the largest in the world. The sabre-rattling accusations of 'economic terrorism' against the minnow nation of Kuwait were a pretext for Saddam to launch a populist war against a weak neighbour.

On 2 August 1990 the Iraqi Air Force started bombing Kuwait, and Republican Guard commando units moved on Kuwait City. Within a matter of hours, the tiny Kuwaiti army was overrun and most of the Royal Family had fled to Saudi Arabia. Over the course of the subsequent days, Iraqi troops ransacked the city, stealing an estimated $1 billion from the national bank, stripping household appliances and fixtures from homes, loading trucks full of meat and other provisions, even making off with a fleet of jumbo jets from the national airline. Torture and humiliation were meted out to captured Kuwaiti soldiers and government officials.

On 8 August, when Saddam declared Kuwait to be the nineteenth province of Iraq, the US Army started to amass a giant fighting force in neighbouring Saudi Arabia. The coalition was drawn from thirty-seven different nations, from Argentina, Bahrain and Canada to Syria, the United Arab Emirates and the UK. After repeated demands that the Iraqi Army retreat from Kuwait, the

United Nations Security Council voted 12 to 2 (China abstained; Cuba and Yemen voted against) to authorise military force to end Iraq's illegal occupation of its neighbour's territory. In spite of the enormous firepower at its disposal, the US military command was hesitant to launch a full-scale ground attack due to its overestimation of the Iraqi Army's strength and their fear that Saddam would resort to the use of chemical weapons, as he had done in the war with Iran and against the Kurds in the city of Halabja. Unlike his impulsive son and the Neocons of the early 2000s, George H.W. Bush was methodical, even cautious in his preparations for war.

Once the fighting actually began, all the historical precedents invoked by the combatants were immediately proved wrong. Talk of the Second World War, Vietnam, the Cold War and the Crusades crumbled in the face of a new kind of high-speed, high-tech warfare. Operation Desert Storm finally began on 16 January 1991 after Bush had issued his last demand that Saddam surrender Kuwait within twenty-four hours, with a vast aerial bombardment of Baghdad and Iraqi forces in Kuwait. On day one alone, US warships in the Gulf fired 116 Tomahawk cruise missiles; 80 B-52 bombers attacked Republican Guard positions throughout Iraq and Kuwait; 300 A-10 sorties were flown against ground troop positions; F-16 fighter jets attacked Iraqi Army command and control positions along the Kuwaiti border; and 250 further sorties were flown throughout the wider Kuwait theatre of operations.

Over the course of the following six weeks, coalition air forces flew more than 1,000 sorties per day. After only a few days of fighting, they had effectively neutralised Iraqi radar-guided surface-to-air missile defences, achieving almost total control of Iraqi airspace above the range of old-style anti-aircraft guns. In effect, the Iraqi Army was defeated from the air before coalition ground troops arrived. A 1994 RAND Corporation report referred to the strategic accomplishments of the coalition air war as 'revolutionary in the history of warfare', the first to convert the battlefield into a 'nonlinear' combat zone in which air command could anticipate, intercept and destroy mobile enemy units in 'real time' and the first to deploy large-scale air power at night with real success.

After a six-week air campaign, the ground invasion of Kuwait lasted a mere 100 hours. Massive American dominance in the skies had blasted a corridor of smouldering tanks and incinerated corpses through the middle of the Iraqi strategic deployment. Almost half of the 350,000 Iraqi troops stationed in Kuwait and southern Iraq defected as soon as the invasion began. The remainder were chased back towards Baghdad and devastated on the 'highway of death', despite pleas from America's allies that the retreating soldiers were 'out of combat' and hence protected by the Geneva Convention. President Bush stood down his troops and put an end to the invasion at midnight on 27 February, stopping short of toppling Saddam from his much-weakened Baghdad fastness. A cowed Saddam, subject to United Nations chemical weapons inspections and economic sanctions, was deemed better for US strategic interests than the potentially chaotic and difficult-to-influence transition to a new regime. Over the course of the conflict, 148 American servicemen lost their lives compared to an estimated 20,000 to 100,000 Iraqi soldiers and 1,000 to 3,000 Iraqi civilians.

Most of the First Gulf War took place at an altitude and speed that rendered US ground troops all but obsolete. In *Jarhead*, his 2003 memoir of life as a US Marine sniper in Operation Desert Storm, Anthony Swofford describes the boredom, heat, camaraderie and anti-heroic nihilism that characterised life in the desert. The majority of the conflict is spent waiting and training, training and waiting, in the impossible heat of a Saudi Arabian base camp. The hours are filled with rifle maintenance, pornography, body-melting runs in 40°C night-time temperatures, letters home and VHS copies of classic Vietnam War movies, which provide imaginative relief in the form of depictions of a real, visceral war in which the combatants can look each other in the eye as they kill and maim for their country's honour. Even when Swofford does make visual contact with the enemy through the sights of his Barrett .50 calibre sniper rifle, it turns out to be a false sighting of a Bedouin camel trader picking his ancient way through the modern conflict zone, rather than an Iraqi soldier. The real action unfolds in the supra-human dimension of air power.

American technological might was so overwhelming as to be faintly embarrassing. The American arsenal included laser-guided Patriot missiles fitted with nose-cone cameras to transmit images back to mission control; satellite 'global positioning systems' to aid navigation in the otherwise featureless expanse of the Arabian desert; heat-sensing night-vision goggles that enabled vehicles and ground troops to move freely under the cover of darkness; synthetic aperture radar surveillance that produced fine-grained images of troop movements from miles above the battlefield at any time of the day or night; missile warning systems that could track where an incoming strike was likely to hit and select which targets to shoot out of the sky; and F-117 Nighthawk stealth bombers, whose dark colouring and angular form made it look like the US Air Force had partnered with a superior, extra-terrestrial civilisation to procure military hardware.

This was in stark contrast to the mainstay of the Iraqi arsenal, the Scud missile, which was first developed by the Soviets in the 1950s for short-range use. The Iraqi military extended the Scud's range and renamed it the 'Al-Hussein' in honour of their great leader. America's military capabilities had been built up during the final years of the Cold War under President Reagan's 'Star Wars' programme, but their power was only now unleashed as their intended target – the USSR – was dissolving itself from within. Under such conditions, it was increasingly difficult for America to maintain its mythic image of itself as the 'rebel alliance' against the Soviet 'evil empire'. With the tin-pot Saddam as a foe, instead of the Great Russian Bear, it was all too apparent with which side the Death Star-style military dominance lay.

⇖⇑⇗

Time magazine's 'Man of the Year' for 1991 was Ted Turner, the billionaire owner of the Cable News Network (CNN). *Time* dubbed Turner 'the Prince of the Global Village', the media potentate who ran the channel that became synonymous with rolling coverage of Operation Desert Storm. Turner inherited his wealth from his father, who had amassed a fortune from roadside advertising billboards during the Great Depression. As a young man in the 1960s and '70s, Turner took his dad's old media business and converted it into what at the time counted as a cutting-edge new media business, branching out first into radio and then cable television. To begin with, Turner filled his channels with cheap content: second-run sitcoms, old movies and Atlanta Braves baseball games (he bought the team in 1976). But in 1980, he came up with the format that would be his lasting contribution to television history: twenty-four-hour cable news. Casting his eye around an increasingly crowded media landscape, Turner settled on current affairs as the only terrain not already dominated by established players. In spite of his antipathy to current affairs broadcasting – 'News is evil. It makes people feel bad,' he once remarked – Turner went all in on a cable network that would be all news, all of the time.

CNN's viewing figures increased twelve-fold during Operation Desert Storm. When the fighting began, CNN was the only American network to broadcast live from Baghdad (CBS had a team in situ but couldn't get its satellite phone to work). As the first Patriot missiles landed on the Iraqi capital, CNN broadcast live footage and commentary from a team of correspondents holed up on the ninth floor of the Al Rasheed Hotel. This was the apogee of 'real-time' media, a live broadcast of a coalition bombing raid direct from the theatre of conflict. For most of the twenty-four hours each day that CNN was on air, it ran pre-recorded shows like *Larry King Live* and *Moneyline*; even during live news broadcasts, most of the airtime was taken up by talking heads, infographics and maps; but during climactic moments like the bombing of Baghdad, CNN put its viewers as close to the source of the action as it was possible to get, short of actually piloting a F-14 Tomcat or huddling in a basement as the bombs fell from above.

The channel became an international hit not only with everyday viewers but also with governments around the world. The always-on stream of ceaselessly updating information changed how governments and armed forces went about their business. Managing the 'narrative' became paramount. Speed of response to unfolding situations was critical. The distance between insider information and public access narrowed. George W. Bush would later observe that 'I learn more from CNN than I do from the CIA … Their reports are still important, but they don't get here in time for the basic decisions to be made.' Before the advent of social media, cable news accelerated the flow of information and shortened the time available for decision making. Whether this newly frenetic pace enabled better decisions to be made was beside the point. In the twenty-four-hour news age, immediacy would often trump considered reflection and long-term strategic thinking.

The success of CNN during the Gulf War paved the way for the explosion of competing cable news services. Jealous of Turner's success, Rupert Murdoch launched Fox News in 1996, just in time for the Clinton–Lewinsky scandal of 1998, a huge ratings booster which had Americans glued to their news screens hungry for each new drop of information from the political scandal of the decade. But twenty-four-hour cable news had more airtime on its hands than there was genuinely new information to broadcast. The extra bandwidth was filled with gossip, speculation, spin-doctored narrative management, strategically leaked details of congressional reports and infinite streams of punditry and partisan comment. The same year that Fox News launched, Microsoft and NBC teamed up to form the imaginatively named MSNBC, a soft-liberal alternative to the Republican red meat of Fox. Shortly afterwards, BBC News 24, Al-Jazeera, RT and France 24 joined what optimists liked to call 'the conversation' but increasingly resembled a brightly lit virtual arena in which ever more outlandish personalities competed to be the centre of attention.

If Vietnam was nicknamed the 'living-room war', then perhaps it was inevitable that Desert Storm should come to be known as the 'videogame war'. During the conflict in Southeast Asia, the Pentagon permitted television camera crews to travel to the frontlines to shoot footage alongside regular ground troops. The footage was then transported from the battle zone via land and airfreight to broadcast studios in the US and elsewhere. In spite of the fact that there could be as much as a two-week delay between shooting and screening, the images had an immediacy that was unparalleled in the history of warfare. Nightly news broadcasts of jungle warfare seemed to bring the war home to ordinary citizens in a way that was simply not possible in the age of the still photograph and the written report. Pentagon strategists believed that television coverage had played a decisive role in swinging public opinion against continued American involvement in Vietnam.

Celluloid reels shipped back from Vietnam had the grainy texture of verité-style documentary; Gulf War footage looked like something out of *Tron* or *Mortal Kombat*. The combination of presentational devices such as infographics, split screens and rolling tickers with 'real-time' updates and battlefield footage via night-vision goggles and nose-cone cameras created a new aesthetic for televisual war reporting. CNN's coverage came with its own branded logo and theme tune. As moody synth music played in the background, the words 'War in the Gulf' in giant orange-red lettering loomed into view from beyond the viewer's line of sight, like a militarised version of the Twentieth Century Fox logo. In the background, an abstract, camouflage pattern was rendered in the same desert sunset hues; the angular forms of fighter jets passed by in silhouette. The logo was clearly designed to whet the appetite for the aesthetic spectacle of techno-accelerationist warfare.

The US military took great pains to avoid the kinds of negative media optics generated by television footage of Vietnam. It was during the First Gulf War that terms like 'surgical strike' and 'collateral damage' were introduced by coalition press officers. This was a form of military 'newspeak' that pedalled the fantasy of a clean, humanitarian war, a war in which advanced technology enabled the US Army to destroy only carefully selected military targets without harming the civilian population. In reality, the US Air Force used a huge number of old-fashioned 'dumb' bombs, which were lucky to get within 500m of their intended target, as well as the headline-grabbing 'smart' ones. Journalists were granted limited access to the battle zone itself. A select group of reporters were permitted to travel together as part of a military-supervised 'pool', who would in turn relay their reports to the press corps as a whole. The US news media colluded in not publishing Kenneth Jarecke's now-famous image of the mummified corpse of an incinerated Iraqi soldier on the 'highway of death', who was caught in the act of trying to escape through the windscreen of his torched vehicle like some latterday inhabitant of Pompeii. Not subject to the same strictures, the British and French press published.

By their very nature, all battlefields are a challenge to visual representation. There is no Archimedean point from which an omniscient observer can survey all of the action as it unfolds in the theatre of combat as though it were a scale model peopled with toy soldiers. The battlefield is always more complex, more chaotic, more fluid than even the most panoramic image can convey. Whether in the form of an eighteenth-century history painting, such as Benjamin West's *The Death of General Wolfe*, which depicted the end of the Seven Years' War, or a modern war photograph, such as the raising of the US flag at Iwo Jima or the 'Napalm Girl' image of Kim Phuc fleeing an American bombing raid in Vietnam, artists must compress the chaos of war into artfully staged tableaux or single resonant moments.

The equivalent visual shorthand for the battlefield during Operation Desert Storm was the video footage transmitted from nose-cone cameras attached to the tips of Tomahawk cruise missiles that were launched at targets in Iraq from warships in the Arabian Gulf. These images were produced by the US military itself using purpose-built hardware, then released to world's press and broadcast on news programmes around the world. Their purpose was to enable civilian viewers to see a small slice of the battlefield from a perspective inaccessible even to most combatants.

Tomahawk footage was like an accelerated version of the films that Thomas Edison and the Lumière brothers made in the first days of cinema when they attached their new cameras to the front of moving trains. These short films were called 'phantom rides' due to the sense of disembodied, ghostly movement that was produced, as though the viewer became a roving eye heading straight into the empty space of the screen. In the Desert Storm version of the 'phantom ride', the viewer was granted a missile's eye view of the conflict. This was the viewpoint that US military strategists chose to broadcast to the world – the pure, anti-sceptic, inhuman perspective of the laser-guided missile. Nose-cone footage was a miracle of hyper-mediated modern warfare, a stage-managed spectacle of high-speed death from above that could be consumed from the comfort of your own home.

↖↑↗

Unlike the Vietnam War, the First Gulf War left little lasting trace in the film and popular culture of the era. Vietnam coincided with the arrival of the

New Wave in Hollywood. Radical young directors like Francis Ford Coppola, Michael Cimino and Oliver Stone turned Vietnam into a series of now-classic movies that combined aesthetic brilliance with fierce anti-war criticism, often to potentially self-contradictory effect. Vietnam was a celluloid war with a rock 'n' roll soundtrack and a sensory palette heightened by ample quantities of heroin, cannabis and LSD. It was spectacular in a very different way to cable news images of Operation Desert Storm. In *Jarhead*, Swofford recounts watching *Apocalypse Now* and *The Deerhunter* with his platoon at base camp in Saudi Arabia and, with a gnawing sense of irony, both recognising the evil of war and delighting in the awesome spectacle of cinematic slaughter.

Movie treatments of the war in the Gulf struggled to come up with a visual language that could capture the experience of contemporary warfare. They tended to be caught between their fealty to the style of classic Vietnam movies and their acknowledgement that the modern battlefield experience came ready packaged in the form of cable TV news and Pentagon-sanctioned nose-cone footage. The conflict was depicted in David O. Russell's *Three Kings* and Sam Mendes's adaptation of *Jarhead*, but neither film has left an imprint on the collective imagination in the way that *Apocalypse Now* or *Full Metal Jacket* has. *Jarhead* begins with a scene in a US Marine training barracks that pays direct homage to Stanley Kubrick's inimitable Gunnery Sergeant Hartman – 'I'll bet you could suck a golf ball through a garden hose' – and Private Pyle, the suicidal grunt. But after the debt is acknowledged, Mendes's film is necessarily a much more tightly focused study of the life of a marine sniper in a combat zone almost entirely dominated by US air power. Mendes reaches for the grandeur of classic Vietnam movies – the towering flames of oil-well fires, troops in gas masks wandering the empty desert – but Swofford is never more than a tourist. He moves through the war at a distance from the action that is both geographical, in that he is always far behind where the real action is, and existential, in that the ancient martial values of honour and courage have been supplanted by high-tech weaponry and strategic planning.

Three Kings plays up the distance from the action even further. The three kings of the title, George Clooney, Ice Cube and Mark Wahlberg, are US servicemen who set out in quest of looted Kuwaiti gold in the days after the war has officially been declared over; they are pursued by a tenacious female news anchor in search of a real scoop, instead of the Pentagon-packaged narrative on offer to the press corps. Unlike Mendes, who nostalgically adopts the visual style of Hollywood golden age 'Nam movies, Russell shot his film in the frenetic style of an MTV music video – all jump cuts, freeze frames, bright filters and loud bursts of thrash metal and hip hop. The adventurers' Humvee even has a Bart Simpson doll attached to its front fender. This is a postmodern movie about postmodern warfare in which the action has already happened elsewhere and the only question that remains is who will make the quickest buck in the aftermath.

Operation Desert Storm inspired no grand artistic statements because it was fed directly into the accelerated churn of popular culture in the electronic media age, registering only as a brief interruption of normal programming, a momentary flicker in the spectacle. Once the war began, the BBC instituted a radio blackout of sixty-seven songs that might be deemed offensive or inflammatory in the context of the war. Listeners had to turn elsewhere if they wanted to hear the Cure's 'Killing an Arab', Desmond Dekker and the Aces' 'The Israelites' or The Plastic Ono Band's 'Give Peace a Chance'. Some artists responded with protest songs, but the conflict was over too quickly to leave much of a mark on popular music. With its anti-war boiler plate about bright young men sent by the older generation to defend someone else's arbitrary 'lines in the sand', Randy Newman's 'Lines in the Sand' could have been written about the First World War. The Geto Boys' gangsta rap, 'Fuck a War', was more to the point: 'Mother fuck a war, that's how I feel / Sending a n***** to the desert to get killed … I ain't getting my leg shot off / While Bush was shown last on TV playing golf'.

The idea of the Gulf War as premeditated spectacle was even picked up on in the wacky world of professional wrestling. In the early 1990s, the World Wrestling Foundation was in its pomp. Weekly matches were broadcast throughout North America and Europe and the slab-like forms of the Undertaker and 'Rowdy' Roddy Piper were folk heroes to millions of children (and a good number of adults too). Wrestling often incorporated current affairs into its outlandish mixture of theatrical performance and sweaty roughhousing, with characters and feuds crafted to tap into mythic archetypes of good and evil, strength and weakness, as well as regional identities and geopolitical allegiances (The British Bulldogs, Jimmy Hart, 'Man of the South', Boris 'The Bolshevik' Zhukov, etc.). During the Gulf War, Sgt Slaughter, a grim-faced former US Marine and Vietnam veteran who defeated opponents with his trademark 'cobra clutch', enhanced his villainous persona by going over to the Iraqi side. Slaughter decried America's lightweight style of humanitarian warfare and instead embraced Saddam's dictatorial barbarism. He teamed up with General Adnan, an Iraqi wrestler and former schoolmate of Saddam Hussein (yes, in real life, not just his ringside persona), as a pair of comic villains who did battle with all-American heroes Hulk Hogan and the Ultimate Warrior.

The most inflammatory satire of American imperial pretensions came from the puckish French philosopher Jean Baudrillard, who in a series of newspaper articles published before, during and after the conflict advanced the mock-serious arguments that 'The Gulf War Will Not Take Place', 'The Gulf War is Not Taking Place' and the 'Gulf War Did Not Take Place'. According to Baudrillard, the war was better understood as pure media spectacle rather than as an armed conflict in the traditional sense that would be recognised by historians of Thermopylae, Austerlitz or Stalingrad. The conflict was meticulously rehearsed by US military strategists; it was planned and wargamed to the last detail; it was executed only after a giant troop build-up equipped with vast and overwhelming technological superiority; the fighting itself was broadcast to the Western world only via carefully stage-managed and edited military footage; all traces of death and atrocity were wiped from the spectacle. According to Baudrillard, this was the very definition of the hyper-real: a simulated event that strove to replace the reality of violence and destruction with its own beguiling spectacle:

> The idea of a clean war, like that of a clean bomb or an intelligent missile, this whole war conceived as a technological extrapolation of the brain, is a sure sign of madness. It is like those characters in Hieronymus Bosch with a glass bell or a soap bubble around their head as a sign of their mental debility. A war enclosed in a glass coffin, like Snow White, purged of any carnal contamination or warrior's passion. A clean war which ends up in an oil slick.

Baudrillard's comments were knowingly opaque and provocative; they were meant to be highbrow and tasteless at the same time; and they seem to have created exactly the effect he intended. Moralists decried his callous indifference to the suffering of the Iraqi people. Realists harumphed that of course the war 'took place', everyone could see that just by turning on the television, which the smirking Monsieur Baudrillard no doubt took as ample proof that he was correct all along.

In many ways, the First Gulf War was the harbinger of developments that would only really come to fruition in subsequent years. As is so often the case, bleeding-edge technologies that were first used by the military would later filter out into the civilian economy. Wide-eyed journalists tended to focus on glamorous death machines such as the F-117 stealth bomber and laser-guided missile systems, but one of the most impactful new devices deployed in the Gulf was satellite-enabled GPS, which in the early 2000s was integrated into mobile phones and would eventually become an everyday tool for hikers and delivery drivers. With its satellite-enabled control of the airspace above the Arabian desert, Operation Desert Storm was a dry run for Google Maps. The hyper-real cable TV experience of 'real-time' battlefield access and digital graphics also anticipated the cyberculture aesthetic that defined later 1990s movies like *The Matrix* (1999), *Existenz* (1999) and even *The Truman Show* (1998), a film about a man who abruptly comes to realise he is the 'real-time' protagonist of a reality TV show.

And, of course, there were the slow-release geopolitical repercussions of the conflict. The decision not to topple Saddam (the UN mandate was for the eviction of Iraqi forces from Kuwait, not 'regime change', as it later came to be known) would store up trouble for the future. George W. Bush and the Neocons were preparing their plans for a Second Gulf War long before 9/11 gave them a pretext for action. In 1991, Osama bin Laden – at this stage no more than a wealthy malcontent who had fought with the Mujahidin against Russia in Afghanistan – watched the build-up of American troops in his Saudi homeland and embarked upon his murderous crusade. In his 1996 declaration of war against America, bin Laden cited the presence of US troops in the Holy Lands of Mecca and Medina as well as the West's exploitation of Gulf oil as justification for violent jihad.

But in 1991, at the end of the conflict in the Gulf, this all lay somewhere beyond the horizon of the here and now. If we look around the wider world of 1991, we will find much that is familiar, but also much that is foreign from today's perspective. There is a sense in which the 1990s as we remember them in popular folklore, the '90s of liberal centrism, techno-optimism and a certain pre-millennial lightness of being, didn't really begin until President Bill Clinton took office in January 1993. The period between the fall of the Berlin Wall and Clinton's election victory was its own mini epoch, which had more in common with the lingering 1980s than with the buoyant boom years of the second half of the decade. America and several other major nations were in recession throughout 1990 and 1991. Oil prices spiked as a result of the war in the Gulf; the savings and loans crisis, which saw the collapse of thousands of co-operative banking associations across America, put a dampener on the world's largest economy. Many countries were still feeling the after-effects of the monetarist economic policies of the 1980s, which had pursued low inflation at the expense of high unemployment.

Urban centres were scarred by the effects of economic depression and deindustrialisation. Somewhat ironically, much of what is now considered the mini golden age of 1990s alternative culture – rave, hip hop, alternative rock, indie cinema, etc. – was spawned in the early part of the decade, before the boom times set in. Alternative culture was fuelled by the oppositional energies of the Reagan–Thatcher years and enabled by the opportunities of cheap rents and pre-gentrification urban spaces. Empty warehouses and boarded-up storefronts could be repurposed as venues for illegal raves and pop-up art galleries. The march of gentrification spearheaded by activist mayors like Rudy Giuliani in New York and associated in Europe with what came to be known as the 'Bilbao effect', after the Basque city in which a new branch of the Guggenheim Museum helped to spark a post-industrial regeneration, was yet to take hold.

In 1991, as the Gulf War came to an end, the form that the post-Cold War geopolitical system would take remained hazily indistinct. When George Bush proclaimed an American-led 'New World Order', his words were aspirational as much as descriptive. Excitement at America's Cold War 'victory' (more like communism's collapse) was tempered by a mood of disorientation and self-doubt. Seeing the chaos caused by economic 'shock therapy' in Eastern Europe – average life expectancy declined by almost four years in Russia between 1991 and 1995, the sharpest drop in an industrialised nation in recorded history – many feared the return of democratically elected communist parties. Bill Clinton would send a secret team of 'advisors' to help ensure that the hugely unpopular Boris Yeltsin won the 1996 presidential election against the opposition candidate of the Stalinist Communist Party.

In the first years of the decade, American pundits feared the economic might of Japan, which was in the midst of a prolonged boom driven by manufacturing exports and the high-tech sector. In the 1993 film *Rising Sun*, adapted from Michael Crichton's bestselling novel, Sean Connery and Wesley Snipes play two LA cops investigating a murder at a cocktail party at the American headquarters of a powerful Japanese multinational corporation. The film makes satirical play of Western stereotypes about the inscrutability of Japanese customs and the fearsome work ethic of Tokyo salarymen. 'We may come from a fragmented, MTV, rap-video culture, but *they* do not', warns Sean Connery in full orientalist sage mode.

In 1991, the internet was still the preserve of research scientists and nerdy amateurs rather than the general public. Tim Berners-Lee announced the advent of the World Wide Web to a handful of users on alt.hypertext.newsgroup and launched the first publicly accessible website from the CERN research centre in Switzerland. He made the source code available for free and has never earned a penny directly from his invention. That same year, the US Congress passed the 'Gore Bill' that would begin the process of opening up the National Science Foundation's internet infrastructure for private ownership. This would pave the way for the massive growth of internet use and the explosion of the digital economy over the subsequent years; but back in 1991, to most people the internet was a futuristic myth rather than an everyday reality. It was not until 1995 and the first public offering of shares in AOL that the dot-com stock market bubble would start to inflate.

A certain social conservatism still prevailed in the mainstream media and public life. It was rare to see openly gay characters on film and television. In the early 1990s, the struggle for recognition and support for HIV/AIDS sufferers was still very much underway. On 7 November 1991, Magic Johnson, the greatest player in basketball history, announced that he was HIV positive and would retire from the LA Lakers, which brought it home to many that it was not just gay people and intravenous drug users who could contract the disease. Attitudes had moved on from the earliest days of the crisis, when police forces raided gay bathhouses on the pretext of suppressing transmission and President Reagan had pointedly refused to mention the word 'AIDS' in public, but the stigma remained. In September of 1991, ACT UP, or the AIDS Coalition to Unleash Power, covered the North Carolina home of Republican Senator Jesse Helms with a giant condom emblazoned with the slogan 'Helms is deadlier than a virus'. Helms opposed federal aid for AIDS treatment on the grounds that 'it is their [gay people's] deliberate, disgusting, revolting conduct that is responsible for the disease'. It is hard to imagine even the most reactionary of politicians using such language in an advanced democracy today.

In Los Angeles on 3 March 1991, a Black man by the name of Rodney King was severely beaten by members of the Los Angeles Police Department on the side of the I-210 highway after being pulled over on suspicion of drunken driving. The incident was caught on video from a nearby apartment building and broadcast on the local, then the national and then the international news. In this case, video footage of a Black man being assaulted by the police triggered a week of rioting in Los Angeles, the worst in America since the Detroit riots of 1968, but not a global protest movement and the stirrings of a worldwide reckoning with the legacies of slavery and racism, as in the summer of 2020 after cell phone footage of the murder of George Floyd by a Minneapolis policeman was shared on the internet.

↖↑↗

I am writing these words in the summer of 2021 as a global pandemic winds towards its final phase and the world waits to discover what will emerge in its aftermath. As I do so, I can't help but be struck by the fact that we are now as far removed from the events of 1991 as my 11-year-old self was in 1991 from the events of 1961, the year in which John F. Kennedy entered the White House, the Algerian war of independence entered its final year and the Beatles played their first gig at the Cavern Club. Not only do considerations of this sort make me feel intolerably old, but they also induce a strange kind of historical vertigo: even if it didn't always feel like it at the time, we've been living through history all these years.

Historical change cannot be weighed in the aggregate as though it were a pile of rice or a bushel of corn. There is no objective measure for the amount of change that takes place in a given period, no external standard by which to compare distinct segments of history. No one can say, 'Ah yes, reading from the chart, I see that 1961–91 yielded 97.31 units of historical change as opposed to the 62.98 units for 1991–2021.' All we can say is that since 1991, that now distant-seeming time, much has changed, and much has stayed the same. And yet, can we say that there has been any revolution in world affairs akin to the Cold War over which Kennedy presided or the decolonisation movement of which the Algerian war of independence was such a prominent part? Has there been any revolution in popular culture akin to the one that began with the Beatles and surged through rock 'n' roll, punk, pop, hip hop and rave music over the subsequent decades?

The world that emerged from the turbulent mini-period at the beginning of the 1990s lasted much longer than a single decade. Unfettered free-market economics, globalised trade and communications, the massive growth of the internet and its incalculable influence on almost all aspects of daily life, ever more libertarian social attitudes towards sexuality, drugs and alternative lifestyles, the contested politics of multiculturalism and national identity: these trend lines have continued to be the dominant influences ever since. Even after 2008 and the worst global financial crisis since the Great Depression, the winning combination of neoliberal economics coupled with libertarian social attitudes – the all-conquering Californian ideology – continued to be the default framework for most democratic nations. But in 2021 the future seems more uncertain than at any time in the last thirty years. It seems that the 1990s are now definitively at an end.

4

Middle of the Road

'CAMPAIGN IN poetry and govern in prose', goes the adage. The poetic highpoint of Bill Clinton's 1992 primary campaign was his acceptance speech at the Democratic National Convention (DNC) at Madison Square Garden on 16 July. In front of a packed auditorium and millions of television viewers, Clinton gave a barnstorming speech peppered with rhetorical grace notes – 'I still believe in a place called Hope' – that helped set the mood music for mainstream progressive politics in the 1990s: uplifting, forward looking, inclusive and perhaps just a little tame when it came to actual policy provisions.

Clinton's primary campaign had been through some rocky moments, including hostile questions from the press about the legality of his Vietnam draft status and the Gennifer Flowers scandal, when a former lover from his days as Arkansas governor went public with the story of their twelve-year-long affair. After an early poll lead evaporated, Clinton's campaign had to be re-ignited with a high-profile interview on the primetime news show *60 Minutes*, in which Bill confessed to his failings and observed that 'character is a journey', while Hillary, transformed from high-achieving career woman to pink-clad helpmeet, promised to 'stand by her man'. After a creditable second place in the New Hampshire primary, Clinton dubbed himself the 'comeback kid' and rode all the way to the nomination as a candidate whose evident flaws seemed to be outweighed, at this stage at least, by his powerful charisma.

In his Madison Square Garden speech, Clinton argued that, with the end of the Cold War and the victory of free-market capitalism around the world, the time had come for domestic renewal. He rejected the conservative orthodoxies of the 1980s and offered a 'New Covenant' with the American people, a promise to use the power of government to guarantee access to high-quality jobs, education and healthcare for all, while also encouraging a renewed sense of individual responsibility. In his most explicit rejection of Reaganite fiscal policy, he declared that 'Trickle-down economics has failed', and offered himself as the champion of the 'forgotten middle class', that vast swathe of the American populace that exists anywhere between the destitute poor and white-collar professionals. Following the advice of his campaign strategist, Dick Morris, who argued that while the 1980s had been about 'me', the 1990s would be about 'we', Clinton reserved his most upbeat lines for a call to unity, urging Americans to:

> Look beyond the stereotypes that blind us. We need each other. For too long politicians told most of us what's wrong with America is the rest of us.

> Them. Them the minorities. Them the liberals. Them, them, them. But there is no them; there's only us.

In the days following the speech, Clinton enjoyed what remains to this day the biggest poll bounce in the history of American elections; it seemed that this was the communitarian reset that many people wanted after the individualistic 1980s.

But underneath the poetry there were clear signs of the prose that was to come when Clinton and his vice-presidential running mate, Al Gore, would take office in 1993. In the same speech in which he called for colour-blind, cross-class unity, Clinton also promised to 'end welfare as we know it', adopting a classically Republican stance on social welfare. In the same breath that he rejected trickle-down economics, he inveighed against the ills of big government and bureaucratic bloat, another traditional Republican position. In fact, Clinton was not proclaiming a radical alternative to the free-market ideology of the 1980s, but instead offering a new political synthesis of traditionally left- and right-wing positions. The aim was to fashion a progressive, centre-left politics that could win elections on the new terrain that had been shaped in part by the conservative revolutions of the 1980s and in part by deeper trends within the global economy. The campaigning poetry of the DNC speech had relatively modest, un-idealistic political goals in sight all along.

When he promised to 'end welfare as we know it', Clinton was practising the political art of triangulation, or the adoption of parts of his opponent's platform as a way to neutralise critique and demonstrate his own pragmatic seriousness. In order to fend off Republican attacks, the Clinton campaign touted its candidate's support for the death penalty and his rejection of 'big government' ideology. During the campaign, Clinton even flew back to Arkansas in order to oversee an execution and press home his tough-guy credentials. The calculation was that by ceding some ground to the opposition, the Democrats would win enough support from moderate voters to be able to enact the central planks of their programme. So, while Clinton talked and acted tough on crime and welfare, he also planned to invest in social programmes, raise the minimum wage and offer tax cuts to middle- and lower-income voters. Triangulation was a political strategy that played defence and attack at the same time. Critics pointed to its self-cancelling nature: accept limited defeat in exchange for limited gains. From 1992 onwards, proponents simply pointed out that, for the first time in more than a decade, the Democrats had won the presidency and were enacting their policies in government.

If triangulation was a cynical election strategy, then the 'third way' was the philosophical justification for this new style of centrist politics. As outlined by the sociologist Anthony Giddens, the third way was a bid to reclaim the mantle of 'modernisation' from the neoliberal insurgents of the 1970s and 1980s who had succeeded in casting market deregulation and individual enterprise as the true engines of social progress. In its most simple form, the third way was an attempt to blend the social conscience of the left with the free-market system of the right. While proponents of the third way conceded that it was impossible to return to the glory days of the post-war period of 1945–70, they argued that at least some of the social democratic values of solidarity and fairness could be salvaged for the new age of globalisation and hyper-individualism.

Crucially, though, left-wing parties could no longer rely on the automatic loyalty of the great mass of working-class voters as they had done in that earlier period. Reagan and Thatcher peeled off votes from the left's traditional support among the upper working and lower middle classes. In general terms, society was more affluent than ever before. Cheap consumer goods, increased home ownership, declining union membership and a mass media diet of glamorous lifestyles and heroic individualism all helped to create a more fragmented electorate that was no longer so respectful of the old political loyalties. So, while the third way stressed the importance of well-funded public services and progressive causes such as racial and gender equality, it also focused on the new imperatives of individual choice in health and education, the promotion of wellbeing and quality-of-life issues and on reskilling workers to compete in the new high-tech global knowledge economy.

In the audience at Madison Square Garden for Clinton's acceptance speech was Gordon Brown, the future UK Chancellor of the Exchequer and one of the chief architects of the modernisation of the British Labour Party in the 1990s. Just as Clinton and his team rebranded their party as the 'New Democrats', Tony Blair and Gordon Brown created 'New Labour', which crafted a new public profile for a party that had come to be associated in many voters' minds with ideological rigidity and a losing battle against Margaret Thatcher's radical reforms. Perhaps more than their specific policy programmes, what united the New Democrats and New Labour was the way in which they sought to prove their electoral seriousness by attacking the left wings of their own parties. Clinton and Blair are still revered by many today as cultural modernisers, who vanquished the radical fringes and converted their respective parties into election-winning machines (at the cost, according to their critics, of genuinely progressive values). In a moment of hubris shortly after his first landslide election victory, Tony Blair went so far as to cast New Labour as 'the political wing of the British people', a telling phrase that suggested a strange mixture of cautious centrism and Leninist vanguardism.

But third-way politics were not just an Anglo-American phenomenon. New Labour learned as much from Bob Hawke and Paul Keating's Australian Labor Party, which won successive elections between 1983 and 1996 on moderate social democratic tickets, as it did from Clinton and his team. The 1990s were a centre-left moment in many parts of the world. Progressive parties were in government in France, Italy, Germany, Greece, Scandinavia and the Netherlands at various points in the decade. And even where the left was not in power, political gravity pulled parties of the right towards the centre ground. The conditions for governing parties were relatively benign. Economic growth was generally strong or fair. The Cold War was over. The shock of 9/11 and the divisions of the Iraq War were yet to come. The 2008 financial crisis and the prolonged period of social and economic turbulence that it triggered was a long way off. The 1990s were a time of relative – because these things are always relative – peace and prosperity, which encouraged a relatively moderate, some might even say dull, political climate in many parts of the world.

↖↑↗

The 1990s were a good time for policy wonks. A mastery of technical detail and certain kind of sober factfulness could still count as political assets. Clinton was renowned as the wonk-in-chief, a former Rhodes Scholar and Yale Law School graduate, who was reputed to be able to complete the *New York Times* crossword in pen each morning before turning to a heavy schedule of NAFTA trade negotiations and private health insurance market regulation. In Clinton's case, the cerebral side of his persona was neatly offset by his down-home Southern charisma and working-class roots. He could play both sides of the aisle, thrashing out the details of welfare reform one minute and joking with an MTV audience about his preference for boxer shorts over briefs the next. Clinton's brand of wonkishness was a new thing in 1990s culture that chimed with breathless magazine articles about the 'information super-highway' and the 'new economy'. Many politicians in the past had demonstrated an impressive mastery of policy detail, but in Clinton's case the perceived mastery was over a newly complex social order that was being rapidly transformed by digital technology and globalised financial markets. Wonkery was a way of showing that you could keep up with the times.

In Britain, many of the new generation of Labour politicians were cut from similar cloth. David Miliband, Ed Balls and Douglas Alexander had all spent time at Ivy League universities in the States and were fans of *The West Wing*, Aaron Sorkin's TV drama about an old-school Democratic president surrounded by whip-smart PR strategists and policy advisors, a liberal wish fulfilment of authentic values pursued via cynical tactics. Gordon Brown was the master of cooking up wonkish-sounding smokescreens in order to conceal his political judgements, such as the grand wheeze of the five 'objective' conditions that had to be met before Britain joined, or more accurately didn't join, the new Euro currency. Dense technical details were thrown up as chaff to blind the public to the essentially political nature of his judgement as chancellor.

The progressive politics of the 1990s were often accompanied by an unstated ethos of managerialism, or a faith in the capacity of very smart people armed with reams of statistics and spreadsheets to manage the complex systems of the modern world in a way that would benefit more or less all members of society. At its heart, managerialism was a belief in the primacy of management over ideology, the notion that competent administration was of greater importance than the ideological struggles of the past. This ethos cut across political lines and extended throughout non-party-political organisations such as the IMF and World Bank, NGOs, think tanks and consultancy firms. The unlikely alliance formed between Tony Blair and George W. Bush during the Iraq War can be explained in part by the two leaders' shared managerialist perspective. In spite of their very different political orientations, both believed that Western-style democracy could be installed in Iraq like a moderately complicated piece of equipment. Indeed, from the perspective of the managerialist, all complex human activities can be ameliorated through more and better management. Not just health, education and the economy, the traditional concerns of government bureaucracies, but also the more rarefied domains of culture, identity and national wellbeing were susceptible to managerialist tinkering.

Managerialism is not quite the same thing as technocracy, or rule by experts. It is similar to technocracy in that it tends to favour expert knowledge and the application of statistical and scientific knowledge to political problems, but it stops short of putting the experts themselves in charge. Managerialists manage based on what they have learned from the experts in concert with their own charismatic leadership and political know-how. Managerialism also thrives on the bureaucratic apparatus of measurable change: league tables, action plans, partnerships, stakeholder meetings, etc., all types of organisation that encourage people to improve their behaviour in relation to some formally expressed goal or target. In fact, when New Labour first took the reins of power in 1997, it set so many targets across its various policy programmes – increasing university attendance, reducing hospital waiting lists, reducing numbers of rough sleepers on the streets, etc. – that it was eventually forced to amend its policy on targets themselves. The sheer number of targets had come to be seen as a distraction from the everyday business of government and a potential source of negative press when those targets weren't met.

Managerialism applied to the practice of politics itself, as well as the actual business of governing. The New Democrats and New Labour applied the full repertoire of managerialist techniques – focus groups, private polling, spin doctors, strategists and consultants – to their party organisations. Bill Clinton once remarked that 'there is no one more powerful than a member of a focus group', which is a revealing statement from a man who negotiated the Dayton peace accords in 1995 with genocidal nationalists Slobodan Milošević and Franjo Tuđman. In the 1990s, politics fused ever more tightly with the media. One of the great political buzzwords of the age was 'spin', or the art of shaping the media narrative via strategic communication and soundbites. With declining revenues and streamlined workforces, newspapers increasingly relied on press releases rather than original reporting as the basis for their articles. The capacity of press officers and spin doctors to manage the public's perception of their political parties increased enormously. The birth of cable news had created an increased demand not just for hard news stories, but also for comment and analysis to fill the empty space of so many hours on air. Political journalism increasingly focused on how campaigns were run rather than on the issues themselves. A new kind of meta-wonkery flourished, a self-conscious turn towards coverage of the coverage, which sought to gauge how effective campaigns were in shaping the media narrative and reaching specific demographic groups and niche voting blocs.

But with greater exposure came greater potential risks. The capacity for gaffes, attacks, gotchas, scandals and just plain old negative perceptions encouraged a strategic hyper-vigilance on the part of politicians and their communications strategists. Policies and soundbites were tested by focus groups and fine-tuned to appeal to specific audiences before they were announced. Bill Clinton's signature welfare reform policy was named the

'Personal Responsibility and Work Opportunity Reconciliation Act', a form of spin doctor's anti-poetry that was just as likely to inspire cynicism and despair as to reassure voters of the president's centrist bona fides. Clinton and Blair were the masters of the endlessly repeated slogan. In Clinton's case it was 'Opportunity, responsibility, community'; in Blair's, 'education, education, education'. This was political messaging boiled down to its simplest essence in order to cut through the noise of the mass media. Politics as earworm.

Of course, political spin was not new to the 1990s. Strategic political messaging goes all the way back to Cicero and the rhetorical arts of the ancient world. As media have changed over time, so too have techniques for managing public opinion. F.D. Roosevelt pioneered the art of the radio broadcast 'fireside chat' during the Depression and the Second World War. JFK was the first president to hold televised press conferences. Professional communications strategists were a staple feature of political campaigns throughout the 1970s and '80s. But the key difference in the 1990s was one of scale and speed. The unofficial motto of the 1992 Clinton campaign was 'Speed Kills, Bush', a handwritten note pinned to the wall of the campaign war room by chief strategist James Carville. The aim was to get 'ahead of the story', to respond quicker than the Bush campaign, to be in the driving seat as the narrative unfolded.

Spin wasn't lying, exactly. It was more a matter of telling the right bit of the story at the right time in order to guide the attention of news editors and the public in the desired direction. And yet, the distance between professional spin and outright deceit was sometimes hard to measure. There is a slippery slope that leads from strategic messaging to the infamous 'sexed-up' intelligence dossier that Blair's team used to justify its support for the invasion of Iraq in 2003 to Kellyanne Conway's infamous remark in 2017 about President Trump's taste for 'alternative facts'. Christopher Hitchens wrote a book about the Clintons, entitled *No One Left to Lie To*, which drew a direct connection between the numerous scandals Clinton was involved in – from Whitewater to Gennifer Flowers to the Monica Lewinsky affair – and the political strategy of triangulation. For Hitchens the two were connected. At a certain hard-to-define point, the subtle arts of spin and triangulation tip over into straightforward moral bankruptcy.

↖↑↗

One of the great ironies of the 1990s was that the victory of the centre left came at the expense of the class struggle. The assumption was that 'we are all middle class now', as John Prescott, the former ship steward and union leader who served as Tony Blair's deputy prime minister, put it. But the yuppification of progressive politics also coincided with a certain fetishisation of working-class identities in popular culture. In Britain, this was most evident in what the critic Owen Hatherley mercilessly dubbed the 'dance, prole, dance' genre of popular cinema. Films such as *Brassed Off*, *The Full Monty* and *Billy Elliot* depicted amiable working-class men from post-industrial northern communities who find a renewed purpose in life through culture and the arts rather than manual labour and the class struggle. Set against the backdrop of Margaret Thatcher's defeat of the unions and mass unemployment in the 1980s, these films stage a series of make-overs on their main characters, as the shabby, outdated men are transformed via the regenerative properties of music, ballet and striptease. The popularity of these films was no doubt bound up with the way in which they allowed audiences to mourn the loss of the old working-class culture while also embracing the newly flexible, creative, classless mood of the 1990s.

One of the most popular TV shows of the early 1990s was *Roseanne*, which was set in the lower middle class, or maybe upper working class, but certainly self-consciously 'blue-collar' home of Dan and Roseanne Conner in small-town Illinois. Dan works in construction, while Roseanne moves from the production line at a plastics company to telemarketer, cashier and bartender before finding a longer-term position as a waitress at a diner. *Roseanne* depicted the economic pressures faced by working people on primetime TV for millions of viewers in America and around the world, and it did so with genuine grace and humour; there was an endearing strain of melancholy and thoughtfulness in the show's depiction of everyday blue-collar life to accompany its more raucous moments. In December of 1990, Roseanne and her husband and co-star, Tom Arnold, were featured on the cover of *Vanity Fair*, a publication whose resurrection in the 1980s had made it synonymous with the glitzy ethos of that decade. The cover feature of Roseanne and Tom was meant to signal a shift toward a new authenticity in the 1990s or, as the editor Tina Brown put it in her diary, 'proletarian chic is all the rage'. The danger was that the interest in working-class life was merely skin deep. One suspects that for Tina Brown 'working class' was a cultural profile, a series of fabric textures and narrative moods, rather than a political concept.

The same sense of fuzzy optimism that Clinton expressed in his DNC speech – the sense that globalisation and technological change could be harnessed for the benefit of all social classes – seeped into the popular culture of the 1990s. This was the era of what the *New York Times* columnist David Brooks dubbed 'bourgeois bohemianism', or the marriage of vaguely progressive values of personal freedom and concern for others with an acceptance of the historical inevitability of free-market economics. Of course, hip capitalism was not invented in the 1990s. Just think of Richard Branson and Anita Roddick, whose Virgin and Body Shop empires converted the currency of counter-cultural cool into vast corporate wealth in the 1970s and '80s. But it was against the backdrop of third-way politics in the 1990s that Boboism really hit its stride.

This was the era of ethical consumerism and concern for the plight of the Amazon rainforest, of upscale yoga studios and ethnic restaurants, of trendy bars decked out in brushed steel and raw concrete, of always having the latest palm pilot or laptop on hand to schedule business meetings while grabbing a cappuccino at Starbucks. It was the era in which we experimented with the term 'metrosexual' and earnestly approved of David Beckham wearing a sarong. To anyone who grew up in the 2000s or after, such blandishments are taken for granted. The media is filled with activist celebrities and socially conscious brands. Multicultural cosmopolitanism is the default mode of popular culture. But in the 1990s, the idea that a holidaying footballer might wear an item of Balinese local dress that resembled a skirt was a matter of great cultural novelty. It scrambled a whole host of deeply held assumptions about class, masculinity, football and beachwear.

Boboism combined the counter-cultural ethos of the 1960s with the self-interest of the yuppified 1980s. Capitalism was the only game in town, but the game could be played in a more elegant, ethically engaged, altogether nicer way if you just knew how, or if you could just afford to shop at the right stores. It was in the 1990s that high-end consumer goods of all kinds started to proclaim their ethical bona fides to customers. Packaging for ice cream, crisps, shampoo and toothpaste was now festooned with lengthy statements of corporate ethics and grassroots community values. In a weird reversal of the logic of commodity fetishism as analysed by Karl Marx in *Das Kapital*, commodities now sought actively to draw attention to their means of production, lavishly describing the humble origins of their CEOs and the artisanal craft practices involved in their manufacture, rather than dazzling the consumer with shiny plastic packaging.

Boboism promoted smooth functioning in the present and gradual improvements over time. It extended the yuppy's fascination with high-end kitchen equipment and sleekly minimalist design – all those black and silver hi-fi systems that seemed so impressive in the 1980s – into ever more areas of daily life. Kevin Kelly, one of the gurus of *Wired* magazine, the bible of the early internet age, wrote a column called 'cool tools', which featured everything from mini-LED torches to custom map-building websites, all of which were Bobo accessories for enhancing, ever so slightly, the functionality of everyday life. The Bobo aesthetic reached its apogee with the release of the Apple iPod in October 2001, the sleek white device that enabled you to transport a thousand songs in your pocket. The Mac product launches were an almost spiritual experience for the most dedicated podophiles, a repeated ritual in which the next incremental step into the digital future was revealed.

↖↑↗

The philosophy of managerialism increasingly applied to the arts, as well as to the traditional meat and drink of government administration, such as healthcare and education. Culture was placed at the forefront of urban regeneration efforts in the wake of the deindustrialisation of the 1970s and '80s. Publicly funded art galleries, museums and performance spaces were built in depressed urban neighbourhoods not only in the belief that culture was a public good, but also as stimuli to economic and social regeneration. First build the glitzy new art gallery, went the theory, then the clusters of restaurants, coffee shops, boutiques, apartments and workspaces would surely follow, converting the decaying spaces of the old manufacturing economy into vibrant and cosmopolitan urban zones.

New Labour was one of the most vociferous proponents – and generous patrons – of the regenerative properties of the arts. Labour poured extra funding into the Department of Media, Culture and Sport and the Arts Council, while Blair and his ministers talked up the 'creative industries' as integral both to economic prosperity and to Britain's identity as a modern, progressive nation. Regional museums sprouted in depressed provincial towns such as Gateshead, Salford and West Bromwich. Indie rock stars and Young British Artists were invited to Number 10 Downing Street for much-publicised summits on youth culture and the arts. Creativity and culture were part of New Labour's self-image as tribunes of modernisation. The non-linear power of the imagination and the invisible glue of culture were touted as essential properties for thriving in the new global service economy. But with government largesse came new requirements to account for the impact of the arts in instrumental and utilitarian terms. Investment in the arts was tied to the government's wider efforts to promote social inclusion, racial diversity, community wellbeing, health and education. The managerialist apparatus of measurable targets and high-fibre mission statements about diversity and inclusion spread through arts organisations, as they were required to justify their new funding streams in terms that suited the government.

One of the great beacons of culture-driven regeneration was the opening in 1997 of a branch of New York's Guggenheim Museum in Bilbao, an otherwise shabby Basque seaport which had suffered greatly from the decline of its shipping and manufacturing industries in the 1970s. The project began in 1986 when Spain joined the EU. The Bilbao city government drew on EU regional development funds to commission high-profile architects to redesign parts of the city's urban infrastructure. Santiago Calatrava did the airport, Norman Foster the metro system and, most famously of all, Frank Gehry conceived the jutting angular forms and undulating reflecting planes of the Guggenheim Museum, which stuck starkly out against the faded nineteenth-century grandeur of Bilbao's docks and boulevards. This was a conscious ploy to use splashy architecture as a lure with which to capture the attention of the world's press and thereby attract tourists and stimulate a depressed regional economy through the alchemy of the global culture industry. The main audience for Gehry's eye-catching design was not the native inhabitants of Bilbao, but instead the global bourgeoisie, the Bobo jetsetters who wanted the reassurance of a named starchitect and the Guggenheim brand while they sampled the regional cuisine and local texture of the Basque region.

By many measures the Guggenheim Bilbao was a success. It generated enough revenue to cover its construction costs within three years and contributed significant tax revenue to the local exchequer, although unemployment rates in the region remained stubbornly high for years to come. Soon urban planners around the world were seeking to re-create the 'Bilbao effect' on their own turf. Abu Dhabi's Saadiyat Cultural District, with its pristine outposts of the Louvre and the Guggenheim, and the West Kowloon Cultural District in Hong Kong, which is home to M+, a museum of modern Chinese art intended to rival London's Tate Modern, both took Bilbao as the inspiration for how to acquire cultural capital and soft power via high-profile regeneration projects. In the last few decades, mini Bilbaos have sprouted in Mecca, Tirana, Belo Horizonte, Perth, Dundee, Liverpool and Margate.

In the week leading up to the grand opening of the Guggenheim Museum in Bilbao, a tense little drama unfolded in the museum grounds that seemed somehow to encapsulate the historical currents that had shaped the institution's birth. Shortly before the opening ceremony, this icon of the new creative economy was visited by a group of refugees from the old world of heavy industry and violent class conflict. Three members of the Basque separatist terrorist organisation, ETA, disguised themselves as gardeners and set about concealing bombs in the grounds of the museum in preparation for an attack on the opening ceremony, which was due to be attended by King Juan Carlos and assorted dignitaries that coming weekend.

As the terrorists went about their work, two passing policemen entered the museum grounds and discovered the 'gardeners' in the process of hiding an explosive device in the fronds of Jeff Koons's giant *Puppy* sculpture, a 40ft-high representation of a Highland terrier made from flowering plants, which high-minded critics have described as a satirical investigation of the relationship between kitsch, artistic value and traditional craft practices in the postmodern era. Seeing the policemen approach, the terrorists opened fire, killing one of the officers, and then fled through the city. One terrorist was arrested later that day but two escaped after they highjacked a car at gunpoint in the city centre; they were later arrested at a remote farmhouse stocked with weapons and explosives.

The incident of the *Puppy* sculpture was a minor moment in the history of Basque separatism. Compared to the Barcelona hypermarket bombing which killed twenty-one civilians in 1987, it was an episode of futility and incompetence that only further discredited ETA in the eyes of the public. By the mid-1990s ETA was deeply unpopular both with Spaniards and Basques; most nationalist politicians were firmly committed to peaceful and constitutionalist means of pursuing regional autonomy. This was the pathway taken by the Scottish, Catalan and Quebecois independence movements of the era with various degrees of success.

But the scene is nevertheless an eloquent vignette of a particular moment in history. This was the last hurrah of a far-left revolutionary movement that was founded in 1959 in order to free the Basque country from Franco's fascist dictatorship and centralised rule. The scenography of a gaggle of Marxist liberation fighters hiding in the fronds of a postmodern flower sculpture on the eve of the opening of an EU-funded cultural regeneration project could have been dreamt up by a satirical novelist or political sketch writer. It is an allegorical image of the past waging war on the future, of left-wing revolutionaries beached on the shoreline of a new world, flailing for purchase, exhausted by history, rendered obsolete by the world-bestriding power of global finance capital, cheap airfares and the allure of an eye-catching but rather vacuous piece of conceptual art.

↖↑↗

If you really want to understand what happens when a decaying regional culture meets footloose finance capital and the global media system, then you should look no further than football, the original working man's sport, which was converted over the course of the 1990s into a multi-billion-pound industry with as many followers in Dar es Salaam and Shanghai as in Derby and Sheffield. Throughout Europe and South America, the sport's historical heartlands, football has traditionally been the preserve of the working class. Rugby, cricket, tennis, polo and yachting were for the nobs, but soccer was for the people. Football clubs were the focus for fierce local attachments, regional pride, ideological or religious affiliation (Roma for the Communisti, Lazio for the Fascisti; Celtic for the Catholics, Rangers for the Protestants), community spirit and a certain sense of everyday elegance, hence the 'beautiful game'. Right from the start, football was more business-oriented than other sports like rugby, cricket and tennis. The working men who played in the first professional teams in the late nineteenth century needed to be compensated for the playing and training time that kept them away from their jobs. For most of its history, player salaries, transfer fees, wealthy owners and a certain buccaneering style of regional oligarchism have all been integral parts of the game.

In the early 1990s, however, football underwent one of the most radical transformations in its one hundred and more years as a professional sport. In 1992, the English Premier League (EPL) was formed. The most successful and well-financed clubs in England would now compete in a stand-alone league, which remained connected to the lower leagues via promotion and relegation, but would have its own separate commercial organisation and, crucially, the ability to sell its broadcasting and sponsorship rights around the world. In 1992, the EPL broadcasting rights were sold to Rupert Murdoch's BSkyB for £305 million. In 2000 the same package cost BSkyB £1.1 billion, roughly a three-fold increase in less than a decade. By 2019 the combined domestic and global broadcast revenues for the EPL were estimated at £9.2 billion, or just shy of the GDP of Mozambique. When the league's founders rubbed the magic lamp and wished for more money and a bigger global profile, they couldn't have imagined the genie's largesse over the coming decades, or the unforeseen consequences of being granted wealth beyond their wildest dreams.

In the season following the formation of the EPL, the new UEFA Champions League kicked off for the first time. In place of the old knock-out competition, in which only the winners of each domestic league were able to compete, the Champions League expanded the number of teams admitted from the most powerful footballing countries and increased the total number of games played. There was now more product to screen on television, more opportunities for branding and sponsorship, more big games between famous clubs, more revenues from ticket receipts and prize money, and more frequent blaring of Handel's *Zadok the Priest* before games to impart, somewhat incongruously perhaps, a soaring sense of the sublimity and grandeur and high European civilisational ideals to the spectacle of twenty-two millionaires kicking a ball around a grassy field.

Football spectatorship was increasingly gentrified over the course of the 1990s, not least because ticket prices climbed steeply due to the growing popularity of the sport both in the UK and overseas. Football's new cultural respectability was signalled by the huge popularity of Nick Hornby's 1992 memoir, *Fever Pitch*, which was made into a successful film starring Colin Firth in 1997. Hornby made no bones about his status as a middle-class, Cambridge-educated football supporter. Rather than a tale of working-class rootedness or violent hooliganism, *Fever Pitch* is an existential drama of fandom, which revels in the rare ecstasy and frequent agony of following Arsenal through the lean years of the 1970s and '80s, followed by their miraculous title-winning season in 1989–90. Critics often credit *Fever Pitch* with single-handedly converting football into the classless leisure spectacle that it is today, largely because it coincided with the first years of the EPL and the new cultural cachet attached to football in the days of Britpop, lads' mags and hedonistic 1990s youth culture. But like many of the more culturally upmarket treatments of football in the 1990s, such as Bill Buford's study of hooliganism, *Among the Thugs*, *Fever Pitch* was a work of *nostalgie de la boue* for a sporting culture that was on the wane. Like *The Full Monty* and the cinema of post-industrial regeneration, *Fever Pitch* looked wistfully back to the pre-gentrification days of the 1980s as much as it defined the new mood of the 1990s.

In many ways, the injection of vast amounts of money into football improved the sport. Grounds became safer and more comfortable. Teams were better coached as a new breed of technocratic manager, such as Arsenal's Arsène Wenger, otherwise known as *Le Professeur*, drilled their players into ever more elaborate tactical patterns. Fitness levels improved as sports scientists and dieticians were included on coaching staffs. More overseas players were employed in European leagues, making the game more cosmopolitan and diverse. The culture became less aggressively macho (although there were still no openly gay players in the top leagues) and less violent. The play got quicker, more athletic, more skill based, more abstract geometric than ever before. The rules of the game were changed (no back passes to the keeper) to encourage this more fluid style of play. There were more games each week. The moments of transcendent beauty and skill and grace came thick and fast. As a consumer entertainment spectacle, the game improved.

But all of this came with significant costs. Tickets got more expensive. Superstar players' wages ate up an ever-increasing portion of clubs' revenues. Power was consolidated among the wealthiest and most famous clubs. The same small cartel of superclubs competed for the biggest prizes each year. Football clubs became the playthings of oligarchs and foreign governments, vehicles for hobbyist enjoyment and the sportswashing of repressive regimes. Financial instability spread throughout the lower reaches of the game. While a handful of clubs floated on the stock market, many more went bust or had to scale back their finances and drop down the divisions. All of the glitz and glamour of the 1990s football revolution couldn't mask the reality of a sport moving decisively away from its history and traditions. Football's heritage as a regional culture embedded in predominantly working-class communities did not disappear, but on top of those roots was grafted a new thing entirely – a globalised, high-finance media spectacle of mind-boggling skill and speed that was, at the same time, just a little bit bland, just a little bit boring.

↖↑↗

In the pages of the *London Review of Books* in April 1994, Edward Luttwak offered an alternative analysis of the mid-1990s socio-economic situation that differed markedly from Francis Fukuyama's liberal-democratic triumphalism and Bill Clinton's third-way centrism. The article was entitled, 'Why Fascism is the Wave of the Future', and from today's perspective it seems a rather prescient reading of the signs of the times.

Luttwak noted two key features of the age of globalisation. First, the forces of 'creative destruction' that defined free-market economics seemed to be accelerating like never before. Joseph Schumpeter, the father of neoliberal economics, coined this resonant phrase in 1942 to capture the way in which innovation and growth within capitalist economies create a ceaseless churn of new technologies, new bodies of skill and knowledge, even whole new industries. This in turn creates an undertow of displacement, as those technologies, skills, knowledges and industries – and crucially the workforces whose livelihoods depend on them and the regional economies in which they are embedded – become obsolete. As Luttwak noted, whereas in the industrial era it might take thirty or forty years, a generation or two, for this to happen, in the age of globalisation the process of creative destruction was gathering pace. Now it might take a decade or less for an industrial sub-sector to come into and pass out of existence. Precariousness and the need for constant adaptation were becoming the norm.

The other feature that Luttwak pointed out was the failure of political parties of both the centre right and centre left to address – let alone to resolve – the sense of dislocation that was produced by this accelerated cycle of creative destruction. While the right offered encomiums to traditional family values and social cohesion, the left sought to mitigate the worst effects of breakneck globalisation with retraining programmes and mild redistribution, neither of which was remotely adequate to the scale of the problem. According to Luttwak, this left a large unclaimed political territory that was fertile ground for what he called a 'product-improved fascism'. Disaffection with globalisation and economic precarity combined with a resentment of ineffectual political elites might not trigger a return to the old style of totalitarian fascism of the mid-twentieth century, but it might be a seedbed for a new media-friendly version adapted to contemporary conditions.

Luttwak's analysis was eccentric, to say the least, in comparison to the avalanche of mainstream punditry proclaiming the miracle of the New Economy and the end of ideology. But even as he wrote, far-right political parties – not yet 'product improved', perhaps, but emboldened by growing support – sought to move onto the terrain he was mapping. In the 1990s Jean-Marie Le Pen in France, Jörg Haider in Austria and Pat Buchanan in the US all made incursions into the political mainstream and helped to 're-normalise' far-right politics. At this stage, the electoral successes of the far right were limited and often at the local level, but they did help to make extremist right-wing politics seem somewhat respectable again, or at least not exclusively associated with skinhead thugs and antiquated revanchists stuck in the mental atmosphere of the 1930s.

Bill Clinton's 1992 election mantra, 'It's the economy, stupid', is often seen as a key part of his winning strategy. George H.W. Bush was strong on foreign policy, but weak on domestic and economic policy, so Clinton's pitch as a charismatic wonk with a neat-sounding economic plan made sense. But Clinton's mistake was to assume that disadvantaged voters would follow their own economic interest purely on its own terms, like a simple equation. Over the course of the 1990s and early 2000s, voter turnouts in many advanced democracies were in decline. This was especially true among the working-class communities that had been the traditional support of the old left. Disaffected with liberal progressivism, struggling to get by in the low-wage, high-precarity economy, and turned off by the relentless spin and bluster of managerialist politics, many voters simply changed the channel. Why tune into politics, when there was football or reality TV on the other side?

In the US, the tribune of the far right was Pat Buchanan, former speech-writer to Nixon and advisor to Reagan, who challenged George H.W. Bush in the 1992 Republican primary on a nativist, anti-immigration platform aimed at winning the white working-class vote for the party of big business and family values. In his speech to the press on announcing his candidacy, Buchanan vowed to protect the nation's 'Western heritage', railed against the UN ('We must not trade in our sovereignty for a cushioned seat at anyone's New World Order') and vowed to put 'Americans first' in all of his policy decisions. In his speech at the Republican National Convention in August, after losing the nomination to George H.W. Bush, Buchanan declared that 'there is a religious war going on in this country. It is a cultural war … for the soul of America'. The liberal commentator Molly Ivins famously quipped that the speech 'sounded better in the original German'. After losing once more in the 1996 Republican primaries, Buchanan eventually won the nomination of the Reform Party in 2000, a far-right political start-up that managed to win a mere 0.4 per cent of the vote in the general election. One of his defeated opponents in the Reform Party primary campaign was none other than Donald Trump, who was just starting to dip his toes into electoral politics. Sensing his impending defeat, Trump pulled out of the race early, calling Buchanan a 'neo-Nazi' and his supporters 'wackos'. Several years and one successful reality TV show later, Trump went on to win the US presidency on a platform that bore a striking resemblance to Buchanan's 1992 campaign.

What was 'wacko' in the 1990s became mainstream in the 2010s. Perhaps the biggest mistake made by liberal progressives in the 1990s was in not taking the threat of the far right seriously, of assuming that history was – and always would be – on their side.

5

Generation X, Y, Z

WHAT IS a generation? Is it a demographic tool for studying trends within the human population? Is it a source of political and cultural identity, a self-conscious label to be worn with pride or shame – 'my generation'? Or is it a marketing device with which to sell products to consumers hungry for a connection with the forces of history?

The classical theory of generations comes from the German sociologist Karl Mannheim, who argued that a generation is not a concrete social identity, like membership of a family or tribe, but instead a 'common location within the social and historical process'. A generation is a kind of historical envelope, or a very large and diffuse historical bubble, within which every member of an age cohort – everyone born within a roughly twenty- to thirty-year period – lives. Everyone who grew up in and around the 1920s or the 1960s or the 1980s formed their outlook on the world in relation to a common set of historical events and social trends. It is not enough simply to live through a particular stretch of history to be a member of a generation. Instead, you have to be young. You have to witness the major events of the day with an as-yet-unformed character, in a state of heightened receptivity, still vibrating to the pressure of the times.

Of course, not everyone responds in the same way to the formative experiences of their youth. As far as I know, no one has yet propounded a theory of generational determinism. The closest we've come is Martin Heidegger's doomy declaration that 'the inescapable fate of living in and with one's generation completes the full drama of individual human existence'. Heidegger's statement seems hyperbolic – the *Sturm und Drang* theory of generations – but it accords with the simple fact that generational membership is involuntary. None of us choose when we live, and none of us select the society and culture into which we are born. Our fate, according to Heidegger, our inescapable destiny as finite human beings, is to be Boomers, X-ers, or Millennials. We are destined to come of age fostered by post-war prosperity or spurred on by neoliberal competition, raised amid Space Hoppers or Tamagochis, listening to the Osmonds or the Spice Girls.

Generation X, the cohort born directly after the Baby Boomers, embraced its fate more with a shrug than a struggle. In the early 1990s, Gen X-ers were in their late teens or twenties, having come of age in the Reagan and Thatcher years. They were the children of divorce, mass media, individual enterprise, conservative retrenchment and renewed nuclear threat in the final years of the Cold War. In many ways, Generation X was doomed to its sense of displacement right from the start, growing up as it did in the long shadow cast by the mythic 1960s, the great age of generational change and youthful radicalism. How could anyone live up to that example? And why hadn't the promised fruits of the 1960s been passed down to the next generation? This is why so many members of Generation X became Marxists – not Karl Marxists, that is, but Groucho Marxists. Generation X was a collection of individuals who didn't want to belong to any generation that would accept them as members. They craved historical meaning, authentic experience, collective struggle, autonomous lives, but they were suspicious of the ersatz forms in which those goods were made available in the age of globalised consumer capitalism.

↖↑↗

Douglas Coupland might not have coined the term 'Generation X', but his bestselling 1991 novel of that name certainly made it into a popular catchphrase, part of the lexicon of cultural analysis wielded by everyone from newspaper columnists to your local video-store clerk. The book was an unanticipated bestseller, which shot to success by describing a previously unrecognised set of demographic trends associated with the rising generation of young adults. In addition to the title itself, Coupland coined a whole new vocabulary of buzzy bon mots to capture this new generational profile: McJob, occupational slumming, legislated nostalgia, historical underdosing, etc. What these terms conveyed was a sense of disaffection coupled with futility, a distaste for consumer capitalism and a simultaneous sense of resignation to its inescapable reality.

The novel is a tale of curated self-marginalisation. Andy, Claire and Dag drop out of their well-paid corporate jobs and retreat to the desert, where they tell each other stories, some fictional, some drawn from life, which encapsulate their sense of alienation and frustrated desire. Crucially, they do not live in the deep isolation of the desert proper. Having fled their careers in Los Angeles, Toronto and Portland, they retreat not to a self-sufficient commune deep in the Mojave, as the prior generation of American dropouts might have done. Instead, they live on the outskirts of super-tacky Palm Springs, in the liminal zone between the sublime wastes of the desert and the liposuction clinics and chain hotels of the city. This is itself a supremely Gen X move. Neither revolutionary nor conformist, the friends choose to live on the outskirts of corporate America, a vantage point from which they can assert their wised-up independence without having to forego the pleasures on offer within the leviathan.

But the desert is always there, a short vintage Saab ride away. The novel's sub-title captures the logic of Andy, Claire and Dag's self-marginalisation: 'Tales for an Accelerated Culture'. By driving out to tell stories amid the sagebrush and cacti, the friends shift down through the gears, retreat from consumerist alienation and bask in a more expansive experience of time and history. The stories they tell combine irony and sincerity, snark and schmaltz, in what would come to be recognised as a typically 1990s way. A whole sequence of stories is set on Texlahoma, a mythic version of middle America set on an asteroid orbiting earth, where it's always 1974, 'the year after the oil shock and the year after real wages in America never grew again'. The novel abounds with precise socio-historical details of this sort. Claire taps her cigarette into an 'overflowing 1974 Spokane World's Fair ashtray'; Andy and Dag wear 'classic Bob Hope Golf Classic robin's-egg-blue windbreakers with white sun hats'. Retro fashion merges with astute political commentary.

But in spite of their snarky repartee, Andy, Claire and Dag are suckers for authenticity. The novel abounds with fleeting moments of belonging. After a late-night storytelling session, Andy wakes up on Claire's bed with his sleeping friends and their pet dogs nestled around him. 'If I could have it thus,' he muses, 'I would like this moment to continue forever.' *Generation X* is a deeply apolitical novel. Its characters exist in a self-conscious state of alienation but place no trust in political activism as a route to salvation. Instead, its world-view is ultimately religious. The solution to alienation is not politics, but the cultivation of moments of Zen-like calm that emerge from expertly selected aesthetic experiences. There is a devotional aspect to the friends' storytelling, a vague air of secularised ritual.

Coupland was originally commissioned to write a work of non-fiction, but the project evolved into a loosely structured novel instead. The traces of the earlier non-fiction project can be detected in the form of illustrated sidebars, which contain pithy definitions of generational catchphrases, and an appendix of demographic statistics, which outline the increasingly precarious conditions faced by young people in the post-1970s free-market economy. Perhaps it was this strange hybrid of feather-light, but 'alternative' fiction and social scientific data that made the book so popular with the marketing professionals of the culture industry. Because predictably – depressingly – *Generation X* was rapidly adopted as an industry guidebook for how to sell things to a demographic group that had proved stubbornly resistant to advertising.

This was the fate of much of the music, cinema and literature associated with Generation X in the early 1990s. What was originally an anti-consumerist stance, a sub-culture rooted in local scenes and independent record labels, radio shows and magazines, was rapidly co-opted as the next glossily packaged youth cultural trend. The culture of Generation X included second-wave punk music like grunge and Riot Grrrl, alternative rock bands like Pavement and Dinosaur Jr, the films of Richard Linklater, Hal Hartley and Kevin Smith, and eventually more mainstream films such as *Singles* (1992) and *Reality Bites* (1994). Generation X was a catch-all demographic term, but the specific cultural variant to be found in indie music and movies was 'slacker', a coinage originated by Linklater in his 1990 micro-budget movie of the same name. *Slacker* meandered its way through the streets of Austin, Texas (after Seattle, the unofficial second city of Gen X), listening in on the cast of eccentrics and dropouts who inhabit its convenience stores, college dorm rooms and dive bars. The very formlessness of the film is an escape from the linear trajectory of the standard American life: school, college, career, marriage, mortgage, retirement.

The ultimate slacker, though, the one true king of the low-key drifters, was the 'Dude', played by Jeff Bridges in the Coen brothers' 1998 film *The Big Lebowski*. The Dude is a becalmed relic of the 1960s counterculture, a signatory of the Port Huron Statement of 1962, one of the founding documents of the student protest movement, who now spends his days in the regional bowling leagues of San Diego, living off welfare cheques and White Russians. Alongside *Withnail and I*, the classic depiction of the melancholy end of swinging London, *The Big Lebowski* must be one of the most frequently quoted movies in recent history. The Dude's litany of catchphrases – 'the Dude abides'; 'that rug really tied the room together', etc. – became part of the vernacular of Generation X, an ironic nod to the noble spirit of a bygone era. But beyond the wacky plot and quotable script, *The Big Lebowski* is also a seriocomic attempt to take the temperature of the present moment and appraise the legacy of the 1960s counterculture. Is the Dude a man out of time or does he have the cure for what ails us?

Generation X was a predominantly white and middle-class phenomenon. Coupland's characters all come from wealthy, college-educated, Caucasian families. Their central problem is how to live good lives under conditions of extreme affluence and security. Their pet anxieties about radiation poisoning and toxic accidents, while plausible, are focused on distant, merely potential threats. Compared to the tales of inner-city pressure – poverty, racism, violence, addiction – that were the staple fare of hip hop, another 'alternative' musical sub-culture that went mainstream in the late 1980s and early '90s, it all seems somewhat affected, maybe even a little precious.

Jeff Chang has charted the fortunes of the 'hip hop generation', a parallel cohort of African Americans and Latinos who were born within the same window as Generation X, but whose formative experiences were of a different nature. Their concerns were not the pressures of affluence, but the shifting socio-political conditions that accompanied the passing of the Civil Rights era: the moral panic surrounding the crack 'epidemic' and the 'War on Drugs', underfunded schools and social services, mass incarceration, the effects of deindustrialisation in predominantly Black communities in Detroit, Los Angeles, Philadelphia and elsewhere. Gangster rap, the militant strain of hip hop that emerged in the late 1980s and early 1990s with artists such as N.W.A., Ice Cube, Tupac and Biggie Smalls, was the inverse image of slacker culture, a Black punk for the 'no alternative' 1990s. Where slackers escaped the system by retreating into a mildly narcotised fog of irony and wonder, gangster rappers tried to beat the system at its own game. With its 'get rich or die trying' ethos, its veneration of the rapper as self-made millionaire, and its hyperbolic enjoyment of conspicuous consumption, gangster rap was a hedonistic parody of the capitalist marketplace.

But even this more nuanced narrative, which avoids turning affluent white experience into an unstated norm, simplifies and excludes large swathes of Black youth culture. Chang focuses on the social history of the ghetto and the hip hop ideal of 'keeping it real'; but hip hop in the 1990s was as polyphonic and multifarious as any musical genre is likely to be. It wasn't all nihilistic gangstas and politically 'conscious' messaging. Nineties hip hop encompassed everything from the wacky humour of the Pharcyde to the soulful R&B of Mary J. Blige to the crunchy naturalism of Arrested Development. Generations contains multitudes, and not everyone wants to represent their social demographic in the same way.

Generations also tend to be nationally specific, although they are becoming less so in the age of globalised mass media. Future historians will study Generation X as a classic piece of Americana, as culturally specific as barber shop quartets, soda jerks and drive-in movie theatres. It was yet another iteration of the abiding American theme of how to balance individual liberty with community bonds. With its alternative groups and hyper-local scenes, it was a morally earnest experiment in living – Henry David Thoreau in ripped jeans. And yet, as one of Wim Wenders's melancholy drifters points out in *Kings of the Road*, his 1976 German road movie, 'the Yanks have colonised our subconscious'. American popular culture is global popular culture. And it's not only the icons of American power, the superheroes and cowboys, who inhabit our fantasies. It's also the slackers and dropouts, the misfits and refuseniks, the gangsters and revolutionaries.

↖↑↗

Does anyone really feel like they belong to a generation? Philip Larkin certainly understood the appeal of generational membership. In his oft-quoted poem 'Annus Mirabilis', Larkin captured both the joyous release experienced by members of the Baby Boomer cohort and his own sense of having been born just too early to enjoy such good fortune:

> Sexual intercourse began
> In nineteen sixty-three
> (which was rather late for me) –
> Between the end of the 'Chatterley' ban
> And the Beatles' first LP.

Larkin plays on the discrepancy between the regularity of calendrical time and the surprising speed of cultural change in the modern world, the sudden, tumbling, headlong momentum of things when the conditions are just right. But did everyone really feel the same way? Did all members of the Boomer generation really get so lucky? Was sexuality really converted, all of a sudden, into a universally satisfying free-for-all, 'a quite unlosable game'? Almost certainly not. Larkin's poem is subtler than you might at first think. It doesn't simply endorse the popular historian's airy generalisations. Instead, it filters those statements through the stifled personality of the poem's speaker, who was born too late to take part in the sexual bonanza and must look on from outside. When you read the poem for a second or a third time, the hyperbolic language of jackpots and money-shots starts to sound more like a pervy outsider's fantasy than the actual experience of a whole generation.

Larkin also gave us one of the canonical statements of generational tension: 'They fuck you up, your mum and dad. / They might not mean to, but they do.' Generously, he notes that his parents were themselves fucked up by their parents, who were, in their turn, fucked up by the previous generation. Generational history, according to Larkin, is an interminable process of mutual fucking up. The fashions change ('fools in old-style hats and coats') and the parenting styles change ('Who half the time were soppy-stern / And half at one another's throats'), but the process of mutual up-fuckery abides: 'It deepens, like a continental shelf.' Generational hurt is built into the human experience. It is hard, like geology.

Generations go way back, but generational *thinking* – the tendency to slice history into generation-sized chunks – is a characteristically modern phenomenon. To be able to think of children, parents and grandparents as representatives of distinct worldviews, as opposed to broadly interchangeable units in a cohesive tribal group or religious order, you must first think of history itself as subject to constant change and sharp discontinuities. This is why generational thinking only really took off in the later eighteenth century, in the wake of the great social upheavals brought about by the age of industrialisation and democratic revolution. In the early nineteenth century, Alexis de Tocqueville observed that the generations were more sharply distinguished in America than in Europe, as the pace of social change was not shackled by aristocratic traditions and manners. 'Each new generation is a new people,' he marvelled.

Today, we seem to be drowning in generations. We're swamped by micro-epochs, stifled by the narrow horizon of each new pop cultural moment, each of which is presented to us as a generationally defining experience. The generation industry is worth hundreds of millions of dollars. Social scientists, demographers, data analysts and trend spotters can make good livings selling generational knowledge to advertising agencies and their corporate clients. Busy journalists with deadlines to meet can concoct new generational categories by following a simple recipe: take a handful of broad-based social trends, add a popular toy or piece of consumer electronics, sprinkle on some economic data, mix in some current affairs, include a soundtrack of popular songs, garnish with some references to film and television, and hey presto! – you've built your own generational identity.

Framed in this way, generations become reductive labels that excuse us from thinking too deeply about history and our place within it. Baby Boomers are affluent, self-absorbed, opinionated and enjoy listening to classic rock. Generation X were disaffected in their youth when they listened to grunge music and wore flannel shirts, but are now more happily embedded in careers, marriages and meaningful lives. They distrust the mainstream, but still want to get ahead. Millennials are sheltered, tolerant, narcissistic and optimistic. They formed their identities in the hothouse world of social media and assume that even the most venerable of institutions should accommodate their oh-so special needs. Then there's Generation Z, or the 'Digital Natives', who were born after the turn of the millennium, the spawn of a fully digitised world. No one really knows yet what their profile will be, but we can safely assume that it will be easily compressed into a few shared characteristics that are useful to marketing executives and policy makers.

Recently, a new micro-generation was invented for those of us who were born slightly too late for Generation X and a bit too early to be Millennials. This is the *Star Wars* Generation, or X-ennials – anyone born between 1977 and 1983, or between the first cinematic releases of *Star Wars* and *Return of the Jedi*. Apparently, members of this generation exist in an ambivalent limbo between the cynicism of Gen X-ers and the optimistic self-absorption of Millennials. We had analogue childhoods and digital adulthoods. Unlike Millennials, we still trust institutions, but distrust social media. We feel nostalgic for the 1990s, as though it were a lost age of light and reason. And yes, of course, we love the *Star Wars* movies. Who doesn't, right? They're epic and exciting, and *The Empire Strikes Back* even had a darkly unresolved ending, so we're prepared to excuse the cute atrocity of the Ewoks, and the fact that George Lucas paved the way for the endless cycle of remakes and reboots that have ruined Hollywood cinema seemingly forever. Such fine-grained generational thinking makes one want to flounce off like Virginia Woolf's Orlando, that gender-swapping and category defying exile from the spirit of the age, whose travels through time were extended up to 1992 in Sally Potter's film adaptation, to write metaphysical poetry under the shade of an ancient oak tree. It makes one yearn for a deeper sense of history, a wider purview on the world.

The greatest purveyors of neatly packaged generational identity are, without a doubt, William Strauss and Neil Howe. Their 1991 tome, *Generations: The History of America's Future, 1584 to 2069*, propounded the first fully generational model of American history, beginning in the Plymouth Colony and stretching ahead to the as yet un-espied future of 2069. *Generations* has all the airtight consistency of pre-Copernican astronomy or Galenic medicine. Where Strauss and Howe depart from Mannheim and the social scientists is with their insistence that generations are not only descriptive but also *predictive*. Mannheim thought generations were useful devices for understanding how history shaped subjectivity at the level of whole populations. For Strauss and Howe, generations became the secret key to history, the golden thread of order and pattern within the grand narrative of the American experiment.

In their system, history becomes a cyclical process driven by four recurring generational archetypes – the Prophet, the Nomad, the Hero and the

Artist – the tensions between whom create the regular patterns of rise and fall, crisis and restitution, that the authors detect in the sweep of American history. Prophets are outward-looking and socially engaged. Nomads tend to be more defensive, as they are responding to the older generation of activist Prophets, and thus have to be pragmatic and resilient. Heroes often live through a time of institutional decline and must therefore trust their own instincts and self-reliance. Artists live in the teeth of crisis when the scope for action is most limited. Along with the four generational archetypes come four historical 'turnings', the authors' term for each twenty-two-year unit of historical time: the High, the Awakening, the Unravelling and the Crisis. At any point in American history, the canny prognosticator can run a finger along the graph and see which generational archetypes are in the ascendant and which are in recession. The ratio of generational types – what, in an unfortunate echo of a tabloid astrologist, the authors call the 'constellation' of generations – determines the more general character of the times, or the spirit of the age.

When it was first released in 1991, Strauss and Howe's book was a huge success. Al Gore was so impressed that he sent a copy to every member of the US Congress. With its grand historical vision, *Generations* stood alongside Fukuyama's *End of History and the Last Man* and Samuel Huntington's *The Clash of Civilizations* as big-picture prognostications of the future of the post-twentieth-century world. What was most striking about Strauss and Howe's vision, though, was its cosinesss, the way in which it sought to humanise history. Its rhythmical patterns were modelled on – and ultimately determined by – the human life span and the inter-generational conflicts to which it gives rise. In their introduction, the authors address the reader in the second person. By reading their book, they claim, 'you may ... gain a better sense of how you and your peers fit into the ongoing story of American civilisation – a long and twisting drama that offers each generation a special role'. We are invited to insert ourselves into this harmonious historical system. We are fixed in place, oriented in time, swept along by a historical process that is both grand and familiar, sublime and beautiful. Strauss and Howe play on the same sensibility that makes genealogy so popular in America and elsewhere. History is a family drama, which has a comfortable place for all of us. This is, ironically, a deeply Boomer-ish view of history, in that it contains the individual at its centre. No wonder Strauss and Howe had such success converting their generational theories into marketable insights for powerful organisations like Nike and the US military.

In an era when politics merged ever more tightly with advertising, it should come as little surprise that Bill Clinton and Tony Blair, two of the most successful political communicators of the 1990s, sought to cast themselves as representatives of a generational shift in the political life of their nations. Greil Marcus claims that the moment Clinton won the 1992 election was when he played saxophone on the *Arsenio Hall Show*. This was the point at which Clinton nudged America into discarding the assumption that presidential politics was the preserve of prep school-educated guys from Kennebunkport and stepping into the post-Baby Boomer age. Clinton was also the first candidate to be interviewed on MTV when he took part in a townhall debate in 1992 with 200 18- to 24-year-olds and answered questions about his star sign (Leo), his favourite painter (El Greco) and his first rock 'n' roll experience ('going nuts over Elvis Presley'). Clinton was not the 1960s radical that his Republican opponents claimed he was; in reality, he was the Boomer moderate who didn't inhale. But his carefully stage-managed media appearances were intended to highlight the historic link between youth culture and progressive political change that had been cemented in the 1960s.

Tony Blair and New Labour made a similar generational pitch, which sought to unite Generation X and the Baby Boomers against what Blair once darkly termed 'the forces of conservatism'. In his speech to the 1994 Labour Party conference, Blair proclaimed his belief that 'rock 'n' roll is not just an important part of our culture … It's immensely important to the future of this country'. Labour published a policy document in same year entitled *Young Britain*, which sought to position the party as the tribune of a new generational sensibility: modern, unstuffy, creative, cool, diverse and all the other rather vague progressive values of the post-1960s youth culture. At the Labour Party conference in 1996, Blair made sure to get a photo with Noel Gallagher, lead singer of Britpop stars Oasis, just as Harold Wilson, the last Labour leader to win a parliamentary majority, had with the Beatles in 1964. Like the Pepsi marketing campaign of the early 1990s, the New Democrats and New Labour claimed to be 'the choice of a generation'.

↖↑↗

The ancient blood libel of 'selling out' has its origins in the left-wing politics of the 1930s. To sell out was to compromise revolutionary principle for personal advancement, often in the form of a cushy position as a union steward or party insider. Even after the term migrated to the cultural sphere in the

1950s and '60s, it retained the association with Stalinist purges and ideological purity. Year Zero for the cultural sell-out was of course 1965: the moment at the Newport Folk Festival when Bob Dylan blew away the purists with a fully electrified set. At the Manchester Free Trade Hall the following year, a member of the crowd called out 'Judas', but it could just as easily have been 'sell out'. It's been downhill – or uphill – ever since, depending on which side of the purity/progress and underground/mainstream divides you find more accommodating.

The ethical dilemma of selling out is one of the features of 1990s popular culture that seems most alien today, part of what marks the decade as a distinct historical era and the hinge point between the analogue electronic culture of the late twentieth century and the new digital universe we now inhabit. In the early 1990s underground acts found it easier than ever to land recording contracts with mainstream labels. The recording industry was flush with cash from the sales bonanza of the new CD format. The charts were dominated by faded stalwarts like Bruce Springsteen, Phil Collins and Sting as well as high-gloss pop acts like MC Hammer and Paula Abdul. Many artists and label owners saw an opportunity and decided to embrace the glamour and riches of the mainstream. Bands like Jane's Addiction, Nirvana, Hole, N.W.A., Cypress Hill, Blur, Oasis, Daft Punk – all acts that had deep roots in underground scenes and had started out on independent labels – sold millions of records and occupied the centre ground of pop music for much of the decade. Many independent labels were bought by multinational corporations and run as in-house boutiques that catered to a more discerning audience in search of niche sounds and experiences. 'Alternative' and 'independent' became marketing labels in their own right.

There were many different versions of the independent ethos, from the punk regionalism of Seattle's Sub Pop, the home of grunge, to the hedonistic brotherhood of Creation, the British label behind Primal Scream and Oasis' ascent to the top of the charts, to the insurgent Black mogul ideal of Def Jam, one of the founding hip hop labels. But in each case there was a guiding belief in the connection between financial and artistic independence. True artistic freedom was only really possible outside the commercial recording industry, free from the influence of corporate executives with their market-research-driven sales plans and niche demographic targeting. In its purest form, though, independence was an existential, as well as an artistic or financial proposition. To be independent was to be true to yourself, to take your destiny in your own hands. Hence the legendary tales of contracts signed in blood and company coffers emptied on colossal drug binges. Within the desire for independence there lurks a hidden potential for self-punishing perversity, a quest for autonomy that might easily tip over into narcissism and megalomania.

For most of pop history there has been a productive tension between the notional realms of the underground and the mainstream. The breakthrough indie-obscurity-to-mainstream-success is one of the great narrative engines of the rock and roll story. The ascent of the Beatles from the Hamburg Reeperbahn to Jonny Carson's *Tonight Show*, of the Sex Pistols from a West London squat to *The Great Rock n' Roll Swindle*, of N.W.A. from South Central LA to the top of the Billboard 100 Chart, all follow similar arcs. The desire to 'cross over' is not just about fame and money and fans and sex and charisma and worship, although those commodities are obviously not entirely unrelated to the process. There are often nobler – and more quixotic – ambitions at work: the desire to communicate and connect with a wider public, the belief that your message deserves amplification, an insurgent campaign to storm the reality studios and disrupt the corporate spectacle, a commitment to the redeeming power of mass art, even the quite blameless desire to make a little money, buy some better equipment and put a little something away for retirement. And yet the tension remains between the purity and authenticity of the underground and the glamorous alienation of the mainstream.

In the post-internet age, that productive tension has slackened. The ground began to shift at the turn of the millennium with the arrival of high-speed broadband and social media. Napster, iTunes, YouTube, streaming services like Spotify and Bandcamp, illegal downloads, Facebook, Twitter, Instagram, etc., have redrawn the topographies of underground and mainstream. We still have corporate and independent media, but the circuitry that connects them has been scrambled. At the top of the pile are the global megastars with their cross-platform multimedia integration strategies and product endorsement deals. Kanye, Taylor, Drake and Rihanna are a new kind of superstar. Instead of a star–fan connection that was cultivated via records, TV appearances, interviews and concerts – all discrete objects and experiences – we now have a constant, real-time stream of updates and micro-intimacies. Stars used to go quiet between albums, retreat to their country mansions, roam their grounds gathering their strength for the next assault on the reality principle. Today the contact is constant, the performance unending. Pop stars are both closer and more distant than ever, the products of a culture of sampling and collage that originated with hip hop and techno and was accelerated by digital technology.

But the internet has also unleashed a very long tail of micro-scenes and niches, each of which exists in its own digital habitat and is largely insulated from the wider cultural ecosystem. New styles and sub-genres spread laterally via discussion boards and social media, rather than being filtered slowly into the mainstream by corporate gatekeepers. It's hard to tell where the centre and the periphery are, and harder still to map the routes by which new genres and styles make the journey between the two. Even in the most recherché sub-cultural scenes you get the sense of constant and furious labour, of everyone working all the time to win followers and make an impression in the general hubbub of social media.

In reality, the process of splitting and sub-division had already begun well before the arrival of the internet. American commercial radio stations were sub-divided by genre and demographic in the 1980s. MTV created shows aimed at specific audience demographics ever since its inception in 1983. It may have traded on the ideal of youth culture as a unitary force, but it categorised audiences by taste, geography and race. For many years, hip hop was entirely absent from the MTV schedule, and it took the success of artists like Run DMC and Public Enemy to prompt the channel to start 'Yo! MTV Raps' in 1987. The idea of a unified popular culture is as mythopoetic as dreams of Arthurian Camelot or the classical Greek fantasy of the golden age. And yet, things were different back then, in that distant time of 1992, when there was a vibrant alternative music press, independent record stores and music venues were dotted throughout the provincial hinterlands, and there was a real sense of insurgency when something new, something unbidden and spiky, made its way into the still narrow channel of the mainstream. We might not have been fully aware of it at the time, but the relative scarcity and difficulty of access enhanced the value of our niche interests. It made a difference that the materials for cultural dreaming and aesthetic self-creation were more than just a mouse click away.

All of this was encapsulated in the now legendary ascent of Nirvana, the reluctant kings of Seattle grunge, from regional indie obscurity to corporate rock mega-success, and the elevation of Kurt Cobain to the dubious office of 'voice of a generation'. It is almost embarrassing to discuss Nirvana in a historical study of the 1990s. Nirvana were so outrageously popular, so freighted with heavyweight rock 'n' roll symbolism, and subsequently so done to death by the heritage rock industry, that they seem somehow unworthy of further comment. Better perhaps to turn the spotlight on the more obscure corners of the early 1990s indie scene – the Shonen Knifes and Sebadohs of the world, deep-scene auteurs who haven't yet been co-opted by the nostalgists and the hacks. But embarrassment is an essential part of the Nirvana story, and Nirvana were the great emblems of the 1990s agon of 'selling out'. When they became the biggest alternative rock band in the world, Nirvana were themselves embarrassed at the sheer scale of their success, discomfited at their newfound fame and wealth, ashamed of their new frat boy fans, and mortified at having chosen to be a part of the grotesque corporate media spectacle.

Nirvana released their global mega-selling album, *Nevermind*, on 24 September 1991, fifteen years after the Sex Pistols' gig at the Lesser Free Trade Hall in Manchester that launched the first wave of punk. You can trace a direct line from the Sex Pistols to Nirvana via Black Flag and the mid-1980s hardcore scene, regional Washington State indie labels like K Records and Sub Pop, the Evergreen College radio station, KAOS, cassette-sharing culture and underground zines. *Nevermind* sold 30 million copies worldwide and Nirvana became one of the biggest bands on the planet, but the source of their appeal lay in their DIY punk ethos and anti-corporate messthetics – their ripped jeans, decomposing sneakers, unkempt hair and mumblecore refusal to play the media game of self-promotion and accessibility.

Make no mistake, Nirvana wanted to cross over into the mainstream as their slacker brethren Sonic Youth and Dinosaur Jr. had done before them. But in doing so they got more – much more – than they had bargained for. In an interview in 1993 Kurt reminisced about the months leading up to the release of *Nevermind*: 'The most exciting time for a band is right before they become really popular. I'd love to be in bands that just do that every two years.' I'm prepared to bet that none of my readers have ever been in a triple-platinum-album-selling alternative rock band; but I'd also wager that many will still be able to recognise Kurt's wistful glance back at the moment just before the wave crested and the band's desires were fulfilled as the point of maximum enjoyment. What is true for indie rock is also true for so much else in life: it is in the pursuit rather than the attainment of our desires that we are most happy. Kurt's statement also captures some of the fundamental ambivalence of Generation X: he is torn between the allure and magic and righteous insurgency of making it big, but also saddened by the hollowness of success on the terms of the market.

Nevermind was designed for populist appeal. Nirvana's first album, *Bleach*, which was released in 1989 by Sub Pop Records, was a thick, treacly paste of heavy punk rock, the musical equivalent of drinking a bottle of cough syrup and beating your head against the wall. *Nevermind* retained the distorted guitars and heavy drums but added a melodious pop sheen and crisp, radio-friendly production – more treble, a cleaner finish, but still scratchy, loud and propulsive. One of the things that made Nirvana stand out from the crowd of alt rock and grunge bands that emerged in the early 1990s was that they were really, really good at what they did. There was a sense on *Nevermind* of a whole range of influences – punk, heavy metal, art rock and even classic pop in the vein of the Beatles – being woven together in just the right way to create something thrilling and new. *Nevermind*'s crossover ambitions were signalled in its ironic cover art, which depicted a naked baby immersed in a clear blue swimming pool, his outstretched arms reaching towards a dollar bill on a fishhook. It is an album cover as instantly recognisable – and as easily comprehensible – as *Sgt Pepper* or *Dark Side of the Moon*: faux innocence, a nod to the 1960s ideal of rebirth and rejuvenation, a hint at the early 1990s cultural mood of going with the flow and casual hedonism, but also an anti-corporate statement on the cover of a corporate-produced rock album. What could be more '90s than that?

On 11 January 1992 *Nevermind* knocked Michael Jackson's *Dangerous* off the number one spot in Billboard's list of 200 bestselling albums. Zoom out just a little bit and the effect of cultural whiplash – of clashing styles and values – is magnified. In America, the bestselling albums of 1990 and 1991 were by Paula Abdul, Sinead O'Connor, Bonnie Raitt, MC Hammer, New Kids on the Block, Vanilla Ice, Mariah Carey, R.E.M., Michael Bolton, N.W.A., Skid Row, Van Halen, Garth Brooks, Guns 'n' Roses and U2. Alongside R.E.M. and N.W.A., Nirvana stick out like a bunch of punks at the school disco. This was a powerful jolt of weirdness and negativity amid the pop pabulum. The climax of 'Smells Like Teen Spirit', Nirvana's biggest hit single, encapsulated this sense of refusal as Kurt hollers over the distorted wall of guitar noise, 'a denial, a denial, a denial'. It was unclear precisely what Kurt was denying – mainstream rock, Reaganism, a new pair of jeans? – but the emotional and sonic power were beyond doubt.

The fun didn't last for long. For Kurt, the ascent from provincial obscurity to a lakefront mansion on the same block as Bill Gates of Microsoft and Howard Schultz of Starbucks was accompanied by a tendency to depressive self-loathing that was only magnified by superstardom. At the peak of Nirvana's success, he and his partner, Courtney Love, a punk star in her own right with a million-dollar contract with Geffen Records, found themselves at the centre of a global media storm. Heroin addiction, intra-band strife, incoherent and evasive public statements, clouds of industry gossip and erratic live shows all fed the tabloid whirlwind. At the eye of the storm, slumped and heavily opiated, Kurt and Courtney seemed to be undergoing a self-imposed deceleration, a fogged and clotted resignation amid the sped-up circuits of the corporate media industry.

The sense of paranoia and antagonism was stoked by a disastrous profile of Courtney in *Vanity Fair*, in which she appeared heavily pregnant and naked from the waist down, and which included anonymous quotes from industry sources claiming that she had used heroin in the early stages of her pregnancy. As a result of the article, the Los Angeles County Child Protection Services department started an investigation; custody of their child, Frances Bean, was granted to Courtney's sister and a prolonged legal battle ensued. The article was also shining proof of the feminist argument that underpinned the Riot Grrrl movement, which sprang from the same underground scene as grunge: that female artists were held to a different standard than their male counterparts. Riot Grrrl was not just about mosh pit ethics – although bands like Bikini Kill and Babes in Toyland first made waves in the punk scene by requiring men to stand at the back of gigs so that women could occupy the centre ground – but a much wider attack on the media's objectification of women and perpetuation of patriarchy. The myth of the apathetic, apolitical 1990s evaporates on contact with Riot Grrrl.

Was Kurt Cobain's suicide on 5 April 1994 a generational event? For the vast majority of young people around the world, probably not. Nirvana were big and the mediasphere was less fragmented than it is today, but their impact was tiny compared to generational super-events like the Apollo moon landing or JFK's assassination or the magical arrival of Elvis in everybody's lives. For Nirvana's devoted fans, though, Kurt's death was very big news indeed, perhaps the biggest in their short lives thus far (it made more of an impression on my 15-year-old self than, say, the fall of the Berlin Wall or the conflict in Bosnia). And for the 10,000 people who gathered at the Seattle Centre when the news broke it was an occasion for public mourning and collective grief. At the vigil, fans listened to Courtney read Kurt's suicide note, which was addressed to his childhood imaginary friend, and denounce him as an asshole for taking the easy way out. They also listened to Krist Novoselic, Kurt's long-time friend and Nirvana's bassist, who asked that people remember the band's commitment to the punk principle that no group was special and no singer a god. Even in the midst of their bereavement, Kurt's loved ones stayed true to the punk values of schism and dissent.

Nirvana were the biggest and most embarrassing expression of the challenge that faced many of the alternative acts that made it big in the 1990s:

what do you do when you arrive? After the initial rush of breaking through has subsided, how do you use your time in the spotlight? How do you remain true to your principles? Is it even possible to have principles when you also have unlimited access to champagne, drugs and groupies?

The history of 1990s alternative music could be rewritten as a series of hare-brained, improvisatory answers to these questions. Kurt Cobain's response took the form of mumbling reticence, heartfelt blues, awkwardness, self-sabotage, heroin and suicide. For the Riot Grrrls, the answers were more explicitly political. Kathleen Hanna and Tobi Vail would sometimes play gigs with 'slut' and 'whore' daubed in lipstick on their bare midriffs. They used the media spotlight as an occasion for a feminist punk performance that reclaimed the language of sexist insult for their own uses. For Richey Edwards of the Manic Street Preachers, perhaps the most high-minded and overtly political British band of the era, the answer was carved into his forearm with a razor blade. In 1991 at a music industry press junket, Edwards carved '4 REAL' into his own flesh in response to a journalist who had suggested that the group's flamboyant punk style was just for show. On the eve of the Britpop phenomenon, Edwards's statement could be read either as a pre-emptive defence against the blizzard of tabloid hype and vacuous claims to zeitgeist-defining relevance that was about to descend upon British indie music, or as the self-harming behaviour of a troubled young man who would famously disappear – presumed to have taken his own life – in February 1995.

When that blizzard did descend, the response from most bands was a lairy, wised-up, more often than not intoxicated, shrug. Blur, Oasis, Elastica, Sleeper and all the lesser lights of the scene made a dash for the limelight only to mince and pout in disdain when they got there. For the luminaries of Britpop, public intoxication took the place of the political and artistic radicalism of prior generations of alternative musicians. This was certainly the case when Jarvis Cocker drunkenly stormed the stage during Michael Jackson's performance at the Brit Awards in 1996. The scuffle lasted little more than a few seconds, but Cocker was taken away for questioning at Kentish Town Police Station after some of the children who were performing on stage with Jackson complained – rather ironically in hindsight – that their safety had been compromised by the gangly indie star's antics. The following morning, Cocker's record label released a statement claiming that he had been protesting the music industry's support of the messianic delusions of an over-indulged pop star. This *ex post facto* rationale was quickly drowned out in the tabloid chatter.

What would you do if you found yourself, even for a brief moment, at the shimmering centre of the spotlight? How would you respond? Would you issue a manifesto, get totally wasted, or throw a bucket of ice water over the head of a government minister, as Danbert Nobacon of the anarcho-pop collective Chumbawamba did when their hit single 'Tubthumping' placed them in the spotlight for a short season at the end of the 1990s? Most of us will never get to find out and, even if we did, it's unlikely that we'd be able to muster the perverse surrealist genius of The KLF, the 'stadium trance' rave act who in 1992 staged their own violent exit from the music industry when they deleted their entire back catalogue, strafed the audience at the Brit Awards with blank-firing machine guns and tossed a dead sheep at the door of the after party bearing the militant vegetarian message, 'I died for you – bon appetit'. In 1994, the group emerged briefly from obscurity in order to stage the ritual burning of £1 million in ready currency (the best part of The KLF's career earnings) in a tumbledown barn on Jura, the Hebridean island where George Orwell had written *1984*. The K Foundation invited a single journalist along to witness the ceremony, which they recorded on a cheap camcorder and later screened at a series of small arts venues around the country. The poster for the screenings posed the following urgent questions:

> Why did the K Foundation burn a million quid? Was it a crime? Was it a burnt offering? Was it madness? Was it an investment? Was it Rock 'n' Roll? Was it an obscenity? Was it art? Was it a political statement? Was it bollocks?

And after that, they disappeared from view. Bill Drummond and Jimmy Cauty, who in 1991 sold more singles than any other band in the entire world, exited the music industry having torched the entirety of their earnings. Of all the statements that were made, of all the poses that were struck when the 1990s underground had its brief moment in the spotlight, this was surely the most radical of all. The KLF violated one of the few real taboos of the age, a moral injunction so subtly present in all of our lives as to be almost imperceptible: get rich, be successful, make your voice heard! Maybe silence and renunciation were the best strategies of all.

6

You Take Me Higher and Higher

PERHAPS THE best way to represent the history of rave music would be in the form of an interactive computer simulation, which would chart the spread of new musical styles and scenes as they travelled through time and space. Something like Google Earth for techno-heads. The user would be able to zoom in on particular locations at different stages in the music's development, such as the Berlin techno scene in 1989, just after the fall of the Wall, or the breakthrough of jungle in London around 1993, or the spread, party by party, of the trance scene in Goa and southern India in the early 1990s. Following a simple key of coded colours and symbols, you'd be able to trace the local networks of producers, DJs, radio stations, record labels, clubs, parties and drug distribution chains that made up each scene. You could follow the lines of flight as they spread through specific streets and neighbourhoods then arrow out to new locations, where they spark a new pattern of interwoven connections as the music scales up from underground niche to regional, national or even international scene.

This method of representing rave's viral spread would be true to the original spirit of the movement, which privileged the collective intelligence of the scene over the ideal of the individual genius or the heroic auteur. Many of the tracks that defined the early years of rave music were made by bedroom producers who made little money and gained meagre recognition for their efforts. Over the course of the 1990s, as 'club culture' grew into a mass-market phenomenon, a star system emerged and people would pay huge sums to see big name DJs in lavish superclubs, but the original ethos of rave was collectivist. The crowd was the star. The scene was the source of energy and inspiration. The technology was a creative force that could be channelled for the enjoyment of swarming crowds of dancers, but never mastered or exhausted.

The music itself celebrated this distributed, linked-up, techno-futuristic way of being: metallic clicks and rasps; the whooshing and whirring of engines; sirens, horns, drills, pumps; scraping, churning, blasting, hoovering; delicate mists of digital information; the sound of a thousand ball bearings dropped on a glass tabletop. The iconography of the scene also drew attention to its wide-eyed futurism. Flyers for early raves depicted cyborg dancers, abstract patterns of grids and lines, fractal geometries and molecular structures, UFOs and spaceships, the sublime vistas of futuristic cities. This was a sub-culture that thrilled to the open-ended possibility of the future and the imminent merging of man with machine. Even the new drug culture that accompanied it, based on the psychedelic euphoria of MDMA or 'ecstasy', sought to convert human neurochemistry into a programmable box of tricks.

Rather than a centre of rational will and action, the self was transformed into a series of chemically engineered intensities, consciousness released into the wider system of the music, the crowd and the club.

The first blips on our interactive map pulse into life in Paris and Milan in the early twentieth century. The European avant-garde thrilled to the possibility of merging man and machine to create a new art form for the twentieth century. Fernand Leger and Dudley Murphy set humans and machines dancing together in their 1924 experimental film *Ballet Mechnique*, but it was the Italian futurist composer Luigi Russolo who was the earliest precursor of techno music. In his 1913 manifesto, Russolo hymned the power of industrial machinery to extend mankind's musical sensibilities and imagined a new 'art of noises' wrought directly from the industrial world itself. Russolo even built a collection of mechanical instruments – including the 'burster', the 'scraper', the 'crackler' and the 'howler' – in order to bring this new art into existence; but in an era before electronic amplification the results failed to match up to the awesome soundscapes of the city street or the factory floor.

A more immediate precursor to rave music, a denser constellation on our growing heatmap, were Kraftwerk, the 1970s synth-pop duo from Dusseldorf. With their cool, sleek compositions about the elegance of the pocket calculator and the joys of travelling on the Autobahn system, Kraftwerk sought to erase the human touch from modern music. In their public personae, they played with the appeal of becoming robotic, of ceding the burdensome human will to the dictates of electronic machinery. And yet, somehow, in their mechanically rigid way, they were also deeply funky. Their tightly wound, minimalist compositions seemed to distil the essence of dance music before it had even been born. On tracks like 'Trans-Europe Express' and 'Robots', you can hear the genetic script of house and techno beginning to coalesce.

The true origin points for rave culture, however, the moment when a whole new musical phylum came into existence, were Detroit and Chicago in the second half of the 1980s. On our interactive map, sometime around 1987, key neighbourhoods, nightclubs and record stores in these two cities start to glow with an intensity not previously seen. In Detroit, the action was centred in Belleville, a semi-rural suburb roughly 25 miles from the downtown core. Here, the Belleville Three – Juan Atkins, Derrick May and Kevin Saunderson – invented techno music. Alongside the Euro minimalism of Kraftwerk, the Detroit pioneers drew their influences from the far-out space funk of George Clinton, the electro hip hop of Afrika Bambaataa, the synth-pop of Yellow Magic Orchestra and the Human League, and the harder, faster edges of disco music such as Donna Summer's 'I Feel Love'. From this mix of inspirations flowed definitive techno tracks like Model 500's 'No UFOs' and Eddie Flashin' Fowlkes's 'Goodbye Kiss'. The Detroit sound isolated and intensified the beat that runs through earlier forms of electronic music. With techno, the beat is harder, faster and more central to the overall structure of the track. On top of this foundation, techno adds a sonic palette that accentuates the alien otherness of machine-made music: claps, rasps, stabs, distorted voices, cascading sheets of metallic noise.

The Belleville Three all came from relatively affluent, middle-class Black families. Their parents worked in management or as shop stewards in the Detroit auto industry. Theirs was not a music of ghetto realism or bluesy complaint, but instead of upwardly mobile aspiration. They were not dancefloor hedonists, as later generations of techno producers tended to be, but cerebral experimentalists, driven by an ideal of techno-futurism, anti-corporate self-empowerment and a certain fantasy of European style and sophistication. The futuristic soundscapes of early techno embodied a subtly political vision: this was an alternative signal that emanated from somewhere beyond the bland consensus of mainstream media. It was a disruption of normal service, a pathway towards a different kind of future.

Techno music was just one of many cultural forms that emerged in the 1980s and 1990s from the interaction between human creativity and new technology, including hip hop, computer hacking, videogame design and cyberpunk movies and novels. In their various ways, these sub-cultures all espoused the cyberpunk ethos expressed in William Gibson's seminal short story 'Burning Chrome': 'the street finds its own uses for things'. In the era of high-tech digital capitalism, freedom is to be found not by escaping from the clutches of the system and rejecting modernity, as many of the countercultural movements of the 1960s sought to do, but instead via the renegade use of technology. Corporate control is challenged by the inventive and often illicit use to which its products are put by samplers, DJs, graphic artists, pirate radio broadcasters and illegal party organisers – anyone who uses the technology for ends other than it was originally intended.

The other new constellation on the map at this early stage is Chicago, where a second strain of electronic dance music was being born: house music. House was named for the legendary Chicago club, the Warehouse, where in the early 1980s DJ Frankie Knuckles mixed disco, funk, electro pop and hip hop for a mainly gay African American crowd. House was built from the same technological and sonic ingredients as techno: the Roland TB 303 and 808 drum machines, the Korg Poly-61 synthesiser, the driving beat and the alien electronic sounds. But there is a tonal difference from techno. House is a music of uplift and celebration. Early tracks such as Steve 'Silk' Hurley's 1986 'Jack Your Body' or Marshall Jefferson's 1987 'Work Your Body' used warmer sounds and incorporated elements of traditional musicianship, such as vocals, piano and saxophone. But these elements were underpinned by a raw, even raunchy beat, an insistent, driving force that urged listeners to cede control, to lose themselves in the physical pleasure of dancing. In its original context of gay African American and Latino dance clubs, house music was a form of spiritual communion for people who might otherwise have been excluded from traditional places of worship, and a refuge from the AIDS crisis of the 1980s.

By 1987–88, our map has a dense grid of connections centred on Chicago and Detroit, the two great cities of the American mid-west. Now that the system has reached a certain threshold it starts to send out shoots across the Atlantic as the new sounds are imported to Europe. New lines of connection can be traced from Detroit and Chicago to Berlin, Frankfurt, Riga, Ghent, Brussels, Ibiza, London and Manchester. New blips appear on our screen as new scenes are formed. The heat map is densest around clubs such as Amnesia in Ibiza, UFO and Tresor in Berlin, Shoom in London and the Hacienda in Manchester, European rave culture's handful of authentic ground zeros. From these points of first contact fresh constellations started to grow. Parties sprung up in disused warehouses, derelict office buildings, commercial river boats and farmers' fields, then melted back into the map, only to be followed by new heat traces that glowed in and out of existence as the weeks rolled on and the scene spread. Over time, more permanent club nights were established. Record shops opened and labels were founded. Radio stations, some legal, but many more pirate operations, broadcast the new sounds from urban hot spots out into the far-flung provinces. Thousands of smaller, fainter, but potentially transformative lines of flight bolted out into the dark spaces of the map, where listeners waited, ready to be plugged into the system.

In Chicago and Detroit house and techno were small scale, local, still marginal scenes, but in Europe the music fuelled a whole new youth cultural movement with its own collective rituals and ideals. In Berlin, the Love Parade, which began in 1989 as a motley collection of fewer than 200 underground party freaks marching to a techno beat in support of 'peace, joy and pancakes', grew within the space of a decade into a million-strong annual street party attracting visitors from around the globe. In southern England in the summers of 1988 and 1989, illegal raves in fields around London's M25 orbital ring road drew as many as 30,000 people. The 'second summer of love', as this was dubbed, saw hundreds of thousands of people flocking to raves and nightclubs throughout the country, in what can only be described as a giant surge of popular psychedelia. Ecstasy became a central part of the experience, a kind of social sacrament that intensified the pleasure of the music and inducted new users into the blissed-out, loved-up vibe. Rave anthems like the D Mob's 'We Call it Acieed' and the Prodigy's 'Charly' started to climb into the Top 40 music charts. The new sonic textures of house and techno shimmered at the edges of a much wider public consciousness, and by the mid-1990s had been adopted by superstars like Bjork and Madonna, who acted as cultural brokers between the underground and the mainstream.

Over the course of the 1990s, as our already busy map glows with ever more nodes and connections, electronic dance music becomes a site of rapid, almost frenzied innovation. A kind of creative misrecognition took place when house and techno crossed the pond. From the original source material sprang hundreds of distinct genres and sub-genres, many of which became self-contained scenes with few if any connections to other parts of the musical ecosystem: house, techno, trance, jungle, garage, gabba, happy hardcore and all of their various sub-sub-genres, such as hard house, hip house, tech house, deep house, etc. Many music critics dismissed this manic proliferation of styles as a sign of rave's ephemerality and the po-faced pretentions of its fans. But the process of splitting and sub-division was driven as much by the technology itself as by the ambitions of its users. The music developed almost with a life of its own, filling previously empty spaces on our map with new sounds and scenes, greedily absorbing energy and influence from the local cultures it met along the way.

Berlin, for instance, embraced the sharper edges of Detroit techno, which seemed to resonate with its rubble-strewn expanses of no-man's-land and the decaying urban infrastructure left over after the fall of communism. Over time, a local variant emerged – harder, faster and more intense than its original source material, a music designed to pummel the body with wave upon wave of abstract machine noise. In the more carefree UK, the Ibiza-inspired acid house sound proliferated. DJs mixed original Detroit and Chicago tracks with a new strain of home-grown music, which often added whistles and sirens, distorted and sped-up vocal samples, acid squiggles, crude but highly effective piano riffs and faster beats to the original DNA. Acid house and its bastard offspring 'hardcore' mixed the far out and the cartoonish, the psychedelic and the zany. The styles of dress and iconography followed the same pattern: flared baggy jeans, high-end sportswear and bright, Day-Glo colours, the smiley symbol, glow sticks, whistles, white gloves. This was yet another of the great British youth sub-cultures, akin to the Teds, Mods and punks of prior eras. Around 1993, hardcore spawned jungle, a hybrid variant built around super-fast breakbeats, Jamaican dub-inflected bass sounds and gangsta-style samples and iconography. Jungle was pioneered by Black British producers, who adapted the hardcore rave sound to their own ends, mixing the buzzy, techno-centric elements of electronic dance music with the sounds and textures of Afro-Caribbean music.

When they were flown over to perform in Europe, the Chicago and Detroit pioneers were often taken aback by the scale of the phenomenon they had helped to spark. Some also shrank from the druggier, more populist tone the scene adopted in some of its new locations, especially in the UK's vast working-class rave mobilisation. There was more sympathy in the early days between Detroit and Berlin, based on a high-minded appreciation for the music and a more politicised understanding of the scene. But most of its more prominent proponents were happy to accept the bookings and build lucrative careers as superstar DJ-producers and legendary fathers of the movement. Throughout the 1990s, the music remained marginal in North America. There were small underground scenes in Chicago and Detroit, neo-hippy rave enclaves in San Francisco and California and a hipster scene in New York, but rave never became the mass youth culture that it did in Europe. Mainstream American tastes were still hooked on grunge, heavy rock, country and hip hop. For many American listeners, dance music was too feminine, too gay, too European.

By the mid-2000s, though, dance music had reached a semi-stable state. The last really new genres to emerge – the last musics that seemed to require a whole new category of their own, rather than a sub-category within an already established genre – were dubstep in the late 1990s and grime in the early 2000s. Both sounds have travelled a long way from the neo-psychedelic hedonism that characterised the birth of the movement not much more than a decade earlier. In fact, some of the best dubstep tracks function as memorials for the end of rave culture, or at least bitter-sweet musings on the time passed and intensity lost since the early 1990s. Burial's 2007 'Raver' and Zomby's 2008 'Where Were U in '92?' entomb early rave sounds in a fog of distortion and crackle, as though rave wasn't just a hazy memory, but a transmission from another epoch, maybe even another world.

↖↑↗

There are two schools of thought about the political significance of rave culture. On the one hand, there are those who see rave as the last flowering of the counter-cultural movements that began in the late 1950s and 1960s. You can draw an unbroken line, so the story goes, from the jazz freaks, beatniks and New Left radicals who sparked the counterculture into life in the 1950s to the warehouse parties and sound systems of the early 1990s. From this perspective, rave culture was a radical alternative to the social atomisation of the post-Thatcher era, a form of political opposition to the market society that flourished unchallenged in the wake of communism's collapse. It may not have had an overtly ideological message beyond a vague will to inclusivity and freedom, but raving did create new forms of social solidarity that were all the more powerful for being site specific and face to face. The sheer physical presence of thousands of people dancing in a field was a challenge to the Thatcherite doctrine that 'there is no such thing as society. There are individual men and women and there are families.' Here was a self-generating series of large, joyous, non-familial collectives which gathered outside the law and in defiance of the age's dominant social philosophy.

On the other hand, there are those who see rave culture as a distraction from genuine political struggle, and perhaps even as an embodiment of the self-interested entrepreneurialism espoused by Thatcher and her followers. From this perspective, the hedonism of 1990s dance music looks more like decadent thrill seeking than political radicalism. Earlier counter-cultural movements had clear political programmes, and their musical expressions – rock 'n' roll, punk, reggae, hip hop, etc. – made explicit reference to wider campaigns for political and social reform (nuclear disarmament, anti-apartheid, Rock Against Racism, etc.). Apart from a few street protests against government attempts to crack down on illegal parties, the energy and resources of rave culture were almost entirely focused on perpetuating the scene itself, on organising and sustaining each new party, not on bringing about lasting political change.

After the miraculous early days in Ibiza, Berlin, London and Manchester, rave culture rapidly grew into a much larger, less idealistic phenomenon. Underground scenes continued to exist, but more commercially minded and opportunistic operators took the music overground. Rather than a radical counterculture, electronic dance music became part of the legal night-time economy, its outlaw origins used as a neat marketing hook to attract new clients. Ultimately, rave became just another sub-system within – or perhaps even a particularly potent expression of – the vast system of global capitalism. For most dance music fans, raving was a weekend escape rather than a campaign for social liberation, a Bacchanalian holiday from the daily grind that ultimately served to confirm the inevitability of that daily grind.

There are elements of truth in both positions, and each can be used to explain different aspects of what was in reality a diverse set of musical subcultures, rather than a single, unitary phenomenon. What the critic Simon Reynolds calls the 'hardcore continuum' stretched from darkcore jungle to Goa trance, and from acid techno to progressive house. The crazy speed of rave's early development spun off a whole cosmos of alternative worlds in the space of only a few years. Some of these worlds were so different, in fact, that their denizens were reluctant to acknowledge their common ancestry.

By the midpoint of the 1990s, fans of acid techno and progressive house were like two separate tribes in my sixth form college in the West Midlands. The acid techno-heads went to free parties in the Welsh hills, organised by anarcho-punk New Age Travellers. In addition to large quantities of ecstasy, they took LSD, magic mushrooms and ketamine – all serious, mind-bending psychedelic drugs. They dressed in a hybridised uniform of combat fatigues and scuffed-up sportswear with nods to the hippy counterculture that still thrived in the 'great green lung' of mid-Wales: t-shirts with fractal patterns, ethnic fabrics, beads and bracelets. The progressive house-heads dressed in box-fresh brand-name clothes. They went to expensive nightclubs in Birmingham, Liverpool and Manchester, where they faced the gauntlet of exclusive door policies which turned away those who didn't look right for the occasion. They hung out in trendy bars rather than fleapit pubs. They tended to be into buzzy, sociable drugs like ecstasy and cocaine, rather than mind-expanding trips on acid and mushrooms. They seemed to bathe more frequently. There were points of overlap between the two tribes – a free party in a disused warehouse on the outskirts of town where the clubbers and the crusties came together – but on the whole, they occupied two separate cultural ecosystems, each with its own set of values and ideals. The acid techno-heads saw themselves as renegade outsiders; the house-heads just wanted to have a good time.

Perhaps it's not possible, in the end, to make a definitive judgement about the political significance of rave culture as a whole. But I can't help but be drawn to the first perspective: the idea that rave harboured some kind of utopian potential. Rave music is a strangely polarising phenomenon. From the outside, without first-hand experience of MDMA-induced euphoria, it can all seem a bit silly, a bit inconsequential. Jarvis Cocker summed up the outsider's perspective in Pulp's 1995 Britpop anthem, 'Sorted for E's & Wizz': 'Is this the way the future's meant to feel? / Or just twenty thousand people standing in a field?' But from the inside, raving can be a powerfully transformative experience. Rave's seemingly apolitical stance was a product of the time in which it first emerged: the post-Cold War, post-ideological, 'no alternative' late 1980s and early 1990s. Rather than a party-political programme, what rave offered was a new take on the politics of joy, the question of who gets to enjoy life to its fullest, and precisely what kind of potential humanity is capable of. Tony Wilson, founder of legendary Manchester nightclub the Hacienda, once described the rave experience as a kind of universal social lubricant, a way of tapping into a fundamental joyfulness in all people: 'You could take any human being, of any sort, to the Hacienda from mid-89 onwards and they would just love it. Human beings love fun and happiness and exuberance, and it was the epitome of that.'

The idea of electronic dance music as a vehicle for human connectivity is the golden thread that runs throughout the scene as a whole, from the illegal rave to the commercial super-club. In *Der Klang der Familie*, a seminal oral history of the early Berlin techno scene, interviewees repeatedly return to the idealistic hope that the sense of ecstatic solidarity generated on the dancefloor would spread throughout society. One of them, Andreas Rossman, talks about:

> The distinct feeling that we were changing the world ... Again and again, you saw how it swept along totally normal people, how the mentality changed, the manner of social interaction. A natural ease spread ... there really was this family feeling about it, and it extended to everyone.

Rossman's observation that a 'natural ease spread' has the ring of Enlightenment experimental philosophy. It could be a line from the radical chemist Humphrey Davy's notebooks recording his famous experiments with nitrous oxide in the 1790s, as though the combination of techno beats, dry ice, laser strobes and MDMA was a new kind of natural element that could reveal previously undiscovered facets of human nature. For the East and West Berliners who came together on the dancefloor after the fall of the Wall, techno music was a way to overcome the trauma of recent history, a blank slate on which to inscribe new and better ways of being together.

In this respect, rave culture was an implicit riposte to Fukuyama's end-of-history thesis. Fukuyama claimed that with the end of the Cold War, the great ideological struggles of the twentieth century had come to an end. History, in the sense of the clash of competing visions of human civilisation, was over. The bourgeois liberal democratic state would now be recognised as the only viable way to satisfy the requirements of human nature in all regions of the world. But rave culture looked forward to a utopian future that would be fundamentally different from the present, and it espoused a vision of human nature – albeit in the rather fuzzy, ill-defined way that stems from ecstatic experiences on the dancefloor – that was less self-interested than the neoliberal vision of *homo economicus* and less susceptible to the drives for recognition and status that Fukuyama saw as potential threats to the stability of the liberal order. The anarchist philosopher Hakim Bey famously included raves as one of his 'temporary autonomous zones', spaces apart from mainstream society where different social laws can operate for limited periods of time.

The total remaking of society never occurred, but rave's wider social impact has been considerable, even if it has rarely been recognised within mainstream histories. In a sense, rave was the final democratisation of the 1960s counterculture. In the UK, the psychedelic sixties were largely confined to an elite group of middle- and upper-class insiders within London's alternative arts and media scenes. The imagery and ideals filtered out into the wider culture, but the scale of flower power's influence has been overstated by a thousand bad documentaries. The impact of rave culture, by contrast, has likely been undersold, largely due to the media focus on the trad guitar sounds of grunge and Britpop. Rave culture was a truly populist neo-psychedelic movement, which was embraced by huge numbers of ordinary people.

Even much of Britpop itself, especially the woozy 'Be Here Now' uplift of Oasis, bears the traces of rave's heady positivity. It wasn't until around 1996–97 that Britpop congealed into the clichés that are remembered today: the Union Jack guitars, the laddish escapades, the drinks with the prime minister. In the early part of the decade, indie guitar rock was more often mixed up with Balearic-style dance music and funk-oriented sampledelia. Primal Scream and the Happy Mondays – as well as less celebrated names like Flowered Up and Transglobal Underground – dissolved indie rock in an acid bath of downtempo dance beats. The most enduring group to emerge from this fertile territory were Saint Etienne, who, on their 1991 album *Foxbase Alpha*, blended their love of classic 1960s pop with the new sounds that could be heard emanating from warehouse parties and pirate radio stations throughout their native London. Saint Etienne were featured alongside Blur and Oasis on the famous cover of *Select* magazine that announced the advent of Britpop in 1993, but in many ways they represent a path not taken for British music culture in the 1990s: Europhile, cosmopolitan, hedonistic, multi-cultural and, most importantly, self-consciously of the moment.

The wider effects of rave's sudden injection of good vibes and loved-up inclusivity were impressive. One of the legends of the early acid house scene was its potential to convert violent football hooligans into smiley ravers in the short time it took to come up on an E. Deeply rooted in gay African American sub-cultures, acid house also helped to dissolve homophobic and sexist attitudes, at least among the members of the younger generation who took to the dancefloor. It's easy to forget today, but in the late 1980s and early 1990s public attitudes to homosexuality were often far from progressive. In the UK, Section 28 of the 1988 Local Government Act explicitly outlawed 'promoting homosexuality' or the teaching of 'homosexuality as a pretended family relationship' in state schools. Across much of Europe and North America, same-sex partnerships weren't granted legal status until the 2000s. Acid house and its many musical children helped to mainstream the ethos of acceptance and joy that had underpinned radical gay sub-cultures throughout the 1970s and 1980s.

The shift from alcohol to ecstasy as the stimulant of choice also helped to change the landscape of heterosexual desire and gender relations. Ecstasy tends to produce generalised, non-specific feelings of love and connectivity, rather than immediate libidinous need. The E'd up dancefloor was home to a thousand micro-affections – smiles, hugs, back rubs, thumbs ups, shared water, etc. – rather than come-ons and chat up lines. 'Fuck sex, let's dance' was the general idea. At its best, you might say, rave culture encouraged a move away from everyday sexism towards a looser, more open-minded sexuality. Even in the slickest, most commercialised superclubs in the late 1990s, clubbers were in touch with a hybridised version of the alternative culture that originally emanated from Chicago and Detroit. Drop into the Ministry of Sound in London, Cream in Liverpool or Gatecrasher in Sheffield circa 1997 and you'd find thousands of otherwise quite ordinary British youths dancing to the sounds of gay Black liberation and indulging, if only for a night, in feelings of collective euphoria and universal good will.

Throughout most the twentieth-century's great age of prohibition, drugs have been secretive, background influences on the culture at large. They might have been absent from official discourse, but we can detect their traces everywhere from the cocaine-fuelled Jazz Age of the 1920s to the art and music of the psychedelic sixties. But in the 1990s, while drug use remained illegal, it became relatively unstigmatised. After the initial moral panic about rave culture died down, public references to ecstasy and other hard drugs became fairly common. Noel Gallagher famously said that taking drugs was as commonplace as 'getting up in the morning and having a cup of tea'. Even the UK government's official drug tsar, Professor David Nutt, later joined in the chorus of normalisation when he declared that, based on all of the available data, taking ecstasy was no more dangerous than horse riding.

While statements like these seem to have bought a kind of familiarity, if not outright respectability, for drug use, they did so at the expense of rendering the process somewhat banal. The whole point of psychedelic experience is that it's not routine, it's not like getting up in the morning and having a cup of tea. The ironic, irreverent style of 1990s popular culture made it all too easy to dismiss drug taking as *mere* hedonism. Looking back on his own drug-fuelled antics in the 1990s, the philosopher Jules Evans takes a more high-minded view, describing himself and his friends not as 'wasted' and 'mashed' hedonists but as 'amateur neuroscientists', who experimented with molecules that harboured the power to radically alter human consciousness without any real clue as to their potential consequences.

The insight applies to the culture as a whole, as well as to the individuals within it. Rave culture was a giant, uncontrolled neurochemical experiment, which released a surge of psychedelic experience in millions of brains around the world. It is impossible to gauge the results of that experiment with any accuracy. But it's worth pointing out that almost all of the characteristic features of psychedelic experience – selflessness, empathy, creativity, open-mindedness, closeness to nature – cut against the grain of modern life, especially in the post-1989 late-capitalist world. Modern human beings are taught to prize self-interest above all else. Subtly, via a trillion tiny signals within our everyday experience, from advertising jingles to political slogans, we are taught to get ahead, compete, achieve, pursue our own interests, realise our individual desires, maximise our own potential. The popular psychedelia of rave culture offered an alternative to the narrow individualism of modern life.

↖↑↗

Perhaps the most ardent believer in the radical potential of rave music was the British state. The story of police versus ravers in the magical summers of 1988 and 1989 has been told many times, but it bears repeating, at least in its broad outlines, not only because it illuminates the wider political significance of rave culture, but also because it's a fantastic story, an antic tale of red-faced coppers and wily outlaws pitting their wits against one another in the rural commuter belt surrounding London.

Acid house prompted one of the last great youth cultural moral panics, which was fuelled by a classic combination of tabloid misinformation and public suspicion of alternative lifestyles. When the tabloids got wind of the acid house phenomenon, they ran incendiary stories about the secretive party scene that threatened to convert the nation's youth into drug-crazed zombies. Headlines like *The Sun*'s '20,000 at Acid Bash. Drug Pushers Galore. Kids of 12 Go Wild' were perfectly pitched both to alarm parents and alert their children to the existence of wild parties with plentiful drugs and no age restrictions. After one of the first reported ecstasy deaths, *The Sun* resorted to its customarily nuanced take on matters of criminal justice: 'Shoot These Evil Acid Barons.' The moral panic quickly filtered up to the highest echelons of government. Questions were asked in Parliament and one Conservative MP wrote directly to Margaret Thatcher, informing her of the distress suffered by his rural constituents when an illegal rave was held in nearby fields.

In response, Kent Police force set up the Pay Party Unit in order to crack down on raves in the countryside around London's M25 orbital ring road. The 'acid house squad', as it was known to cheeky ravers, grew into a nationwide taskforce whose sole purpose was to disrupt the underground rave scene. Officers seconded to the unit tapped phones, shut down pirate radio signals, printed fake flyers to confuse partygoers, deployed rapid response units to close down potential rave sites and sent helicopters to monitor existing parties from the air. The rave organisers fought back with their own counter-tactics: on-site lawyers to stall the police with flashy legal arguments and writs for harassment, fake flyers and radio announcements to send police officers on false trails and a constantly shifting network of mobile phone numbers and pirate radio frequencies to stay one step ahead of police surveillance.

Against this backdrop, raves were seen by many as part of a wider threat to Britain's social and political order. The Pay Party Unit drew on the same repertoire of not-quite-legal policing tactics that had been deployed during the miners' strike in the mid-1980s, including unlawful stop and search and equipment seizures. The chief officer was Superintendent Ken Tappenden, a wily old fox who had spent most of 1984 devising ways to prevent Kentish miners forming flying pickets to support their NUM brethren at pit mouths in Yorkshire and South Wales. Rave was the largest unauthorised mass mobilisation since that strike. Scenes of police officers chasing ravers through farmers' fields invoked images of the Battle of Orgreave in the summer of 1984, when roughly 8,000 picketers had battled 5,000 police officers in fields surrounding the South Yorkshire smoking plant.

It is no coincidence that rave music emerged from the decaying industrial heartlands of North America and Europe. In Chicago, Detroit, Berlin, Rotterdam, Ghent, London, Manchester and Sheffield, illegal raves took place in empty warehouses and factories whose production operations had been shifted overseas by multinational corporations seeking cheaper labour markets and lighter regulation. In many cases, the Pay Party Unit deployed their officers against the sons and daughters of the very working-class communities whose livelihoods had been decimated by the industrial decline of the 1970s and '80s. The artist Jeremy Deller captures this sense of historical continuity in *The History of the World, 1997–2004* (2004), a sprawling thought diagram that demonstrates the hidden connections between brass bands, those staples of northern working-class culture of the early to mid-twentieth century, and acid house music. In the form of sketchy thought bubbles and radiating lines of connection, Deller invites the viewer to trace the cultural connections between the miners' strike, electro, civic pride, Chicago and Detroit, deindustrialisation, Ecstasy, parks, melancholy, the summer of love, advanced capitalism and sound systems. By placing rave culture in the wider context of twentieth-century working-class identity, Deller makes the case for acid house as a kind of post-industrial folk music, a way of using new technology to forge a sense of community and identity in opposition to the destabilising effects of global capitalism.

Beneath the measured language of public order and safety that was used by police spokesmen, there was a more atavistic impulse behind the crackdown on raves. There is an instinctual sense of unease that stirs in the breast of public officialdom when confronted with large unlicensed groups of people. Especially at the outlaw fringes of acid house, there was an air of almost military organisation – of rave culture as a nomadic war machine, the sound system as a kind of heavy artillery and of ravers themselves as a mobile marching army of loved-up troublemakers. The paramilitary overtones were most apparent in the first years of the 1990s, when rave culture formed a temporary alliance with the New Age Traveller movement. New Age Travellers were semi-nomadic dropouts from urban society, a loose coalition of back-to-the-land hippies, anarcho-punk squatters, radical anti-road campaigners, environmentalists and assorted ne'er-do-wells who joined a convoy at the promise of cheap drugs and good times. New Age Travellers

– or 'crusties', as they were more frequently known – dressed in a style that can only be described as Mad Max goes to the Albion Fayre, a kind of post-apocalyptic hippy punk comprised of scuffed biker boots, leather jackets and dreadlocked hair. In the early 1990s, the hippy festival circuit that had been running since the 1970s started to host increasingly large-scale raves, where sound systems like Tonka, DIY and Spiral Tribe introduced a harder-edged acid techno sound to match their more confrontational style.

The scene reached its apotheosis at Castlemorton Common in the summer of 1992 with a giant five-day festival, during which the police were powerless to stop upwards of 30,000 ravers inhabiting what amounted to a temporary city built on a classic bit of English common land in the lee of Worcestershire's Malvern Hills. The sheer scale and duration of Castlemorton ensured that rave culture was headline news for the first time since the summer of 1989. The public outcry led to the passage of the notorious Criminal Justice and Public Order Act of 1994, a wide-ranging piece of legislation which, among other things, outlawed groups of people gathering in public to listen to 'repetitive beats'. The fuzzy attempt to legislate based on musical genre – did 'repetitive beats' include African drumming and military tattoos, as well as house and techno? – was what really gave the game away. These sections of the bill were aimed squarely at alternative lifestyles that the authorities found both morally distasteful and vaguely threatening.

New Age Travellers were the great 'folk devils' of the age. In his speech to the Conservative Party conference in May of 1992, Prime Minister John Major blustered, 'New age travellers? Not in this age. Not in any age,' as though he were announcing an inter-dimensional time war against the crusty menace. But political rhetoric of this sort only burnished the travellers' dark charisma. In most provincial town centres in early to mid-1990s Britain you'd often see a disorderly group of travellers hanging around, possibly accompanied by a couple of flea-bitten dogs and a gaggle of teenagers looking to score some weed. In among the heritage buildings and the bustling chain stores, there'd be a band of outlaws who seemed to have wandered in from another world, a wild frontier somewhere far beyond Middle England. I can still remember the jolt of astonishment and jealousy I felt when I heard in the summer term of 1992 that a boy from my boarding school had run away to join a traveller convoy. It was a moment of heart-stopping romantic glamour, as though he'd stowed away on board a pirate ship or signed up for the French Foreign Legion. There was a genuine sense at that time of being no more than a few steps away from a radically different way of life. There was a fairly easily accessible pathway from a respectable middle-class adolescence to a nomadic world of anarcho-punks, hippy dropouts, drug dealers and bums, an off-ramp from normal society into the wide-open spaces of the underground.

↖↑↗

Today, electronic dance music scenes span the globe, from Malawi to Melbourne and from Mexico City to Manila. In many cases, though, it seems as though the sounds haven't changed that much since the mid-1990s. The music has plateaued. The social ritual has become mundane, just another part of the global leisure economy. New tracks are released and new DJ names appear on flyers alongside the elder statesmen of the scene, but the goal now seems to be curation and preservation, rather than innovation. Go to a techno club today, and you'll find old heads dancing alongside newer recruits. Some of the younger ravers might have been born after the music itself, but they still want to tap into the sonic, social and neurochemical possibilities first discovered thirty years earlier.

We have entered the era of rave as museum piece, rave as respectable chapter in official cultural history. In 2019, in order to commemorate thirty years since the fall of the Wall, the Alte Münze gallery in Berlin staged a multimedia exhibit, which enabled visitors to immerse themselves in the 'legendary Berlin of the 1990s', complete with vintage club flyers, a re-created section of the Wall and eyewitness testimony from DJs and club promoters. Like many earlier counter-cultural movements, from the swinging sixties to punk, the history of rave has become a form of cultural capital which city governments can convert into tourist visits and boosted revenues. In the same year, the Saatchi gallery in London, once associated with the rebel postures of the YBAs, staged 'Sweet Harmony: Rave/Today', an exhibition of photographs, posters, artefacts and sound installations that explored the impact of rave music on British popular culture over the last thirty years. Artists such as Jeremy Deller and Mark Leckey have brought rave culture out of the club and into the gallery in the form of artworks that memorialise the lost possibilities for community and identity that have passed away with rave's demise.

It is a great irony that for many people who grew up in the late 1980s and 1990s, house and techno music are surefire ways of being transported into the past. What was once the sound of the future is now fodder for middle-aged nostalgia. To this day, when I'm listening to old rave tunes while I make dinner for my family, there are certain triggers in the music – some mathematically precise combination of synth stabs, arpeggiated piano riff, acid squiggle and throbbing bass – that activate a signal buried deep within my central nervous system, the source code for a delirious state of euphoria that I once experienced on a dancefloor sometime in the 1990s. This is the closest thing to time travel that I know of. The large and frequent doses of MDMA that I took as a teenager seem somehow to have permanently altered my neurochemistry, seeded my brain with little slivers of lost time, which blossom into life when the alchemical combination of wine on an empty stomach and old rave tunes hits the blood stream. For a brief but vivid moment, I come untethered from my daily routine and float through the strange seas of my own bio-hacked brain. But it's never more than a brief interruption of normal service, a slight flicker in the force field of everyday life.

Rather than giving into the lure of nostalgia, perhaps it's wiser to ask what it was about rave culture that we so miss in the present, what set of possibilities it embodied that have been closed off today. Rather than the individual feelings of pleasure that it generated, perhaps it was what the Berlin scenester Katie Schwind called the 'social architectures' that rave enabled that we yearn for today. Where in today's popular culture can we find an equivalent sense of collective euphoria, an equivalent social technology for gathering people in a space to celebrate the joy of the present and the promise of the future. That experience of collective ecstasy is available to us via sports events and music festivals, but only in ever more heavily commercialised forms. Mass political gatherings are on the rise, but what unites us in that case is often a sense of embattled outrage and resistance, rather than celebratory joyfulness. The hedonism of the late 1980s and early 1990s was enabled by material conditions that no longer exist. Rave culture emerged before the introduction of university tuition fees in the UK, before house prices spiralled beyond the reach of most first-time buyers, before the financial crash and political austerity accelerated economic inequality, before young people were taught to think of themselves as human capital, as walking CVs stuffed with the experience and qualifications necessary to scrape a living in the new digital economy, before smart phones and social media immersed us all in a web of constant self-surveillance. The late 1980s and early 1990s were certainly not a golden age of youth-friendly social policy, but they at least contained the space and materials for non-utilitarian cultural experimentation – that is, for play, for goofing off, for un-self-conscious hedonism.

7

Moore's Law

MOORE'S LAW, which was formulated in 1965 by the computer scientist and future CEO of Intel, Gordon Moore, states that the number of transistors that can fit onto a silicon chip will double every two years. It has not been proved wrong yet. Since the 1970s, the power of integrated circuits has increased at roughly the rate Moore predicted, driving one of the greatest technological revolutions in human history: the advent of the digital age.

It was in the 1990s, with the spread of the internet and the rapid growth in personal computer use, that this technological revolution burst into public consciousness. At the beginning of the decade, the internet was a closed network accessible only via government or university log-ins. Public internet service providers, or ISPs, offered consumers access to local area networks via modems that transmitted information through analogue telephone lines, often at punitively high prices. The internet was predominantly text based, oriented towards specialised fields of knowledge, such as aeronautical engineering or Grateful Dead bootlegs, and was mainly the preserve of academics, government researchers, geeks and amateurs. Even by 1995 only 0.4 per cent of the world's population had internet access, and over half of those people were in America.

By the turn of the millennium, the internet was well on its way to becoming the all-encompassing global super-brain and attention-devouring surveillance machine that it is today. Hundreds of millions of daily users around the world had access to millions of web pages, almost all of which were available via free but enormously powerful search engines. Increasingly, computers connected to the internet via high-speed broadband, which enabled the transmission of high-resolution images and video. Wi-Fi networks were being rolled out across cities and towns, so that users could log on while moving around in physical space. Increased bandwidth would usher in 'Web 2.0', a whole range of new platforms that enabled file sharing, interactivity, mobile connectivity, and the mass harvesting of users' data to enable governments and businesses to track the online habits of private citizens. The NASDAQ tech stock bubble was fit to burst with the animal spirits of over-excited investors keen to own a multi-billion-dollar slice of the digital future.

In the 1965 article in *Electronics* magazine in which he formulated his famous law, Gordon Moore speculated on what the future might look like if he was right: 'Integrated circuits will lead to such wonders as personal computers – or at least terminals connected to a central computer – automatic controls for automobiles, and personal portable computer equipment.' The arrival of the internet in the 1990s was one of those rare moments in history when science-fiction-tinged predictions about life in the future actually seemed to be coming true. Even back in the distant dark ages of dial-up internet connections, when many of us logged on for the first time, most likely on a boxy desktop PC with a dial-up modem that ground out that bouncy metallic *ne-nah, ne-nah* as you waited ... and waited ... for your page to load, there was a sense of making contact with the future, of living on the cusp of a profound transformation in human civilisation.

But since its first formulation, Moore's Law has exceeded the bounds of its original mandate. No longer purely a theorem of computer science, it has become a shorthand for society's almost mystical belief in technological progress. In its popular, folkloric version, Moore's Law expresses our assumption that computers will steadily increase in power, encompass ever more aspects of our daily lives and yield ever more elegant and necessary solutions to the problems of human existence. While this secular religion originated with the hackers and geeks who built the internet in the 1970s and 1980s, it went nuclear in the 1990s. The explosion of internet use didn't just send packets of information around the world, it also spread myths and fantasies, visions of the digital millennium in which humanity would be transfigured and society transformed by the sacramental flow of zeros and ones. In their various ways, these prognosticators and visionaries were all votaries of Moore's Law.

Many of these fantasies are still with us today, but in general we are less credulous of techno-utopian visions than we were in the wide-eyed 1990s. The promises of instant communication, global connectivity and revolutions in work, commerce and leisure made by the first wave of digital prophets have remained unfulfilled or been severely tarnished. Social-media-driven anxiety, fragmented attention, online hate speech, the decimation of print media, the rise of the gig economy, the monopolisation of the web by a handful of giant corporations, mass surveillance, the first Twitter troll to occupy the White House: the digital optimism of the 1990s seems almost quaint today. From our vantage point in the 2020s, we can look back on the techno-futurist visions of the 1990s as one might survey the Jetsons-style projections of the 1950s – the future of jet packs, flying cars and picnics on Mars that never came to be.

↖↑↗

The origins of the internet date back to the Cold War military-industrial complex and the first heroic age of computer science – when computers were the size of university classrooms, had names like 'Colossus', and the process of 'debugging' involved hand-picking fried moths out of vacuum tubes.

The world's first computer network was built in the late 1960s by scientists working for the US military's Advanced Research Projects Agency (ARPA), which was founded by President Eisenhower in 1957 in response to the Soviet Union's Sputnik rocket and satellite programme. ARPA's main task was missile defence, but in order to calculate nuclear blast forces to one hundredth of a second the agency required vast amounts of computational power. By the late 1960s, ARPA had created a local network of mainframe computers – bulky, cabinet-sized machines housed in universities and other government research institutions – through which scientists could share and comment on each other's work. In 1969, the network connected four universities: Stanford, UCLA, UC Santa Barbara and the University of Utah. In 1970, it was extended to Harvard, MIT, the Bolt, Beranek and Newman technology company, and the RAND corporation. By 1972 it had twenty-five nodes. At this stage, ARPANET, the direct forerunner of the public internet that would encircle the globe a mere thirty years later, was buried deep within the bureaucratic world of Cold War military research.

Over the course of the 1970s and 1980s, members of this specialised community helped to build the underlying technology of the internet: packet switching, file transfer protocol, transmission control protocol, ethernet and data transmissions via high-speed coaxial cables, packet satellite transmission. As more and more universities built their own supercomputing centres, the US government's National Science Foundation (NSF) saw the need for a durable infrastructure to connect these disparate networks together. In 1986, the NSF launched what came to be known as the 'backbone' of the internet, the underlying architecture that transmitted data between the individual parts of the system and articulated it as a whole. This 'network of networks' bundled the original ARPANET, as well as universities, government agencies such as NASA and private companies such as the Dow Jones stock exchange, into eleven regional networks throughout the US.

The other great stepping stones towards mass internet use also emerged from deep within the worlds of academic research. In 1989 at CERN, the European Organization for Nuclear Research, Tim Berners-Lee invented Hypertext Transfer Protocol, or HTTP, the underlying set of rules that enabled clients (search engines) and servers (websites) to locate each other and exchange information without a central organisation or authority. Berners-Lee also invented hypertext links, with which users could highlight words or passages in their own documents and link them to other documents online. If the internet is a network of computer networks which facilitates the transmission of data between distant computers, then the World Wide Web is the vast archive of documents, a kind of planetary database, that we can all access from the comfort of our homes via those networked computers. In the form of hypertext, Berners-Lee moved a step closer to one of the ancient dreams of mankind, a dream that had previously been expressed in the form of the ancient library of Alexandria, Diderot and d'Alembert's Enlightenment *Encyclopédie*, and Vannevar Bush's post-Second World War plans for the analogue Memex machine: a total architecture for the world's information.

The project began when Berners-Lee started looking for a way to enable the multinational and multidisciplinary researchers at CERN to share documents with one another on the institute's internal computer network. The results of that investigation, Berners-Lee quickly saw, should be scalable to other networks for maximum efficacy. What was required was a minimal set of rules that would enable users around the world to share their information. Or, as Berners-Lee put it in his autobiography, *Weaving the Web*, 'anything potentially connected with anything', an infinitely proliferating series of possible connections that 'brings the workings of society closer to the workings of our mind'. The combination of mind-numbingly boring technical detail and visionary utopianism expressed in Berners-Lee's writing is characteristic of much early 1990s internet discourse. For Berners-Lee and many of his colleagues, HTTP was not just a technical feat of coding; it also expressed a vision of how humans might build a more perfect world.

The other great leap forward was the launch in 1993 of Mosaic, the first genuinely user-friendly web browser. Mosaic's design incorporated features that we now take for granted but were not part of the clunky web browsers of the very early internet: images and clickable icons. This was a step change in interface design that helped to convert the web into a multimedia experience, rather than simply a repository of specialist information. The most important thing about Mosaic was that it was actually pleasurable to use for people who had no interest in the technical features of computers. Without having to fiddle about with website addresses or typed commands, users could simply enter a search term and then scan results, click on interesting items, follow hyperlinks and look at images. The web became an immersive environment, rather than a collection of documents. In this respect, Mosaic paved the way for the familiar internet of today, the internet as leisure experience, entertainment platform and mildly psychedelic alternative world.

It was in the first few years of the 1990s that the internet, a government-funded, institutionally embedded, research-oriented communications network, was transferred to private ownership and public use. In 1990, the NSF announced that it would gradually withdraw funding so as to enable private companies to take over both backbone operations and service provision to individual users. The .gov and .edu domain names were now joined by the .coms. This unleashed a swarm of competition as large telecoms and media companies, as well as what journalistic cliché now insists on calling 'plucky' start-ups, sought to invent the internet business more or less from scratch. Mosaic, for instance, was first developed by Eric Bina and Marc Andreessen at the University of Illinois' National Center for Super Computing, a government-funded research institution that had been one of the earliest members of ARPANET. The program was originally written for the large and expensive Unix machines used by computer science researchers, but Bina and Andreessen also made it available for Windows and Mac users via a free download from the NCSA servers. Between September 1993 and June 1994, more than a million everyday citizens had their first experience of 'surfing the web' in the form of a free gift from the US government's supercomputing agency.

By mid-1994, the race to develop the commercial internet was in full swing. Riding the success of Mosaic, Bina and Andreessen left the groves of academe for the more dynamic – and much better remunerated – pastures of Silicon Valley, where they became part of the new 'digerati' class of tech industry multi-millionaires and billionaires. Mosaic was bought by Netscape and incorporated within one of the most successful early web browsers. Netscape was itself part of the flotilla of now defunct and largely forgotten enterprises that helped to extend recreational internet use beyond the self-enclosed worlds of academic research and geek-driven bulletin boards to the great mass of American – and shortly worldwide – consumers. For most mid-90s internet users, the first points of contact with the digital future were AOL, Mosaic, Compuserve, Prodigy, Genie, Lycos, Netscape, Webcrawler, Infoseek, Magellan and their ilk. These were the intermediate species, the soon-to-be missing links, in the evolution of the megafauna that now dominate the online environment: Amazon, Google, Facebook and the rest of the advertising-surveillance industrial complex.

Between 1995 and the end of the decade, the public internet spread like wildfire throughout America and the affluent nations of Europe and East Asia. Major milestones were passed on an almost daily basis. In 1994 the White House launched its first web page and Netmark completed the first e-commerce transaction online. In 1995 Microsoft launched Windows 95, which became the standard PC operating system and, in the form of Internet Explorer, the standard web browser for Middle America. In 1996 Amazon sold its first book online. Jeff Bezos announced his ambition to create the online 'everything store' and everybody scoffed at his hubris. In 1997 and 1999, Intel released its Pentium II and III microprocessors, which become synonymous with the rapid acceleration of processing power for desktop PCs in everyday homes. In 1998 Larry Page and Sergey Brin launched Google, which enabled users to search a database of 518 million hyperlinks, a number that rapidly increased as the company's algorithms continued to search and archive the endlessly proliferating strands of code on the World Wide Web. There were 16 million internet users in the world in 1995 and 361 million at the turn of the millennium. By 2018 half of all the humans on planet earth were plugged into the system.

⇖⇑⇗

Throughout the 1990s, digital technology was one of the few genuinely avant-garde movements in popular culture and society. At the same time that the public internet was taking off, large swathes of music, film and fashion were turning to the past for inspiration. In many ways, the 1990s were an era defined by retro cool and self-aware irony. There was a vague sense that the great cultural innovations lay in the past, somewhere in the ferment of modernism in the 1920s or the rock 'n' roll revolutions unleased between Elvis's arrival in the 1950s and the exhaustion of punk in the 1980s. The internet promised exactly the kind of radical transformation of culture and society that in prior eras had been the preserve of avant-garde artists and political revolutionaries. As Michael Wolf puts it in *Burn Rate*, his memoir of his time as an early internet entrepreneur, 'all technology is transitional'. In the short term, start-ups scrambled to build the first internet service providers, web browsers and online magazines. But these were merely stepping stones to the next wave of innovation. And then the next, and then the next. The most wide-eyed tech entrepreneurs saw themselves as riding the ever-rising curve of Moore's Law into an open-ended and quite possibly utopian digital future. Today the web browser, tomorrow virtual reality cybersex. Today email, tomorrow global telecommuting.

Unlike prior radical movements, though, the 1990s digital avant-garde was capitalist to its core. Business itself became revolutionary. Tech innovation and entrepreneurship were to the 1990s what Cubism or free jazz had been to earlier epochs. In the digital realm, the old hierarchies ceased to operate. Established companies were weighed down by the excess baggage of internal bureaucracy and outmoded methods. It was the smaller, nimbler operators who could move fast and break things. The 1990s tech business invented its own modernist lexicon of neologisms and buzz words: angel investor, mezzanine fix, burn rate, digerati, etc. Language was stretched and deformed in order to capture the new reality that was in the process of emerging. Company finances were transformed into a higher form of non-Euclidean mathematics. Profit was a distant, highly speculative possibility. Costs were met by investors betting on the shape of a future yet to be invented. As Wolf puts it: 'It was ground zero: no rules, no religion, no canon, no bullshit.'

It was against this backdrop that the 1990s futurology business was born. According to the seers and prognosticators who wrote the endless stream of think pieces describing the shape of things to come, there was seemingly nothing the internet would not revolutionise in the near future. First on the horizon was the transformation of the workplace and economic life. The paperless office, telecommuting and the weightless economy were all on the cusp of being born. Business gurus and tech journalists (a newly glamorous profession in the 1990s) predicted that more and more workers would be able to live in remote locations and do their jobs entirely online. Digital computers would do away with the need for inter-office memos, typed minutes of meetings, printed manuals and guidelines – all the papery impedimenta of mid-twentieth-century office work. Soon, videoconferencing would enable face-to-face contact from distant locations. Offices would shrink to skeleton-staffed hubs and workers would video or email in from their homes in rural locations. In the ideal version of the digital workplace these newly footloose telecommuters would live in chic country retreats – Telluride, Colorado, say, or the highlands of Scotland – where they would enjoy high-speed internet access, efficient transport connections and plenty of spare time to indulge their passions for sky diving or raising heritage-breed cattle. The vision was one of global mobility and quality of life, rather than of isolation and carpal tunnel syndrome.

With its decentralised structure and principle of universal access, the internet seemed to many early enthusiasts to threaten the entrenched powers of large corporations and national governments. Some championed the internet as an escape from the dead hand of corporate America. The new platform would empower small firms and individual enterprises, which could respond better to the needs and desires of their clientele. Others claimed the digital revolution would empower citizens to hold their elected officials accountable and demand better results from their governments. Why have elections every four or five years when you could have regular e-referenda on specific issues? Peer-to-peer networking would enable citizens' coalitions and single-issue pressure groups to challenge governments from below without having to rely on biddable representatives. The increased flow of information would usher in a golden age of transparency, empowering the wised-up digital citizenry to scrutinise every line in every budget brought by their politicians. Beyond the reach of repressive governments, free speech would flourish in the wide-open spaces of the internet.

The promise of the digital economy was underpinned by a vision of the world as composed, at its most fundamental level, of information. Inspired by the science of cybernetics, or what the field's founding father, Norbert Wiener, called the study of 'control and communication in the animal and the machine', the digerati saw human beings, societies, economies and ecosystems as woven together by interlocking patterns of information. In 1992 Kevin Kelly, prominent cyber-guru and soon-to-be editor of *Wired*, the in-house journal of the 'digital generation', published a 500-page tome on 'the new biology of machines, social systems and the economic world'. Kelly argued that the internet was the product of the same underlying processes – feedback, distributed control and emergence – that enabled self-organising systems like ant colonies and biological cells to function in the absence of a central authority. According to Kelly and other advocates of the 'New Economy' or 'bionomics', networking was an inherent feature of complex systems; thus centralised control worked against the grain of nature itself. Implicit within Kelly's book was an alluring vision of a deregulated, tech-enhanced free-market system that would liberate individuals from needless government regulations and enable cathedral-like patterns of social and economic order to emerge from their networked creativity and enterprise.

One of the most successful works of internet futurology, both in terms of sales and accurate predictions, was Nicholas Negroponte's *Being Digital*, which extrapolated from current trends to a near-future world of e-books, e-newspapers, smart watches and phones, in-car GPS systems, the death of the CD-ROM, and always-on twenty-four-hour work schedules – that is, a near-future world that looks a lot like life today. But beyond its specific predictions, Negroponte's book was significant for how it helped to establish the mood music for the digital future. The broader trends underlying these particular technologies would be 'decentralisation', 'globalisation', 'harmonisation' and 'empowerment'. The members of the coming 'digital generation' would improve their lives and enhance their identities by plugging into the global network. A certain lightness of being, a vague air of existential uplift, would spread among the populace like a cooling mist. Negroponte and his fellow 'digerati' presented themselves not simply as engineers and technocrats, but as philosophers of the near future. Where Heidegger gave us 'Being and Time' and Sartre gave us 'Being and Nothingness', Negroponte gave us Being Digital – a release from the existential cares of human life via smart technology and global connectivity.

Not all commentators were so blithely optimistic about the coming digital revolution. In a now infamous piece in *Newsweek* in February 1995, Clifford Stoll sought to burst the techno-futurist bubble: 'The truth is that no online database will replace your daily newspaper, no CD-ROM can take the place of a competent teacher and no computer network will change the way government works.' Stoll was, of course, spectacularly wrong, but we should spare him our retrospective jeers.

The early days of the public internet were a ferment of innovation, competition, speculation and bullshit, but they were also, by definition, open-ended. Just like any slice of historical time, the mid-1990s were a multidimensional possibility space, a garden of forking paths, out of which many possible futures proceeded, only one of which would come into being. Just as the era was characterised by futuristic speculation, so too was it a time of lost possibilities and roads not taken. It could have been different. There is, for instance, an alternative timeline in which Tim Berners-Lee chose to make hyperlinks bi-directional, as he was encouraged to by Doug Engelbart, the early internet pioneer, a feature that would have enabled a system of micro-charging, as was suggested by Jaron Lanier, the early 1990s virtual reality guru, which would in turn have enabled online publications to generate revenue from sources other than advertising, which might have prevented the collapse of the regional newspaper industry that has occurred over the last two decades, which could have acted as a bulwark against the spread of misinformation and conspiracy theories online. Might, maybe, possibly, perhaps. The line between counterfactual history and idle speculation is notoriously thin. And yet, ruminations of this sort help us to grasp the oft-forgotten fact that technology is not destiny and the internet is not simply the product of natural laws and human nature, as some techno-utopians suggested.

↖↑↗

Beyond the predictions of civic and economic progress lay a more visionary possibility still – the glittering, almost transcendent domain of 'cyberspace', which, to many wide-eyed early adopters, seemed to hold out the promise of personal freedom and fulfilment on a scale never before seen. There is a particular type of nerd, more often than not a ponytailed man who works in software and collects replica samurai swords, for whom knowing the exact origin of the term 'cyberspace' is an issue of the utmost importance. Should the first attribution go to the Danish designers who worked under the name 'Atelier Cyberspace' in the 1960s? Or maybe to Bruce Bethke, the science fiction writer who used the term 'cyberpunk' in a piece in *Amazing Science Fiction Stories* in 1983? Suffice it to say, the term was catapulted into the zeitgeist by William Gibson's 1984 novel, *Neuromancer*, in which 'cyberspace' is the name of the global computer network and immersive virtual environment through which Case, the novel's hacker anti-hero, is chased by corporate spies and underworld assassins in his quest to reunite the divided halves of a rogue artificial intelligence.

In the novel, Gibson describes cyberspace as a 'consensual hallucination' and 'bright lattices of logic unfolding across that colorless void', giving a sublime three-dimensional appearance to the underlying technology of digital computation: the orderly pulse of electrons through silicon circuits. In an interview with the *Paris Review*, Gibson recalled the moment in the early 1980s when he saw a group of kids playing videogames in an arcade and instantly came up with the idea for *Neuromancer*:

> Even in this very primitive form, the kids who were playing them were so physically involved, it seemed to me that what they wanted was to be inside the games, within the notional space of the machine. The real world had disappeared for them – it had completely lost its importance. They were in that notional space, and the machine in front of them was the brave new world.

For many internet users in the 1990s, Gibson's science-fictional vision of cyberspace seemed to be almost within reach. The reality of mid-1990s internet use was still a long way from the sublime vistas of *Neuromancer*. Online sub-cultures thrived in the form of Multi-User Dungeons, or fantasy role-playing games, early message boards, such as the WELL and Usenet, which enabled users to share information and enthusiasms at a distance, and rudimentary webpages, but these were largely text based and often fairly static experiences. And yet, the same desire that Gibson saw in the arcade gamers of the early 1980s, the desire somehow to enter the machine, to live in a three-dimensional realm inside the computer, was what drove many early adopters. Somewhere beyond the blocky graphics and text-heavy interfaces, users imagined a transcendent realm of pure information and unbridled personal freedom.

The very idea of the online world as a three-dimensional space is a relic of a prior era. Today, we spend more time online than ever before, but in the age of social media and streaming it is much harder to imagine these experiences taking place in a single coherent space. In place of cyberspace we now have a handful of 'platforms', the social media and e-commerce giants that have staked out their claims to the online world. Our online experience is of a much higher resolution than the clunky interfaces of the 1990s and yet, paradoxically, that very seamlessness has dampened our imagination of what the internet is and could be. For many early users, cyberspace was really out there, a 'notional space', as Gibson put it, into which we could escape from the drab reality of everyday life. Now it's just more television.

In the ideal visions of the first cybernauts, logging on to the internet enabled the user to cross over into a new domain, a virtual elsewhere beyond the here and now. The user left his or her body behind in the 'meatspace' of the home or office and roamed freely as a disembodied consciousness, untrammelled by the categories of gender, race and class. In cyberspace, you would be defined by your interests and choices alone. You could create your own avatar, revel in anonymity, find your true tribe in a free space beyond nation and geography. One of the most popular discussion forums was Usenet, a seemingly endless series of threads and sub-threads where users could exchange information, discuss niche topics and make friends with other pseudonymous users who might be located on the same street or on the other side of the world. The site had the branching structure that we have now come to associate with online discussion. An infinite range of possible topics – cybersecurity, chaos theory, *X-Files* fandom, haute cuisine, BDSM, libertarian politics, virtual reality, hot stock picks, crochet clubs, etc. – could be divided into an infinite series of sub-topics and sub-sub-topics. This was a new medium that seemed to open up a series of glowing portals to other worlds, rarefied branches of knowledge, connections to like-minded others, specialist sub-cultures, all accompanied by the sense of creating one's own tailor-made identity in the accelerated flows of information and code.

Cyberculture drew its inspirations from a range of different sources, including the 'hacker' ethos of self-empowerment through coding skills and technical know-how, a radical commitment to freedom of speech and open-access publishing, and a belief in technology as a means of self-transformation and even altered consciousness. In February 1996, John Perry Barlow, former lyricist with the Grateful Dead and prominent spokesman for the 1990s digerati, issued 'A Declaration of the Independence of Cyberspace' in response to the US government's Telecommunications Act, which included provisions to enable the federal government to censor obscene material online, as it already did for other broadcast media. 'Governments of the Industrial World,' it began:

> You weary giants of flesh and steel, I come from Cyberspace, the new home of mind. On behalf of the future, I ask you of the past to leave us alone. You are not welcome among us. You have no sovereignty where we gather.

Barlow's text encapsulates many of the key principles of cyber-utopianism: that cyberspace is a real place that exists beyond the laws and sovereignty of nation states; that cyberspace is the natural 'home of mind', a new dimension that enables human beings to transcend their physical beings and supersede the outdated era of flesh and steel; that cyberspace is the point of contact between the present and the future, a portal through which radical newness enters the world.

But if you trim away the pie-eyed cyberbabble, what you are left with, at the heart of Barlow's declaration, is a form of ideological mystification. Or, more simply put, you are left with a lie. In the full flight of his speechifying, Barlow states: 'Cyberspace does not lie within your borders. Do not think that you can build it, as though it were a public construction project. You cannot. It is an act of nature and it grows itself through our collective actions.' Of course, Barlow knew full well that the internet originated as a 'public construction project' in the form of ARPANET and the NSF's internet backbone. It was funded by the US taxpayer and built with both public and private goals in mind. By casting that publicly funded infrastructure project as 'an act of nature', a kind of digital life form that unfurls spontaneously like the tangled creepers of the Amazon delta, he sought to transfer the internet from the domain of democratic oversight and public ownership to that of individual enterprise. Barlow echoes the techno-libertarianism and hyper-individualism of much of 1990s cyberculture. It seems all too fitting that the Declaration of the Independence of Cyberspace was issued from Davos, Switzerland, home of the World Economic Forum and the high Alpine retreat of the new global super-elite that was best positioned to flourish in – and profit from – the libertarian utopia of cyberspace.

↖↑↗

Cyberculture wasn't just the preserve of specialist online message boards of the kind John Perry Barlow frequented. It also made its way into the culture via the analogue media of the day, the magazines, newspapers, movies and TV whose business models would be thrown into turmoil by the new digital technology. The most popular and long-lasting cyberculture publication was – and still is to some extent, although with less of an aura of visionary cool these days – *Wired* magazine, which was founded in 1991 by Louis Rossetto and Jane Metcalfe. *Wired*, as its writers proudly proclaimed at every possible opportunity, was the in-house guide to the rapidly emerging digital age. Its founding editors and star writers, including high digerati sages such as Kevin Kelly, Nicholas Negroponte and Barlow himself, weren't simply reporters who chronicled events from the outside but central players in the emerging Silicon Valley culture industry.

Wired treated technology as a cultural experience, rather than just a technical or economic concern. In keeping with the ideas of the magazine's patron saint, Marshall McLuhan, the form of the magazine was just as important as its content. While the public internet was still in its infancy, *Wired* helped to define the look and feel of an online world that was made up of equal parts fantasy and reality. John Plunkett and Barbara Kuhr's designs favoured bright, saturated colours, pixellated fonts, skeins of text that overflowed on to images and across borders, abstract grid patterns and fractal designs, pages covered in glitchy static. It is striking how frequently *Wired*'s cover art featured the human form subsumed in some kind of computer-generated code or graphics. In its most visually striking early manifestations, *Wired* conveyed to everyday consumers the delirious sense of being swamped by the new technology, immersed in data. Go with the flow, it seemed to be saying, turn on, plug in, and let yourself be transformed by the new possibilities of the digital age.

Wired was cool but mainstream, equal parts cyberpunk style sheet and infotech trade magazine. It drew much of its inspiration from the edgier *Mondo 2000*, which was founded in 1984, but continued to define the bleeding edge of cyberculture well into the 1990s. In their first editorial, R.U. Sirius and Queen Mu, the presiding geniuses of *Mondo 2000*, laid out their programme for the magazine:

> Mondo 2000 is here to cover the leading edge in hyperculture. We'll bring you the latest in human/technological interactive mutational forms *as* they happen.
>
> We're talking Cyber-Chautauqua: bringing cyberculture to the people! Artificial awareness modules. Visual music. Vidscan magazines. Brain-boosting technologies. William Gibson's cyber-space Matrix – fully realized!

The central appeal of *Mondo 2000* was the promise of living in the future as it happened, a real-time experience of the cyber-revolution that was equal parts reportage and science fiction. Inside the covers of the magazine, articles about the latest consumer tech products and developments in computer science sat alongside features on electronic music, esoteric religion, smart drugs, figures from the 1960s counterculture such as Sun Ra and Timothy Leary, and rhapsodic treatments of the coming revolution in 'cybersex' and 'teledildonics'. Editorials mixed esoteric cyber-discourse with references to global events – the fall of the USSR, the LA riots, congressional hearings on copyright law – to create a sense that digital technology was bound up with the dawning of a new era in world affairs.

Sometimes the gap between reality and imagination was all too apparent. A 1993 feature titled 'R. U. a Cyber-Punk?' offered readers a visual guide on how to accessorise one's wardrobe in cyberpunk style. At the centre of the full-page spread, beneath a handy definition of the term 'cyberpunk' – 'a hardboiled hacker with anarchist inclinations' – we see a long-haired man clad in black leather, who is festooned with the gadgets and accessories that enable him to surf the wave of the future. Instead of the mind-bending gadgets promised in the first issue of the magazine, the vidscans and AI modules of the science fiction imagination, the reality of the 1990s cyberpunk seems somewhat prosaic, even a little dweeby. In addition to a minidisk player, handheld scanner, cellular phone, portable CD-ROM player and Apple Powerbook, our cyberpunk carries with him a 'combination briefcase' and 'non-digital paper variety' money. Rather than emanating from the depths of the cyber-underworld, most of these gadgets were available from Radio Shack or PC World. Readers might have been justified in their suspicion that 'cyberpunk' style was just a handy way to market consumer electronics.

Of course, it was only a matter of time before Hollywood caught on to the new new thing. Between *The Lawnmower Man* in 1992 and *The Matrix* in 1999, Hollywood studios produced a series of cyber-thrillers that sought to spin cinematic gold from the otherwise prosaic experience of logging on to the internet. In the 1990s, the movie industry was on the cusp of its own digital revolution. A hundred years after the Lumière brothers had invented the cinematographe, the celluloid strip was gradually being discarded in favour of digital video and the magic box of computer-generated imagery that was on display in blockbusters such as *Jurassic Park* (1993), *Titanic* (1997) and the world's first fully digitally animated feature film, *Toy Story* (1995). In contrast to the mega-spectacle of the CGI blockbuster, cyber-thrillers sought to tap into the edgy, sub-cultural worlds of hackers and cyberpunks in a bid to claim some of their up-to-date street cred for the ageing movie industry. The results ranged from the techno-sublime to the techno-ridiculous.

The cyber-thriller genre came in a variety of different flavours. *The Lawnmower Man* (1992) was a Frankenstein reboot, in which a renegade computer scientist seeks to cure his mentally disabled gardener with an experimental VR therapy. 'Virtual reality holds the key to the evolution of the human mind,' enthuses Pierce Brosnan's Faustian Doctor shortly before the Lawnmower Man's super-charged brain causes him to take his revenge on the local rednecks and do battle with FBI investigators. In *The Net* (1995) Sandra Bullock played a charmingly nerdy cybersecurity analyst who stumbles upon a shadowy conspiracy involving a group of online terrorists and a digital master-key to all of the encrypted information in the US. Cue a series of chase scenes in picturesque locations throughout North America and repeated episodes in which Bullock stares into a brightly lit screen and types furiously.

Hackers, which was also released in 1995, the *annus mirabilis* of the cyber-thriller, altered the template by focusing on a group of heroic cyber-nerds, rather than the maverick individual favoured by Hollywood tradition. The group embodies the most cherished values of the rising cyber-generation: youth, freedom, democracy, multiculturalism and impeccably chiselled good looks. Jonny Lee Miller and Angelina Jolie's onscreen chemistry was dampened by the fact that whenever they came within touching distance of each another, their diamond-sharp cheekbones threatened to draw blood. *Johnny*

Mnemonic (1995), based on a short story by the godfather of cyberpunk, William Gibson, and *Strange Days* (1995), directed and written by Hollywood action supremos Kathryn Bigelow and James Cameron, were the edgiest of the bunch. Both drew on the full panoply of cyberpunk scenography: VR brain implants, underworld gangs, black-leather-clad extras, near-future settings and a general air of fin-de-civilisation weltschmerz.

For all of their differences, these films shared at least one trait in common. They all hurled themselves with puppyish enthusiasm at the aesthetic challenge posed by computation: the fact that it is inherently boring, maybe even anti-cinematic. The dull truth of the matter is that for the great mass of knowledge workers who ply their trade in the post-industrial information economy, computation is banal. What do we do all day except hunch over our desks in featureless office complexes manipulating abstract symbols on glowing computer screens? Underneath the plastic casings, somewhere deep within the insulated wires and integrated circuits, electrons pulse in orderly procession. Documents are processed, accounts are tabulated, figures are shifted from one column to another. Rather than wigging out on trippy graphics or hacking into secret domains, we get on with our jobs, order products, chat with friends, read articles, etc. We don't look at the machine, we look through it. But in the early days of the internet, before the technology had been assimilated into our daily routines, the Hollywood cyber-thriller sought to make computation cool.

The apotheosis of 1990s cyber-thrillers was, of course, *The Matrix*, which begins in a featureless office cubicle in a plate-glass skyscraper somewhere in the dead centre of corporate America and then catapults the viewer, via a series of techno-mystical awakenings, into the hidden reality that lies behind our mundane existences. In this case, the matrix turns out to be a *non*-consensual hallucination that has been foisted upon the human species by a future race of artificially intelligent machines. Humans have been encased in womb-like pods that extract our life force as energy for our machine overlords, who have tricked us into thinking that we're still living in the glory days of *Friends* and Windows 98. Or something like that. I suspect that for most viewers, the techno-mythological narrative was of secondary interest to the hyper-kinetic action sequences and edgy cyberpunk style.

The Matrix succeeded where prior cyber-thrillers had failed due to the seamless grace with which it wove together live-action stunts and CGI. It was a great leap forward in digital filmmaking, the point at which digital effects became indistinguishable from photography. Kung fu battles, flying bullets, a helicopter crashing into a skyscraper, the blank white space of the training construct: all had the same degree of photo-realistic precision. Before *The Matrix*, cinematic depictions of cyberspace had looked exactly like cinematic depictions of cyberspace. The blocky geometric forms and screens filled with shimmering lines of code were a Hollywood production designer's idea of the digital future. *The Matrix*, by contrast, made cyberspace indistinguishable from our current reality. It suggested a higher order of computation by taking our everyday experience as the content of the simulation.

The Matrix also played it cool. Neo, Trinity, Morpheus and the gang were Mods rather than hippies. Their sleek tailoring and black leather trench coats suggested ascetic self-control rather than trippy hedonism. Instead of enjoying the sensory riches of cyberspace, their aim was a mastery so complete as to be able to bend the system to their own uses, to see beyond the simulation. *The Matrix* was equipped with a techno-millennarian vision of real grandeur, one that made the government conspiracies and underworld plots of prior cyber-thrillers seem like small potatoes indeed. In preparation for his role as Neo, the Wachowskis insisted that Keanu Reeves read three key works of cyber-theory: Kevin Kelly's *Out of Control*, Jean Baudrillard's *Simulacra and Simulation* and Oscar Zarate's *Introducing Evolutionary Psychology*. Three whole books in preparation for a $63 million movie – now that is dedication to your craft. It was from this mixture of cyber-theory, postmodernism and bioscience that the Wachowskis wove their mythic tale of Neo, the chosen one, who would lead an enslaved humanity out of the matrix and towards enlightenment.

The choice that Keanu has to make between the blue pill of forgetting and the red pill of enlightenment has since become a digital age meta-meme, a meme that expresses our distrust of the world of information glut and ever-proliferating memes. Is it better to remain in a comfortable simulated reality, one where we can enjoy the pleasures of steak and red wine, as Joe Pantoliano's treacherous Cypher chooses to, or to awaken into the harsh light of a reality in which it's gruel for dinner every night and humankind must fight for its freedom against the machine overlords? If this was simply a conversation starter for first-year philosophy students all would be well. But the red pill motif has been adopted by online conspiracy theorists and political extremists of various stripes as a shorthand for ideological demystification. Adrift in a flood of information, uncomfortably wired into the global network, QAnon supporters, incels, neo-fascists, the militia movement, anti-vaxxers, or whichever gang of crackpots first manages to capture their eyeballs via YouTube or

Facebook's algorithms, urge us to choose the red pill and cast off the shackles of globalisation, liberalism, multiculturalism, modern science, or just plain old common sense. They offer the comfort of simple binary choices in an age of unfathomable complexity.

Pretty much everyone recognises *The Matrix* as the ultimate expression of 1990s cyberculture, a status that is confirmed both by its vast box office success and its influence on the culture at large. But there is a strong case to be made for another late-90s Hollywood film as capturing the true spirit of the coming digital era, a film in which there is nary a black-leather-clad cyber-ninja in sight. In Nora Ephron's *You've Got Mail* (1998), Tom Hanks and Meg Ryan, America's sweethearts, play a pair of well-heeled Manhattanites who embark on an online romance unaware that in real life they are rival bookstore owners. Kathleen owns the quirky indie store, The Shop Around the Corner, and Joe runs Fox Books, the corporate megastore that is trying to drive out the competition and homogenise the high street. (Meanwhile, in the real world of 1998, Jeff Bezos's Amazon is gearing up to eat both operations for breakfast.)

On the face of things, these two films could not be further apart. Where *The Matrix* took its inspiration from postmodern cyber-theory and hacker sub-cultures, *You've Got Mail* looked back to the easy glamour of golden age Hollywood and Ernst Lubitsch's 1940 romantic comedy, *The Shop Around the Corner*, from which Nora and Delia Ephron adapted their script. Where *The Matrix* immersed its viewers in science fiction spectacle, *You've Got Mail* ambled its way around a gentrified Manhattan of well-maintained brownstones, beige chinos and tasteful coffee shops.

But scratch the surface and these two films are in fact remarkably similar. Both are relics of an era when it was still possible to see cyberspace and the real world as two separate domains of reality that were connected only via complex, non-linear pathways. In *The Matrix*, Neo wakes up to the real reality of 2199 and the struggle for humanity's future in the age of the machines. In *You've Got Mail*, Kathleen and Joe find love online, but can't make things work in the tricky dimension of the here and now. Both films are also about the threat posed to civilisation by the supra-human forces of technology and commerce, the first embodied in the form of a race of artificially intelligent machines that wish to convert humankind into a natural resource, and the second embodied in the form of Jeff Bezos and the 'everything store' (so no real difference at all). *You've Got Mail* is that rare Hollywood creature, a romantic comedy about the inflexible law of the marketplace. By the end of the film, the indie store has closed, its staff have either retired or found work at the conglomerate down the road, and Kathleen pursues her dream of becoming a children's author (presumably with the financial support of her new chain-store-owning partner). Ultimately, *The Matrix* and *You've Got Mail* were the two sides of the same bitcoin. The digital revolution was built from equal parts black-leather-clad ninja hackers and chino-wearing corporate executives.

⇱↑⇲

The historian Fred Turner has pointed out the remarkable change in cultural meaning that digital computers underwent between the 1960s and the 1990s. In the 1960s, when ARPANET was first coming online, the computer was a symbol of mass bureaucratic society and the subordination of the individual to 'the machine'. Computers were part of the Cold War military-industrial complex, emblems of the technocratic alienation against which the 1960s counterculture rebelled. By the mid-1990s, that set of associations had been completely reversed. Computers were now seen as tools for personal liberation, a means of enhancing individual agency by plugging into a decentralised global network of instant communications and universally accessible knowledge.

This complete revaluation was enabled in large part by the miniaturisation and acceleration of computer technology that took place in those years – the shrinking of the computer from the size of a room to something that could fit on your desk and shortly in the palm of your hand. But Turner also explains how the values of a certain strain of the 1960s counterculture – in particular, the strain that valued personal freedom and the transformation of consciousness via psychedelic drugs and alternative lifestyles, rather than the Marxist politics of the New Left – were projected on to computers. The 1990s cyber-revolution was built by a loose coalition of ex-hippies, research scientists and good old-fashioned American capitalists. Spokespeople such as Kevin Kelly and Nicholas Negroponte helped to synthesise the values of the libertarian, far-out counterculture and the free-market economics of corporate America. For a short while in the mid-1990s, it looked as though this strange amalgam of the culture of the hippies and the economics of the Reaganites might be the answer to everyone's problems.

In 1995, Stewart Brand, one-time Merry Prankster and central player in the new Silicon Valley intelligentsia, wrote an article in *Time* magazine with the characteristically boosterish title, 'We Owe it All to the Hippies'. Brand's article briefly traces the same line of development that Turner does in his book, from the hippy counterculture to the freewheeling, decentralised early internet. But from his vantage point in 1995, riding the cresting wave of mid-90s digital optimism, Brand looks forward to a bright digital future of yet further empowerment via 'freeware' and 'shareware', open-access software that promotes technical know-how and participatory culture. He also notes with the optimism of the ageing hippy that the internet is the preserve of the young and the open minded, and that the rising generation will carry forward the values of the counterculture into the digital future.

Brand looked into the future and got it completely wrong. In reality, the utopian ideals of 1990s cyberculture proved no match for the laws of the marketplace and the opportunism of investors. In the 1990s, cyber-utopianism was shielded from contact with reality by the speculative excesses of the NASDAQ stock market bubble, during which vast amounts of finance capital sloshed around in search of the technologies that would define the future. In the days of the bubble, the hard questions of how to generate long-term profits and durable business models could be left until later. When the bubble burst, however, internet companies were forced to think much harder about those questions, and the answer, as we all now know, was advertising. But what Google and Facebook sold to advertisers was not simply access to consumers' eyeballs, as TV and newspaper ads had done for decades, but something of much greater potential value: the consumers themselves, or at least fine-grained data about how those consumers behaved in every aspect of their lives that could be recorded via laptop, smart phone, credit card or any device hooked up to the internet.

This is what Shoshana Zuboff calls 'surveillance capitalism', a new twist on the old trick of extracting surplus value from productive labour. What data companies like Google and Facebook offer is not just vast amounts of information about our online habits, but also the capacity to predict and influence those habits in the future. Or, as Zuboff puts it, what the industrial revolution was to nature in the nineteenth century, the digital revolution will be to human nature in the twenty-first. We are the raw materials. Our heedless, acquisitive, curious, kind, fearful, paranoiac, bored, majestic, utterly mundane and now highly predictable behaviour has become the ore out of which some of the world's largest companies spin their gold. Surveillance capitalism was effectively invented in 2001 by Google, a company whose founding motto was 'Don't be evil' and which grew out of the open-minded research culture of Stanford University. It is an irony of mind-boggling proportions that this new global architecture for the modification of human behaviour was born out of the 1990s ideals of decentralisation and individual empowerment.

If the cultural meaning of the computer shifted from a tool of bureaucratic alienation to one of personal liberation between the 1960s and the 1990s, then what shift has occurred in the subsequent thirty years? Computers have shrunk to the size of atoms and have been infiltrated into every part of our daily lives. Many of the features that early adopters in the 1990s found so miraculous – all the world's knowledge at my fingertips; instant connection across geographical distance – we simply take for granted. The shine has worn off the internet and we are now more likely to complain about fragmented attention, siloisation, misinformation and online hate speech than to marvel at its magical powers. The 1990s idea that computation enhances personal liberty is in seemingly terminal retreat. Perhaps the cultural meaning of the computer today has shifted once again; this time it is a symbol of nervous exhaustion and irritation, a desire to switch off, slow down, reclaim the rhythms of perception and thought of earlier, less hyper-mediated times.

And yet the promise of the 1990s was real. Today, Tim Berners-Lee devotes much of his time to what he calls the 're-decentralisation' of the internet. This takes the form of lobbying governments to regulate data monopolies and protect whistleblowers, while also developing technologies that will enable users to control all of their own data online. The godfather of the World Wide Web, a man who gave away the original html source code for free and has never profited directly from his invention, is embarked upon a quest to restore some the web's original spirit of empowerment and openness. Sometimes the way forward and the way back are one and the same.

8

Into the Void

EVERYONE WHO grew up in the 1990s knew someone like my friend Dave. When I first got to know him, Dave was a cheerful, slightly awkward but highly sociable member of the group of friends I met in my first year at university. He was studying aeronautical engineering and hoped one day to work for NASA, but his main passions were mountain biking, kite flying, bong arcana and videogames. We were all caught up in the hurly burly of undergraduate life – the social round of pubs, clubs, concerts, house parties and the occasional last-minute essay crisis. But even in the midst of this hectic activity, Dave's favourite pastime was sitting on the dilapidated sofa in his basement flat, smoking weed and playing videogames. This was the basecamp from which all of his missions were planned and to which they all returned. The flat, the couch, the screen and the bong.

Halfway through our second year at university, Dave underwent a strange transformation. The change began when he broke up with his girlfriend, but it went well beyond the fall-out from a brief undergraduate love affair. Gradually, Dave retreated into himself. He spent more and more time at home engulfed in a cloud of weed smoke with his twitchy fingers glued to his joypad. To begin with, it was a partial retreat. Occasionally, he'd come around for dinner or show up at a party, but eventually he just disappeared. We tried to maintain contact, but the spark of friendship seemed to have been extinguished. He was sullen, ill at ease, couldn't look us in the eye.

Dave's horizons had narrowed. He shuffled back and forth between the couch, the fridge and the toilet, with occasional sorties to the grocery store to buy rolling papers and junk food. He had tapered his desires down to the thinnest of edges: the dopamine reward cycle of the videogame and the THC hit of the skunkweed. After a while, we stopped going to his house. It was too awkward, this business of trying to rekindle a friendship with someone who wasn't really there. Eventually, Dave got kicked out of university and he moved back into his parent's house. We lost contact forever.

Doctors and psychotherapists have a number of ways to describe what happened to my friend and many other young people like him. Addiction, depression and cannabis psychosis are all plausible candidates for what went wrong. There are ample clinical literatures on each of these conditions that could throw light on the situation. In the 1990s, there was also much less general awareness about mental health; my friends and I were too caught up in our own heedless ways to be properly alert to Dave's problems. But there was also something larger than one young man's individual psychology in play. Dave's mind, like all of our minds, was embedded in a new kind of ecosystem, one that was composed of the accelerated digital media of the internet and videogames as well as the hybridised alkaloid molecules of the new strains of super-skunkweed bred by Dutch marijuana growers in the late 1980s. Our brains were lit up with intensities, our synapses super-charged with repeated loops of stimulus and slump, that would have been unknown to a young man fifty or a hundred years earlier. No doubt Dave's psychology would have been fragile whatever era he was born into, but the environmental triggers for his psychosis were unique to the age in which we lived.

↖↑↗

The game that Dave played more than any other was *Doom*, one of the best-selling titles in videogame history and one that did more than most to make gaming a ubiquitous feature of the cultural landscape in the 1990s. *Doom* is about a space marine who is stranded on one of Mars's moons and has to fight his way through a plague of radioactive space zombies (the gates of hell having been thrown open by an ill-fated teleportation experiment) in order to save humankind and return to planet earth. Mercifully, the narrative is not the main point of *Doom*; most players are barely aware of its existence as they blast their way through level after level of space zombies. This is because the gameplay unfolds entirely from the first-person perspective of the space marine, known to regular players as 'Doomguy', as he glides through abandoned moon bases and power plants in his quest to rid the universe of radioactive demons.

At the bottom centre of the screen is Doomguy's hand, which holds a variety of different weapons, including a pistol, a shotgun, a machine gun, a rapid-fire plasma rifle and, as a reward for those who progress furthest in the game, a chainsaw. Occasionally, the hand jerks upwards and to the left in recoil at a shot or in order to reload the weapon. Beneath the hand, running in a thin strip across the bottom of the screen, is a band of infographics with a constantly updating read-out of Doomguy's ammo, health, armour and weapons levels. The rest of the screen is filled with the environment itself, rendered in what was at the time cutting-edge graphical detail. Columns, staircases, carpet, sky, earth, wood, stone, metal, flame, blood, viscera: the player's field of vision is filled with the contents of the space marine's consciousness. As in reality, so in *Doom*: we move through the world that lies just beyond our heads; but in the game we move with an uncanny, weightless glide, as though the world inside the computer runs on a system of physics just slightly less refined than our own. If *Doom* can be said to be about anything at all, it is only in a secondary sense that it is about radioactive space zombies and the fate of mankind. In a more immediate sense, *Doom* is about how we perceive the world: our existence as a roving consciousness for whom the world is an endlessly receding horizon of uncertainty.

Doom was released in December 1993 with little fanfare in the mainstream media and zero advertising budget. The first version of the game was available in the form of 'shareware' that could be downloaded for free; when users became well and truly hooked on the gameplay, they could pick up the telephone and pay for access to further levels. The full version of the game was sold via mail order, and it was not until 1995 that it was available in bricks-and-mortar retail outlets. *Doom* was the product of an alternative culture industry, one that was housed far away from the red-hot centres of the American mediasphere in Los Angeles and New York. The underlying technology for the game had been designed in a dingy industrial park in Shreveport, Louisiana, and later in a student apartment in Madison, Wisconsin.

News of this next-level gaming experience spread via word of mouth among enthusiasts, as well as in online chatrooms and discussion boards. It is estimated that the shareware version was played by as many as 20 million users, and an additional 6 million hardcopies were sold in North America and Europe by 1999. When *Doom* was first made available for download, the entire AOL network seized up due to the scale of demand. Suburban America's internet portal of choice was laid low by nerds preparing to do battle with the space zombie hordes. *Doom* began life as a PC game, and one of its most popular features was the multiplayer option, which could be played online via Local Area Network connections. Groups of players fought one another over the internet in real time, all the while screaming obscenities and glorying in wreaking spectacular ultra-violence on their foes. For many early users, this was the most fully realised version of cyberspace currently available. An immersive, three-dimensional, fully networked interactive experience, a step change in mankind's capacity to simulate alternate realities and glory in synthetic amusements.

But what kind of alternate reality was this? *Doom* was striking both for the sheer speed of its gameplay and the visceral nature of the violence it depicted. On his ill-fated quest, Doomguy faced a veritable cornucopia of satanic beasts, all recently unleashed from the bonds of hell, including Dark Lords, Hell Spawns, Pain Elementals, Cacodemons, Vulgars, and Barons of Hell. Each of these beasts loomed out of the depths of the screen and had to be blasted or chopped into submission in order for the player to move deeper into the world. With its simulated ultra-violence and cartoonish gore, *Doom* was often associated with other kinds of 'extreme' popular culture in the 1990s: the films of Quentin Tarantino and Abel Ferrara, the ghetto aesthetics of gangsta rap, the sonic onslaught of grunge and heavy metal. A whole sub-cultural ethos grew up around first-person-shooter videogames, a predominantly masculine culture based on the enjoyment of simulated violence, techno-gothic fantasy worlds, gross-out humour, profanity and verbal jousting.

John Carmack and John Romero, the designers of *Doom* and its even more successful sequel, *Quake*, were two of the most prominent public faces of the 1990s videogame revolution. Carmack was the next-level programming ace, Romero the charismatic showman and designer. Feted at gaming conventions and profiled in *GQ* and the *New York Times*, they were the poster children for gaming as the 'new rock 'n' roll'. In fact, it wouldn't be too difficult to craft a rock 'n' roll biopic out of their story, one that pulled off the classic biopic trick of highlighting its subjects' bad behaviour and moral failings, while also taking vicarious pleasure in their antics.

Act I would trace the pair's rise from the undersexed nerdery of teenaged Dungeons and Dragons fandom, including the time when Carmack broke into his high school computer lab in the middle of the night in order to get extra time on the servers, through their first steps into the mail order software business, to the moment when *Doom* is about to launch. The creation of *Doom* itself would be dramatised in the form of an extended montage sequence of hunched male bodies, brightly lit screens, incessantly typing fingers, Eureka moments of geek camaraderie, and a gradually mounting pile of discarded pizza boxes and soft drink bottles. *Rocky* for software programmers.

Act II revels in the moment of runaway success, when *Doom* crashes the AOL servers and the dollars start rolling in. A legend is born. We witness the two young nerds metamorphose into two slightly older nerds, who trick out their new Dallas office like a geek pleasuredome and invest in several Ferraris each. They enjoy the adulation of fans and critics alike. They get laid more frequently than before. But, of course, there is trouble in paradise. As in all rock biopics, Act III depicts the fall from grace, the expulsion from the garden. Tensions flare between Carmack and Romero. Who deserves most credit for their success? Is engineering or design more important? Whose Ferrari has the coolest paint job? Who is responsible for the failure of their bloated samurai epic, *Daikatana*, which is released years behind schedule and fails to capture the zeitgeist like their previous titles? Egos inflate, suspicions creep, ill communication reigns. Tensions are further inflamed by the media furore surrounding *Doom* and *Quake*'s potential role in spurring copycat violence and school shootings. Carmack and Romero receive hate mail from critics, as well as the adulation of fans.

In the hands of a canny director, *The Doom Story* might be made to show how Carmack and Romero's success was emblematic of the new world created by those other geeks triumphant, Zuckerberg, Jobs and Gates. *Doom* was part of a mass digital culture that came online over the course of the 1990s, a culture that took a huge variety of forms, from websites and online communities to CGI movies, and from the sampladelic cultures of rave music and hip hop to the 'digital pet' toy, Tamogotchi, which encouraged kids all over the world to care for a rudimentary simulated lifeform that could be carried in their pencil cases at school. These are very different kinds of cultural experience that share an underlying technology – the almost magical capacity of zeros and ones to simulate lifelike beings and immersive alternative worlds. So much of popular culture in the 1990s was derived from the new possibilities opened up by digital computation. And yet so many of the forms this culture took bore the stamp of their creators' youthful, male, emotionally limited obsessions – fantasy worlds, stylised violence, competition, the desire for status, the reduction of the world's complexity to a series of binary choices and rigid categories. Or maybe it was just a harmless way of goofing off after work.

↖↑↗

The origins of the videogame industry can be traced back to the penny arcades and fairground amusements of the 1920s. This is where the first coin-operated pinball machines were introduced to a mass public keen for cheap thrills and interactive entertainments. With their flashing bulbs and tactile interfaces, pinball machines were the forerunners of arcade games like *Pac Man* and *Pong* that were so popular in the 1970s and '80s. They also generated a similar atmosphere of moral panic to the one that would later descend upon videogames – fears about technological hyper-stimulation and the erosion of moral character by excessive absorption in simulated environments. This was the gilded age's version of our own fears about post-literacy and wasted childhoods.

But the computational machinery that set videogames apart from earlier amusements emerged from the same Cold War research infrastructure as the internet, with its ample government funding and freewheeling approach to innovation and experiment. *Space War*, one of the very first videogames and the inspiration for arcade classics like *Galaxy* and *Space Invaders*, was invented by students at MIT in 1961. Nolan Bushnell, who converted *Space War* into an arcade console that was played in bars and restaurants in the 1970s, first played the game via ARPANET, the forerunner to the internet, while studying at the University of Utah. Even before that, in the days of the room-sized behemoths like ENIAC and Colossus, researchers built simple programs to play chess, Go, and even ping pong against one another. As the computer industry developed in the 1970s and '80s, what began as a sideline for curious researchers developed into a full-grown industry in its own right.

Unlike the commercial internet, however, videogames did not come freighted with high-minded ideals about organising the world's knowledge and empowering global citizens. Videogames were about thrills and spills; goggle-eyed, white-knuckled adventures, rather than self-improvement. When Tim Berners-Lee invented the World Wide Web in 1989, he envisaged the new technology as an extension of the human brain and an expression of humankind's fundamental nature as a rational animal. The invention of videogames from the same underlying technology was an expression of a different facet of human nature, our status as *homo ludens*, the playful animal which likes to disport itself in entertainments that have no purpose beyond themselves. Pong's squelchy back and forth of simulated tennis, Jumpman's struggle to scale the construction site and save his girlfriend from Donkey Kong, Super Mario's adventures in wonderland, even Doomguy's bloody path towards the hellmouth: all are expressions of the deep human urge to play.

And yet, all things contain their opposites, and too much of a good thing can do you harm. Just as Berners-Lee's vision of the world brain finds its nightmarish antithesis in the form of our contemporary plague of disinformation and surveillance, so too can the promise of the infinite space of gameplay contained within the compact form of the console – the shiny plastic casing of the Xbox or PS4, which glows with such sleek and agile promise – produce its own antithesis in the form of the sullen, obsessive, basement-dwelling bong head, like my friend Dave. For some, the human urge to play led not into the wide-open spaces of a digital utopia, but into the slumped ennui of the kid who couldn't get off the couch.

Doom was part of a wave of now-classic 1990s titles such as *Street Fighter*, *Mortal Kombat*, *Gran Turismo*, *Sim City*, *Grand Theft Auto* and *Goldeneye* that helped to make videogaming into a mass cultural phenomenon. But even as recently as the early 1980s, the rise of videogaming was far from a foregone conclusion. In 1983, the nascent market for home videogame consoles, which was dominated in America by Atari's Video Computer System and its smaller competitor, the Fairchild Video Entertainment System, collapsed almost overnight, losing 97 per cent of its revenues in a single year. This was partly due to competition from the first wave of desktop PCs and the poor quality of many of the games, such as Atari's notoriously bad *ET: The Extra-Terrestrial*, in which players guided an ET avatar that looked like he'd been built from Duplo by a not particularly precocious 3-year-old through a series of levels, almost all of which were designed in a uniform palette of green and yellow blocks. Instead of flying off the shelves and into consumers' homes, an astonishing 700,000 copies of *ET: The Extra-Terrestrial* and assorted Atari titles were dumped in landfill. After the 1983 market crash, many American retailers dismissed videogames as a passing fad. There was a tendency to see videogames as a sub-sector of the toy industry, as electronic entertainments for children rather than as a new medium in their own right. At this early stage in their development, the cultural framework for understanding what videogames meant and were capable of was not in place.

Today, most people are comfortable with the idea that videogames are a respectable way for a civilised human being, child or adult, to spend at least some of their leisure hours. Videogames are reviewed in broadsheet newspapers. You can study them in universities. They are exhibited in art galleries. Some even have secret lines of code embedded in them by government agencies seeking to recruit whizz kid hackers as cybersecurity specialists (converting poachers into gamekeepers). The US military used *Doom* as a training simulation for recruits to learn battle tactics. In fact, videogames come in so many different forms and are used in such a wide variety of social settings that to discuss them as a single entity is to betray one's ignorance. It's a bit like asking a literary critic whether books are good or bad in general. Throughout the 1990s, however, this cultural status was yet to be earned. Videogames hadn't been gentrified.

It was the arrival in 1986 of Nintendo's Entertainment System (NES) and *Super Mario Brothers*, the ready-to-play game that came packaged with each new console, that sparked the videogame revolution. The gameplay in Super Mario was fast compared to previous titles. Mario caromed around with a sprightliness and elasticity of such grace that his energy seemed to transfer to the players themselves; the fantasy landscape of drainpipes, magical mushrooms and skittering turtles that he explored bore the stamp of its creator Shigeru Miyamoto's off-kilter imagination. This was a game of sufficient complexity and speed to generate that twitchy need for more and yet more hours of play that characterise the very best in the medium. NES was a giant commercial success. It is estimated that by 1990, 30 per cent of American households had one.

The history of videogame consoles is often told in terms of 'generations'. The NES was the most successful of the third generation of consoles, which was made up of 8-bit machines like the Commodore 64 and ZX Spectrum. Beginning around 1990, the fourth generation of 16-bit machines were released, the most popular of which were the Super Nintendo Entertainment System, the update on the NES, and the Sega Genesis (or Megadrive if you were playing in Europe and elsewhere). Many an early 1990s childhood was defined by the icons of these two corporations, Super Mario and Sonic the Hedgehog. Sega presented itself as the edgier, slightly more punk-ish alternative to Nintendo. Sonic had spiky blue hair and lived for the thrill of speed, while Mario was a more whimsical, easygoing figure who bounced around his magical landscape. Both sold vast numbers of units. Beginning in 1994–95, the fifth generation of 32- and 64-bit machines was launched with the Sony Playstation and Nintendo 64, and then the sixth around the turn of the millennium with the Xbox, Playstation 2 and Gamecast. Meanwhile PC gaming took giant leaps forward with the release of new graphics cards and chips to enhance visuals and increase processing speeds.

It is worth pausing for a moment to think about the nature of the changes that occur at each step of this process. An 8-bit videogame console can process eight pieces of information at the same time. Each bit of information is a binary value, either 1 or 0. So an 8-bit machine has 256 possible states, or 2 to the power of 8 states. These are the underlying hardware conditions that set the parameters for how memory, colour graphics, music, picture resolution and gameplay can operate within the game. Programmers can utilise the possibility space created by these 256 potential combinations, but they can't add a 257th. A further set of constraints is added by the fact that each console is designed in different ways, which means that those 256 operations are configured differently within each machine. The NES, for instance, contained a palette of 256 possible colours, while the Commodore 64 had only 16 colours, a trade-off that opened up other possibilities such as greater storage capacity. The games that could be played on each machine were the product of the interactions between the imaginations of the programmers and the hard limits imposed by mathematics and technology.

With each new generation of consoles, that possibility space expanded exponentially. The 16-bit consoles were capable of 65,536 operations. That's enough to give you the speedy thrills of Sonic the Hedgehog and Super Mario, graphics that simulated the play of light upon metallic surfaces, movement that approximated the torque and acceleration of a rally car, albeit in heavily pixellated, block-like forms. The 32-bit consoles were capable of 4.29 billion operations. That is a change of oceanic magnitude, one that enabled the shift to 3D polygonal graphics, or the ability to simulate objects from complex meshes of polyhedral shapes. What this means is that the designer can much more closely approximate the flowing organic forms of the real world by using multiple flat planes, the joints and weaves of which are barely visible to the user's eye. This is what enabled the shift from *trompe l'oeil* 3D effects, like the ones used in *Doom*, to something approaching a believable alternative world. It gives you the shimmering translucence as Lara Croft dives into a jungle lagoon or the undulating distortions as a submarine approaches in *Metal Gear Solid* or the murky snowscapes of *Goldeneye*. This is the point at which videogaming starts to edge towards computer animation and virtual reality.

Videogames weren't just about speed and violence and psycho-kinetic thrill seeking. Games could be compelling for all manner of reasons, including problem solving, complex narrative, quirky design and fascinating ideas, the compulsive desire to fit the falling blocks into the available space. The best-selling handheld videogame console remains to this day the Nintendo Game Boy, which was first released in 1989. In this case, the portal to another world came in the form of a 4.7 x 4.3cm green and white screen with a 160 x 144 pixel resolution; or, in other words, a tiny little fuzzy rectangle. But in keeping with Nintendo's company motto – 'lateral thinking with withered technology' – the Game Boy was technologically unsophisticated but imaginatively and ludically brilliant. The simple geometric forms of *Tetris*, *Mario Tennis*, *Legend of Zelda* and *Kirby's Dreamland* kept children away from the temptations of literacy and the natural world for hours on end.

The other great symbol of the new possibilities of videogaming in the 1990s was *Sim City*, which was first released for PC in 1989 but spawned a whole series of sequels and spin-offs in subsequent years, including *Sim Ant*, *The Sims* and *Sim Earth*. In the Sim games you didn't shoot space zombies or explore fantasy worlds or battle street punks or race sports cars. Instead, you managed a complex system, such as a city, an ant colony, a family or the earth. The player used the levers at his or her disposal – budgeting decisions, the allocation of public services, zoning laws, etc. – in order to set the parameters within which the system could grow. When you left a Sim game to its own devices, the city, ant colony, family or earth would continue to evolve (or devolve) of its own accord. There was no way to win at *Sim City*. There were no points tallies, no levels to conquer, no final bosses to defeat.

Sim City's designer, Will Wright, drew his inspiration from the science of complex adaptive systems and James Lovelock's Gaia hypothesis, rather than death metal and horror movies, as in the case of *Doom*, or Japanese myth and stereotypes about Italian plumbers, as in the case of *Super Mario*. If *Doom* was lifelike in that it mimicked our first-person perspective on the world, then *Sim City* was lifelike in that it mimicked the way in which humans are always embedded within complex systems over which they have limited control. *Sim City* was the ideal game for the network age.

Computational time unfolds at a different pace than that of ordinary historical time, with its regular generational cycles every twenty-five years or so. The pace of technological innovation in the 1990s meant that we passed from the third to the sixth generation of games machines in the space of ten years. But in that same period, a single generation of young people were coming of age, many of them growing up immersed in the exponentially expanding space inside the machine. As they grew, videogames ceased to be seen purely as toys; instead, they became a vast cultural ecosystem in their own right, which gave birth to a range of sub-cultures and forms of life the likes of which most people born before the 1980s are blissfully unaware. By the end of the 1990s, videogame launch parties were being held at the Ministry of Sound nightclub in London. Flyers for the newest releases with perforated strips to be torn off and used as roaches for spliffs were being handed out at music festivals. For many of us who grew up back then, the sensory details of low-res graphics, tinny soundtracks and calloused fingers from hours of joypad abuse exercise a kind of techno-Proustian magic over our now middle-aged minds; these triggers are capable of transporting us back, for a fleeting moment at least, into the past.

↖↑↗

Doom was released early in this process of exponential growth, but it arrived like an arrow pointing directly into the future. One of the most striking things about *Doom* was the speed at which the game unfolded. Doomguy raced into the void and the monsters loomed out of the depths at a speed that was both thrilling to experience and challenging to keep up with. This was one of the great triumphs of Carmack's game engine, the underlying computational architecture upon which Romero and his design team grafted their bestiary of demons and sprites. Players of *Doom* and its successor, *Quake*, for which Carmack refined and enhanced the original game engine, often refer to the sense of proprioceptive 'rightness' about the game. The combination of first-person perspective and self-directed forward motion seems to create a shadow sensation in the player's brain of real-life tactility and presence. *Doom* and *Quake* are games that you don't just see unfolding on the screen, but feel within your central nervous system, as your internal sense of motion and balance torques this way and that in relation to the gameplay. It was as though the game engine had directly harnessed the accelerated electronic signals within the computer chip. *Quake III Arena*, a stripped-down version of the game designed for multiplayer battles, which was released in 1999, was the first title to be played by professional e-sports gamers. Out of Carmack and Romero's mid-1990s innovations would grow a multi-million-dollar global industry with accredited tournaments, professional players, an avid fanbase and, as of the early 2020s, a campaign for Olympic accreditation.

It will come as no surprise that both Carmack and Romero were avid science fiction fans; both were captivated by the idea of the holodeck in *Star Trek: The Next Generation*, a room-sized virtual reality simulator which can produce a seemingly infinite number of alternative worlds, almost all of which demonstrate the limitations of network television budgets by resembling familiar genre fiction settings, such as film noir or the Western. Immersive simulation is not just a staple of science fiction, but also hovers as a dreamlike possibility over new media technologies in the real world. When he was confronted with the development of Technicolour movies in the 1950s, the great French film critic André Bazin looked forward to a future of 'total cinema', the point at which the movies, enhanced by unforeseen technological developments, would become indistinguishable from life itself. This, claimed Bazin, was the hidden logic of all media, an urge towards the exact replication – and perhaps, ultimately, replacement – of everyday reality.

Eventually, John Carmack left id Software to work for Oculus, the technology development company, on its virtual reality project. In interviews, Carmack spoke of virtual reality not simply as a fiendishly difficult engineering project, but as a 'noble goal' and a 'moral imperative'. This is the transcendental aspect of digital culture and the videogame industry that is not often recognised by everyday gamers. Beyond the geek aesthetics and impenetrable jargon, there lies an almost supernatural belief in the value of ever more complete simulations of reality. Strip away the vast depths of knowledge and skill, the business acumen, the technological innovation, the millions of hours of coding experience, all of the software programmer's armoury of technical know-how, and there remains a perverse desire to re-create the world in its entirety. Shigeru Miyamoto, the legendary inventor of *Donkey Kong, Super Mario* and *Legend of Zelda*, and the closest thing that videogame culture has to a Shakespearean Bard-figure, described his goal in designing the fantasy landscape of Zelda in the following terms:

> The spirit, the state of mind of a kid when he enters a cave alone must be realised in the game. Going in, he must feel the cold air around him … If you go to the cave now, as an adult, it might be silly, trivial, a small cave. But as a child, in spite of being banned to go, you could not resist the temptation. It was not a small moment then.

Videogames are emanations of humankind's god complex, our desire to rebuild the world from scratch, to recover the lost Eden of childhood and see the world as if for the first time.

Throughout the 1980s, videogaming was a mostly flat experience. *Pacman, Pong, Space Invaders, Super Mario*, etc., all unfolded within two-dimensional environments. The most immediate precursors to Doom were *Hovertank* and *Wolfenstein 3D*, which Carmack and Romero developed in the early 1990s. Carmack's great innovation for Hovertank was to illustrate only the walls and floor but not the ceiling of the environment, which conserved processing power and enabled smoother gameplay. And yet in both games the environment was composed of flat, featureless blocks of colour. The great innovation of *Doom* was to render the world inside the computer more 'cinematic', more replete with minute textural detail that contributed little to the actual gameplay but helped to convince the player that he was in an alternative universe similar to our own.

Rather than illustrating the entire environment, the game engine would simulate only a thin strip of architecture from a single, mobile perspective, as though a ray of light was being projected on to an otherwise dark world. This convention saved processing power and came up with an elegant visual solution to the problem of how to create a sense of perspective within the flat plane of the screen. Another perspectival trick was 'parallax scrolling', or instructing the game engine to make objects further away from the player's perspective seem to move slower than objects that were closer. This meant that the sense of realistic perspective was maintained even as the character moved around the environment. 'Texture mapping' meant that instead of illustrating surfaces as uniform blocks of colour, the game engine could project variable patterns on different parts of the same surface, which gave the impression of texture and detail. What in *Hovertank* appeared as a uniform grey plane could become in *Doom* a recognisable approximation of a stone wall covered in patches of moss. Variable lighting techniques added to this sense of textural reality, in which the environment was illuminated by a range of clearly identifiable light sources.

With *Doom*, the devil really was in the details. Players didn't just enjoy the experience of blasting space demons into little pieces; they also enjoyed the hyper-real rendering of the little pieces themselves, the flecks of gore and pools of blood that were animated in such loving and unnecessary detail. This was the videogame equivalent of what the literary critic Roland Barthes called the 'reality effect', or the way in which the great realist novels of the nineteenth century included descriptions of material objects that had no actual bearing on the narrative events or symbolic meaning of the story itself. The classic example that Barthes gives is the barometer that hangs on the wall of Madame Aubain's apartment in the opening paragraph of Flaubert's novella *A Simple Heart*. The barometer does not feature in the narrative nor does it symbolise Madame Aubain's social status or moral character. It is a 'narrative excess' and a 'residue' that plays no substantial role in the text's meaning. What it does, though, is signal a reality that lies beyond the text, the reality of reality itself. It was the reality effects in *Doom* that made it such a significant leap forward and solidified the appeal of the first-person-shooter genre. The texture of moss on stone walls. The mottled grey pattern of the mountains that loom in the distance. And, most strikingly of all, the residues of blood, guts and dismembered corpses that litter the screen. The ooze of the real.

↖↑↗

'It's going to be like fucking *Doom*.' This is one of the lines that Eric Harris delivered to camera in his suburban bedroom shortly before he and Dylan Klebold walked into Columbine High School on the morning of 20 April 1999 and murdered twelve students and one teacher before taking their own lives. Harris's online moniker was 'Rebdoomer'. His personal website was a foul stew of violent screeds against school bullies and 'mission logs' preparing for the attack, but it also hosted the new *Doom* levels that he made with the game's popular 'mod packs', software plug-ins that enabled hardcore players to create their own environments and monsters. It is impossible to determine the ultimate cause of Harris and Klebold's murderous rampage. Psychologists have identified Harris as a clinical psychopath with a messianic superiority complex. Klebold was a submissive who wrote in his diary about his 'infinite sadness' at his lack of success with girls. Harris was on the anger management drug, Luvox, and Klebold was on anti-depressants. Both were bullied at school. What is clear, though, is that the murders were bound up with – not caused by, necessarily, but somehow connected to, rendered imaginatively possible by – the feverish fantasy lives that the two boys lived out through videogames and movies. In their diaries, they referred to the planned attack as 'NBK', or *Natural Born Killers*, after the 1994 Oliver Stone movie about a pair of serial killers who stage their attacks for the national media.

The Columbine Massacre re-ignited a debate about violent movies and videogames that had been underway for much of the 1990s. *Doom* was first released on 10 December 1993, the day after US senators Joe Lieberman and Herb Kohl held a congressional hearing on the social effects of violence in the media, the main focus of which were two-dimensional fighting games such as *Mortal Kombat* and *Lethal Enforcers*. As a result of the hearings, games companies agreed to a rating system similar to the one used for movies. Some also toned down the gorier features of their forthcoming titles in order to avoid scandal, but demand for and supply of violent game content barely abated in the following years. In fact, it likely accelerated as gamers got older, graphics got better and the total videogame market expanded. *Doom* became a grisly cause célèbre when a new round of congressional hearings was called by Senator Sam Brownback in March of 2000 in the wake of Columbine. Harris and Klebold's references to *Doom* and the saturation of the media with still images taken from the school's security cameras as the massacre unfolded prompted journalists and politicians to question whether violent imagery in videogames could directly cause copycat violence. The fact that the two most prominent voices in that debate were Sam Brownback, a conservative Christian senator from Kansas, and Marilyn Manson, the lead singer of a goth metal band, tells you something about the quality and tone of public debate in America at the end of the twentieth century.

It would be all too easy to dismiss Senator Sam Brownback of Kansas as a caricature of fin-de-millennium American conservatism, with his granite-hard commitments to American exceptionalism, flag and faith pieties and the extreme fiscal policies that helped to bankrupt his home state when he served as governor in the 2010s. To be sure, his reflections on the Senate floor about the causes of school shootings entirely failed to mention both the long history of violent media that stretches back through the Marquis de Sade and Jacobean tragedy, with its flayed corpses and poisoned skulls, and the more salient fact of America's perverse gun culture that enabled two disturbed teenagers to amass an arsenal of military-grade weapons. But even a stopped clock can occasionally capture the zeitgeist. 'Unfortunately,' mused the senator, 'there have always been, and there always will be, youth who are drawn to extreme behaviour, but what qualifies as extreme depends on what's normal. If the entire norm changes then the extreme changes with it.' Brownback's comments capture the sense of historical vertigo that many of us feel when confronted by the horror of Columbine-style massacres, the sense that the very ground beneath our feet has shifted, that we have entered a terrifying new normal.

Another target of the post-Columbine moral panic was Brian Hugh Warner, otherwise known as Marilyn Manson, the lead singer of the eponymous glam-goth-thrash-punk-metal band. In the days following the massacre, false reports circulated that Harris and Klebold had worn make-up and clothes directly modelled on Manson's during the attack. Those reports were eventually debunked, but only after the story had taken on a life of its own in the ceaseless churn of cable news, tabloid reportage and internet commentary. Marilyn Manson band members were subject to death threats and political denunciations; their US tour had to be cancelled for their own safety. But rather than accepting the role of America's scapegoat and slinking quietly off beyond the city walls, Manson made a series of media appearances in which he offered an alternative take on the killings. The scapegoat turned media critic. In *Rolling Stone* magazine, he argued that 'times have not become more violent, they have just become more televised'; and on *Fox News* he observed, 'those kids ended up on the cover of *Time* magazine. The media gave them exactly what they wanted.'

The man in the white face paint and blue eye make-up was surely right. They did it for the cameras. Irrespective of the psychological triggers that enabled Harris and Klebold actually to go through with their plan, and irrespective of how much they enjoyed playing *Doom*, the obvious function of the attacks was to create a spectacular event that would light up screens around the world. Harris and Klebold wanted to be recognised. They wanted to become part of the spectacle, to cross over to the other side of the screen.

Their website and notebooks can be read as precursors to the toxic online sub-cultures that emerged on platforms like 4chan and Reddit in the early 2000s. Many of the cultural touchstones are the same: *Doom*, *Quake* and first-person-shooter videogames, edgy 1990s movies such as *Fight Club* and *The Matrix*, Japanese anime and extreme pornography, all wrapped up in a self-declared 'nerd' identity that was bolstered by volleys of violent misogyny and rhetorical bombast. Their writings were not overtly political, but they were steeped in the same brew of resentment and vainglory that drives the alt-right and neo-reaction movements today. With his complaints about his 'infinite sadness' at not having a girlfriend, Klebold might even be an early member of the involuntary celibate, or 'incel' movement that rails against feminist empowerment and the unfairness of sexual selection. Their praise for radical free speech ('This page explains the various things in the world that annoy the SHIT outa me. God I just LOVE freedom of speech') and social Darwinism ('getting rid of all the stupid and weak organisms ... but its all natural!!! Yes!') foreshadow the anti-politically correct, pseudo-scientific, hyper-individualism that can be heard in the echo chambers of alt-right social media.

In the years since Columbine, the mass shooting event has become a grotesque cultural meme, a template that can be followed by other lost boys desperate for recognition in a hyper-mediated and profoundly alienating world. Between 1999 and 2012, there were 140 school shootings in America. Many of the perpetrators of those attacks – and many would-be perpetrators whose plans were foiled – explicitly cited Harris and Klebold as their inspiration. In his notebooks, Harris proclaimed his desire to 'kickstart a revolution', but he never formulated a specific ideology or cause to fight for. The motivations of subsequent school shooters are just as opaque and confused. Many express a diffuse sense of resentment cobbled together from the stews of online reaction, the grievances of incels, alt-right deplorables, white nationalists, neo-misogynists, quack-eugenicists, videogame purists, doxxers and conspiracists to be found on obscure subreddits, 4chan and later 8chan threads. The sense of dark purpose conveyed by Harris and Klebold's 'mission logs' and military-style planning, the sense of a luminous meaning that hovers just beyond the bland consensus of everyday life, collides with the petty resentments of little men.

No doubt this kind of stuff has been around for a long time. Hatred, resentment, stifled desire, status anxiety: ugly feelings run deep in the human heart. But when they are fed on a diet of 'extreme' popular culture and juiced up by a constant stream of confirmation in the form of response and repostings, the suppression valves that held the Underground Men in check in prior epochs crumble away. Our horror at mass shootings like Columbine is an intensified version of that low-grade, but widespread anxiety many of us feel about screen culture in general, the fear that as a culture, as a species even, we are losing our grip on the line between reality and simulation.

9

Shock, Horror!

'SATURDAY NIGHT LIVE' —
STILL WILD & CRAZY AT 25
ShowTime

SCRATCH
& MATCH
GAME CARD INSIDE

SPORTS ★ ★ ★ ★ FINAL

DAILY NEWS

$1.00 www.nydailynews.com NEW YORK'S HOMETOWN NEWSPAPER Sunday, September 26, 1999

RUDY'S ART WAR

WHAT'S WRONG WITH THIS PICTURE?

Detail from 'Holy Virgin Mary' by Chris Ofili

Showdown looms over Brooklyn Museum

MICHAEL DALY & STORY ON PAGES 6-7

WHAT IS the difference between art and pornography, except maybe a few zeros at the end of the price tag? This was one of the questions posed by the most successful visual artist of the 1990s. Jeff Koons shot to art world acclaim – and public notoriety – with his 'Made in Heaven' series, produced between 1989 and 1991, which depicted the artist and his then wife, the Italian-Hungarian porn star Ilona Staller, in a variety of sexual poses and a range of artistic media, including oil on canvas, lithograph billboards, glass and plastic sculptures and silkscreen canvases.

Some of these works are very rude indeed. *Blow Job*, *Couch*, *Ilona on Top*, *Jeff Eating Ilona*, *Kiss*, *Position Three* and *Violet-Ice* are all small-scale glass sculptures (on average around 50 x 40cm) of Jeff and Ilona having sex in a variety of positions from the *Kama Sutra*. *Dirty – Jeff on Top* is a life-size plastic cast of Jeff and Ilona on a rocky platform made from a mixture of what seems like granite and coal, so that their bodies are smeared with dirty black streaks. *Red Butt (Distance)* is a large silkscreen print that depicts Jeff and Ilona performing anal sex. *Red Butt (Close-Up)* is a large silkscreen print of the same image but now from a much narrower angle, so that all we can see is Jeff's groin and half of his penis, Ilona's butt and splayed vagina, her red-PVC-clad thighs and a red-velvet-gloved hand playing with her clitoris. This one sold for $520,000 at Christie's in New York in 2005. Not too shabby for an image that is all but indistinguishable from a page torn from a porn mag.

Silver Shoes is a hyper-realistic photograph printed in oil inks on a mounted canvas that depicts Jeff and Ilona in a corner of his studio (you can see a blank canvas, a ladder and some more porn-art in the background). Jeff is naked, his penis at half-mast by Ilona's right buttock. Ilona is in white fishnet stockings with a lacy hem at her upper thigh. She also wears gloves of the same lacy white material, a coronet of pink and white flowers, and a pair of silver high-heeled shoes. She is laid out on her back, her legs held aloft in Jeff's arms, so that her labia are near the centre of the picture's formal composition (this one sold for $800,000 at Sotheby's in 2007). Perhaps it was in reference to this picture, the one with Ilona's vagina framed as the image's implied centre of meaning, that Koons remarked: 'Ilona is one of the greatest artists in the world. She is a great communicator, a great liberator. Other artists use a paint-brush. Ilona uses her genitalia.' The question, though, was what did those lips want to say? What brush strokes did they want to make? What was the point of displaying hardcore porn in a prestigious New York gallery?

One thing that Koons wanted to communicate by way of Ilona's genitalia was that judgements of taste are relative. One man's pornography is another man's art. Or, as D.H. Lawrence put it in his essay 'Pornography and Obscenity', 'what is pornography to one man is the laughter of genius to another'. In addition to the porn images, 'Made in Heaven' included non-explicit works, such as *Bourgeois Bust – Jeff and Ilona*, a marble bust of the artist and his muse in the style of a nineteenth-century academician, *Mound of Flowers*, a tacky glass sculpture of a bouquet in lurid reds, blues and yellows, and *Yorkshire Terriers*, a polychromed wood sculpture of two cute-as-a-button terriers, one with a blue and one with a pink bow in its hair. That one sold for £855,000 at Sotheby's in London. With its mixture of styles and allusions – the *Kama Sutra*, Masaccio's *Expulsion from the Garden of Eden*, Madame Tussaud's waxworks, junk-shop kitsch, hardcore pornography – Koons was making what was by now a rather traditional pop art move, which was to erase the boundary between high art and low culture by placing radically different kinds of objects in the hallowed space of the gallery. Koons's main contribution to a tradition that included Duchamp, Warhol, Rauschenberg and Lichtenstein was to add hardcore porn to the mix.

But that was not all that those mute lips had to say. Koons wanted to make a point about human identity and sexual desire. In spite of his relativistic view of culture, Koons was no nihilist. Just because tastes and beliefs change, does not mean there are no ultimate values. In interviews, Koons often talked about the emotional and spiritual struggle that went into the production of the 'Made in Heaven' series. 'I went through moral conflict,' he said, 'I could not sleep for a long time in the preparation of my new work. I had to go to the depths of my own sexuality, my own morality, to be able to remove fear, guilt and shame from myself.' What do you get when you remove fear, guilt and shame? You get desire itself, unmediated by false consciousness. You get a return to the garden, before the moment of expulsion depicted with such solemnity by Masaccio in fifteenth-century Florence.

In this respect, Koons was less of a postmodern trickster and more of a new age spiritual guru. 'Made in Heaven' urges us to cast off all restraint, all good taste, all well-educated opinion, and to embrace our true desires, our real selves. Ilona's floral coronet and white, lacy shrouds invoke the pastoral innocence of the flower power generation. The quest to discover the authentic self and its pure desires chimes with the 1960s ethos of personal liberation and belief in sexuality as the key to identity. Koons used obscenity not only as a way to reverse conventional artistic values, but also as a kind of aesthetic battering ram with which to break on through to a new perspective on the self and its desires. 'I'm interested in love, I'm interested in reunion, I'm interested in the spiritual, to be able to show people that they can have an impact, to achieve their desires,' he claimed. His goal was 'transcendence – to help people find something of greater interest than the self'.

Like many a self-help guru, Koons was not averse to becoming spectacularly rich. 'Made in Heaven' wrestled with weighty spiritual themes – or, at least, that's what its creator said it did – but it was also cannily designed to capture the media's attention and place Koons himself in the spotlight. The Koons–Staller marriage was a calculated career move on both sides, as well as an amorous adventure. If the porno shock tactics of 'Made in Heaven' weren't enough to grab the public's attention, then the tabloid tale of the love affair between the artist and the pornographer, as well as the subsequent scandal of the divorce and the international custody battle over their son, Ludwig, most certainly was. Over the course of the 1990s, Koons became the world's highest-grossing art star and a ubiquitous figure in the media. His multi-million-dollar artworks floated like bubbles on the speculative tides of the global financial markets, surging upwards in price after the recession of 1989, then tumbling downwards in the early 2000s after the dot-com crash. Today, Koons is the public face of his own art corporation, which employs over 100 craftspeople in his Manhattan studio. He still holds the record for the highest sale of a work by a living artist – $58.4 million for an orange balloon dog sold at Christie's in New York in 2013.

In many ways, though, Koons was the least interesting half of this art/porn power couple, and yet he was still the one who got all the artistic credit and most of the royalties. Born in Budapest in 1951, Illona Staller was an eccentric product of the Cold War. In her autobiography, she claims to have been an informant for the NKVD, or the Soviet secret police, while working as a part-time model and courtesan in a grand Budapest hotel frequented by Western businessmen and diplomats. In the 1970s, she escaped to the West – or, more accurately, the south, as she was travelling from Hungary – to Italy, where she embarked on a high-profile career in pornographic cinema, starring in such titles as *The Ingenue*, *Private Vices, Public Pleasures* and *The Rise of the Roman Empress*, the last of which influenced some of Koons's compositions in 'Made in Heaven', and was also perhaps a source of personal anxiety, as Ilona's co-star was none other than Big John Holmes, he of the legendary appendage. But La Cicciolina (her porn name) was more than just a woman who appeared in dirty movies. With her floral crowns, long blonde locks, gauzy outfits and increasingly plump plastic lips, she cultivated a larger-than-life persona as a kind of neo-pagan sex goddess, at once a kitschy, fabricated character out of a

Russ Meyer fantasy land and a powerful force of nature, who was the mistress of her own desires.

Staller also took the idea of sexual politics seriously; so seriously, in fact, that she stood numerous times as a candidate for the Italian parliament and, in 1987, won a seat as a member of the Radical Party. Her successful election campaign included much public nudity, frequent stripteases and the handling of a large snake on the hustings. As an MP, Staller referred to her fellow parliamentarians as 'cicciolini', chubby little boys, insinuating that they liked to play among – and most likely with – themselves. During the build-up to the First Gulf War, she publicly offered to have sex with Saddam Hussein as a way to defuse the mounting tensions in the region. She made the same offer to Osama bin Laden roughly a decade later. Her antics were crude and embarrassing, but didn't they also contain at least a few grains of truth? Staller articulated the blunt reality of power and politics, both in Italy and around the world. Politics is about status and competition, implicit and actual violence. Politics is, in the crudest terms possible, a dick-measuring contest: my Scud missile's bigger than yours. La Cicciolina offered herself up as a one-woman bomb disposal squad, who would resolve the conflict through a sublime act of sexual healing. Beneath the political theatre – which had a characteristically Italian *opera buffa* quality – was the same post-1960s belief in the redemptive power of sexual desire and the restorative properties of a really good fuck.

↖↑↗

'Made in Heaven' was certainly novel and definitely obscene, but it was also very much of its time. The 1990s shock art moment began before 'Made in Heaven' made its debut. In 1987 Andres Serrano's *Piss Christ*, a photograph of a small plastic crucifix submerged in a jar of the artist's urine, provoked the ire of Republican senators, who wanted to shut down the National Endowment for the Arts for funding this piece of degenerate art. On the floor of the Senate, Republican congressman Jesse Helms thundered, 'I will not even acknowledge that it is art. I do not even acknowledge that the fellow who did it was an artist. I think he was a jerk.' His colleague Alfonse D'Amato tore up a picture of Serrano's artwork and denounced its 'deplorable, despicable display of vulgarity'. In 1990 Robert Mapplethorpe's exhibition at the Cincinnati Art Gallery was closed down by the police and the museum's director was charged with two counts of 'misdemeanour obscenity'. Most of the images in *The Perfect Moment* were beautiful, inoffensive and sad (the show opened shortly after Mapplethorpe died of an AIDS-related illness): still lives of lilies and orchids, self-portraits, group portraits, nudes, memento mori. They expressed a distinctive sensibility and documented the queer sub-cultures of Downtown New York. Maybe not your cup of tea, but far from obscene, pornographic or illegal. What provoked controversy were the handful of images which contained explicit depictions of gay sex and fetish practices: Mapplethorpe shot from behind, his torso twisting around so he can meet the camera's gaze, with a bull whip inserted in his rectum; a sideways-on close-up of a male posterior, the body bent forward at the waist, with a large black dildo inserted in the rectum; a standing man, his face covered by a leather mask, urinating into the mouth of a kneeling man (*Jim and Tom, Sausalito*). These images were designed to provoke. That's why Mapplethorpe contorts his body and meets the viewer's gaze: upon whose authority do you judge me?

'Made in Heaven' was launched during the same tense moment for American art. The Berlin Wall had recently fallen and the Soviet Empire was dwindling. What else was the American right to do but turn its attentions to the enemy within: degenerate artists sponging off government agencies. And yet, while Koons's 'Made in Heaven' garnered plenty of bad reviews – banal, unoriginal, too eager to shock – it drew none of the outrage that religious conservatives had directed towards Serrano and Mapplethorpe. The art historian Lauren DeLand puts this down to the ultimately quite conventional romantic ideals that Koons wove into the work. He and Staller got married shortly before embarking on the project. They were framed in a variety of hardcore tableaux, but these were images of happily married heterosexual love, with none of the queer marginality of Serrano and Mapplethorpe's work, and free from the shadow of the AIDS epidemic which was still associated in many people's minds with gay sex and moral degeneracy.

In Britain, a new generation of visual artists adopted Koons's strategic combination of shock tactics and art world business savvy. The Young British Artists (YBAs), as they came to be known, got their start at the beginning of the decade, when they were still fresh from their theory-heavy art degrees and the recession had tanked the global art market. YBAs like Damien Hirst, Tracey Emin and Sarah Lucas staged their first shows in disused warehouses in the East End of London. These were the same post-industrial spaces that were taken over by sound systems and ravers on the weekends; yet another way in which the hip cultural industries came to replace the manufacturing base of earlier decades. One early show staged by Hirst and Lucas was even raided by the police in the mistaken belief that an illegal rave was underway.

The rise of the YBAs from London's edgelands to the heights of the global art scene unfolded at breakneck speed, propelled by the cultural accelerants of speculative finance and tabloid scandal. In 1993, Emin and Lucas were opening 'The Shop', a tatty, magnolia-painted storefront on the largely boarded-up Brick Lane, the heart of London's Bangladeshi community, where they sold t-shirts with 'Have You Wanked Over Me Yet' and 'I'm So Fucky' scrawled on them in magic marker. By 1997 they were exhibiting at the Royal Academy and were the official face of British contemporary art. In large part, it was the patronage of Charles Saatchi that propelled them to such heights. Saatchi was the co-founder of the famous advertising agency Saatchi and Saatchi, which had masterminded the 'Labour Isn't Working' billboard campaign that helped Margaret Thatcher win power in 1979. Saatchi was forced to sell off most of his collection of established American and European modern artists in the recession of the late 1980s and made a conscious decision to re-invest in much cheaper works by local artists with more scope to appreciate in value. Saatchi was the first of a new breed of artworld 'speculectors', wealthy connoisseurs who acquire and sell contemporary art collections in very short time frames in order to ride the shifting tides of the market.

But the YBAs achieved a prominence that went well beyond the rarefied worlds of the international art market and the culture pages of the better newspapers. In 1997, when the Royal Academy's planned show of modern classics fell through, Saatchi stepped into the breach and offered his own collection of contemporary British art as a replacement. Thus was *Sensation* born, the group show that cemented the YBAs as both establishment insiders and tabloid demons in one fell swoop. Much of the work combined high-concept visual tricks with obscene materials drawn from the most lurid reaches of popular culture. The art critic Julian Stallabrass referred to it as a form of 'High Art Lite' or 'fast food modernism', which combined extreme content with easily digestible statements on the commodification of art and the debasement of popular culture. It was slick, crude, designed to make you think, and aimed at a decidedly mass audience.

As with Koons's art-porn crossovers, it was meant to shock. Sarah Lucas made collages of topless pin-up girls alongside surreal headlines from the British tabloid press, filling otherwise respectable galleries with cheap, misogynist gags to show how everyday sexism reduced women to their bare physical attributes. 'Two Fried Eggs and a Kebab' and 'Chicken Pants' were among the most mordantly bathetic. Chris Ofili made glowing devotional images of a Black Virgin Mary, who was partly composed of elephant dung and surrounded by butterflies made from female genitalia cut out of Afro-Caribbean porn mags. In the 'Disasters of War' series, Jake and Dinos Chapman created gory battlefield models, which teemed with undead Nazi biker gangs, roadside lynchings and piles of mutilated corpses – an infinite regress of violence and degradation. In *Zygotic Acceleration*, they exhibited life-sized models which seemed to depict some kind of deranged genetic experiment: agglomerations of multiply conjoined siblings, some with penis-noses, some with anus-mouths, all sporting the latest in branded sportswear.

Marcus Harvey's *Myra* used children's handprints to compose an 11 x 9ft image of Myra Hindley who, along with her partner, Ian Brady, murdered five children on the Saddleworth Moor in the early 1960s. With its combination of child-generated content and a series of grotesque murders whose perpetrators were still alive in prison, that one was real catnip for the tabloids. Tracey Emin exhibited her unmade bed, along with the snotty tissues, condom packets and overflowing ashtrays that surrounded it. Emin's tent was a faux-naif confessional, a seedy bare-all disclosure of all of the one-night stands, failed relationships, assaults and abortions from the artist's past. It was an exercise in over-sharing, of rubbing the viewers' noses in it.

Mat Collishaw's *Bullet Hole* was a photo-realistic image of a bullet wound in a scalp. The image is shot at such close range that the wound has become estranged, as though it were some kind of undiscovered erotic aperture, glistening with pinkish-red menace. The thick parted hair makes the scalp look more like a Wookiee's erogenous zone than an identifiable part of the human anatomy. The image is divided by a regular grid pattern, which invites our detached, almost scientific gaze, as though the viewer were a detective inspector trying to crack a case. Damien Hirst went in for gory 'vitrines', large glass cases that displayed a variety of pickled fauna: a great white shark; the skinned head of a cow; a sheep sliced down the middle into two halves; a rotting cow's head, with thousands of flies, two bowls of sugared water, and an Insect-O-Cutor arranged around it. Hirst was the Jack the Ripper of 1990s conceptual art, a slasher-artist who exhibited a series of enclosed existential horrorscapes within the antiseptic, vaguely scientific space of the vitrine.

In many ways, the public outcries of the 1990s testified to how far the boundary between acceptable and obscene had been pushed. The '90s were a very late stage in the history of obscenity. By the time Koons and Hirst came along, there had already been centuries' worth of provocative modernist art, so many years' worth, in fact, that the modernist equation of shock tactics and cultural progress was beginning to wear a little thin. After De Sade's

120 Days of Sodom, Courbet's *L'Origine du Monde*, Manet's *Déjeuner sur l'herbe*, Duchamp's *Fountain*, Joyce's *Ulysses*, Nabokov's *Lolita*, Réage's *Story of O* and Manzoni's *Artist's Shit*, was there really any mileage left in outraging bourgeois taste and morality? What frontiers were left to be pushed? In a sense, it is a testament to the ingenuity of 1990s shock artists that they managed to discover new horizons of shockability, new terrains of the obscene. In order to get a rise out their audience, many of these artists had to turn the dial up to eleven. Hence the Piss Christs, the elephant-dung Madonnas, the pope languishing beneath a fallen asteroid, the rotting cow heads, the Day-Glo displays of abjection and perversity.

The ideal audience for 1990s shock art was divided into two distinct sections. On the one side were the hip and the wised-up: those discerning viewers who were familiar both with Bauhaus and blaxploitation movies, or Titian and top-shelf porn mags. On the other side were the stuffy conservatives, who thought all real art consisted of eighteenth-century paintings of horses and whose stomachs turned at the mere mention of pornography. No wonder that the exhibition of YBAs that opened at the Royal Academy then transferred to the Brooklyn Museum was called *Sensation*. Sensation as in public scandal, but also sensation as in direct sensory experience. This was shock art for a culture already saturated with intense visual stimuli, a culture already numbed by the everyday shock effects of top-shelf magazines, video nasties, sensationalist news stories, confessional chat shows.

When *Sensation* transferred to the Brooklyn Museum in 1999, it provoked the ire of Rudy Giuliani, New York's high-profile mayor, who was making headlines around the world with his crusade against the strip clubs and flea-pit porn cinemas of Times Square in his bid to gentrify the once-rotten Big Apple. Giuliani denounced what he saw as the anti-Catholic bias of Ofili's Black Madonna paintings, froze the museum's funding and threatened to have it evicted from its city-owned premises. In response, pro-free-speech protestors took to the streets and the museum sued the city for violation of its First Amendment rights. When the judge ruled for the museum, Giuliani denounced him as 'totally biased' and 'part of the politically correct, left-wing ideology of New York City'. Curators at the museum hit back by placing a yellow stamp next to the more provocative works, an ironic trigger warning that stated that they may 'cause shock, vomiting, confusion, panic, euphoria and anxiety'. During the culture wars of the 1990s, it was the radical artists who stood up for the right to free speech in art galleries and the conservatives took offence. A mere twenty years later and the tables seem to have turned.

↖↑↗

Koons's work was hardcore, but wasn't mainstream culture in the 1990s also becoming more explicit, maybe even more hardcore? Part of the general intensification of popular culture was the appearance in otherwise respectable venues of ever more extreme depictions of sex and violence, ones that would previously have been deemed beyond the pale of mainstream cultural debate. Pornography, fetish and BDSM imagery, video nasties, horror films, true crime monstrosities: these illicit materials were adopted by serious artists as vehicles for questioning the distinction between high and low culture and pushing the boundaries of what could and could not be said in public. Sometimes the resulting works were tame attempts to court scandal in the most obvious places. Madonna's 1992 *Sex* book, a glossy coffee-table tome containing pictures of the singer and her celebrity friends in a variety of artfully shot and not particularly explicit poses, can only have been shocking to the most determined of Heartlands conservatives. To everyone else it seemed like an attention-grabbing ploy, and a straight rip-off of Robert Mapplethorpe and Helmut Newton. But for all of its lame posturing, *Sex* was emblematic of a mediascape where shock tactics were still associated with radicalism and progress.

It wasn't just artist provocateurs like Koons who were pushing the boundaries. The late 1980s and early 1990s were the heyday of the Hollywood erotic thriller, glossy blockbusters in the vein of *Fatal Attraction* (1987) and *Indecent Proposal* (1993) that combined edgy plots about adultery and gender politics with steamy sex scenes that might titillate a 13-year-old boy at best. The apex of the genre was Paul Verhoeven's neo-noir thriller, *Basic Instinct* (1992), which tells the story of a glamorous blonde thriller writer whose murder plots are being acted out in real life. Verhoeven pushed the limits of the genre with his infamous 'gratuitous beaver shot', in which Sharon Stone, the glamorous blonde thriller writer in question, uncrosses her panty-less legs in an all-male police interrogation room in order to demonstrate who really has the biggest balls. The nadir was Verhoeven's follow-up, *Showgirls* (1995), the story of a plucky outsider who climbs the greasy pole of the Las Vegas stripper industry, a film of such startling badness that it prompted some critics to ponder whether the director was in fact making an intentional comment on the debased nature of contemporary culture by producing such a wilfully bad film. Either way, *Showgirls* contained enough nudity to garner the most restrictive NC-17 rating from the American authorities, which generated a welcome storm of publicity and enabled it to make a handsome profit through VHS rentals, the domestic onanist's format of choice.

Jonathan Demme's *Silence of the Lambs* (1991) relied on mood and atmosphere more than explicit depictions of sex and violence, but with its semen-flinging inmates, hyper-cerebral and unrepentantly evil anti-hero, Hannibal Lecter, and deeply perverted villain, Buffalo Bill, the film was a uniquely intense psychological horror. There was a kind of aura surrounding the film, as word of mouth reports about its scary intensity made their way around school playgrounds. The climactic scene during which we watch Clarice Starling groping her way around a pitch-dark basement from the perspective of Buffalo Bill's night-vision goggles places the viewer in the position of pervert-voyeur extraordinaire. We might contrast this scene with the damp squib of an orgy depicted in Kubrick's *Eyes Wide Shut* (1999). Kubrick is trying for the same effect, the moment where we cross over into the secret world of the obscene: Buffalo Bill's night-vision world, *Pulp Fiction*'s gimp dungeon, *Twin Peaks*'s Black Lodge, a secret place where all of your darkest, most unspeakable desires can be fulfilled. And what does Kubrick show us? A Victoria's Secret commercial, a fantasy of well-groomed, all-female nudity that takes place in what seems like a hedge fund manager's Long Island estate. *Eyes Wide Shut* might be the last work of a cinematic master; but against the cultural landscape of 1999 it also seemed a bit vanilla.

The pinnacle of 1990s cinematic obscenity would have to be David Cronenberg's *Crash* (1996), his adaptation of J.G. Ballard's 1973 novel about an obscure group of car-crash obsessives – it's hard to tell whether they're a club, sub-culture, a cult, or some kind of renegade therapy group devoted to the amplification of perversity as a route to spiritual health – who have a sickly fascination with celebrity auto disasters and the erotic possibilities generated by the violent meeting between flesh and machinery. Cronenberg's film contains lots of nudity and many sex scenes, which is no doubt why it was given an NC-17 certificate by the American film censors, but it is not so much the contents of the film that render it so shocking, as its style and tone. *Crash* is a mid-budget Hollywood film that obeys the narrative logic of pornography; which is to say that there is no narrative arc to speak of, only a series of more or less flimsy scenarios, each of which leads to an extended sexual encounter or car crash or, from the perspective of the film's protagonists, ideally both.

The 1990s were the latest phase in the commercialisation and democratisation of the sexual revolution of the 1960s. This was an era of equal opportunities raunchiness, vulgarity and libido for all. In her 1997 experimental novel, *I Love Dick*, Chris Kraus argued that 'the sheer fact of women talking, being paradoxical, inexplicable, flip, self-destructive but above all else public, is the most revolutionary thing in the world'. Kraus's novel was filled with abstruse discussions of the New York literary theory and conceptual art scenes, but her embrace of the messy reality of female desire was echoed in popular culture from *Sex and the City* to the Spice Girls. Unvarnished sexuality came with an air of progressive uplift, a sense of liberation from the stale gender archetypes of the past. Eve Ensler's *The Vagina Monologues* wove together the testimonies of hundreds of women about their relationship with their most intimate parts. *Puppetry of the Penis* was a stage show in which a pair of Australian dudes made funny shapes out of their cock and balls. Ensler and the Aussie dick guys might have started out in the artistic underground, but in the 1990s their work became resoundingly mainstream. Mothers and daughters would happily spend an evening in an off-Broadway theatre listening to women talk about their vaginas or watching men wrapping their penises into funny shapes. This was wholesome entertainment for the discerning, liberated family.

The sociologist Angela McRobbie identified a new 'post-feminist' strain within 1990s popular culture. A new generation of young women were coming of age who felt that they could take many of the social gains won by earlier campaigners for granted. Access to education and careers; financial independence both inside and outside of marriage; the social acceptability of platonic friendships with men; dwindling tolerance for sexual double standards: so secure did many of these freedoms seem that the right-on rhetoric of the 1970s and '80s was seen by many young women as obsolete, or just plain uncool. This post-feminist ideal is most clearly on display in *Bridget Jones's Diary*, the bestselling novel and film that sparked the 1990s 'Chick Lit' boom. Bridget drinks to excess, responds positively to her boss's sexual banter, confides in her close circle of male and female, gay and straight friends, accidentally exposes her arse on national television, and, contrary to the established canons of feminist politics, finds happiness in a conventional marriage to a handsome human rights lawyer. In a sense, it was the self-conscious desire for a traditional happy ending that was the crudest part of the film.

Politics got raunchy too. In 1991, during her testimony in Clarence Thomas's contentious confirmation hearing for the Supreme Court, Anita Hill was called upon to describe the sexual harassment that she alleged Thomas had subjected her to during her time at the US Department of Education. Via televised hearings from the floor of the Senate, the American public learned not only of Thomas's persistent unwanted advances, but also of how he liked to regale Hill with details of the bestiality and orgy porn he watched at home and his claim to resemble the legendary 1970s porn star 'Long Dong Silver'. Whether you believed Anita Hill, as the liberal t-shirt slogan put it, or whether you bought Thomas's claim that the hearings were 'a high-tech lynching for uppity Blacks', it was impossible to ignore the disparity between the low comedy of Thomas's alleged utterances and the high ideals of the chamber in which they were scrutinised.

As it turned out, however, the Thomas confirmation hearings were only a teaser for the main event – the latest sullying of American presidential ideals – that was the Clinton–Lewinsky scandal of 1997–98. I am loath to retell the story of this grand, all-consuming presidential scandal with its the obvious power imbalance between the leader of the free world and the recently graduated intern, the glib presidential lying, the stage-managed support role ascribed to Hillary, and the salivating opportunism of Newt Gingrich, the leader of the House, and Kenneth Starr, the Department of Justice's lead investigator. For a significant portion of 1998, the world's news media was consumed with a debate about whether fellatio constituted sexual intercourse. Clinton famously claimed that he 'did not have sexual relations with that woman' on the unstated grounds that he had confined himself to the occasional blow job and inserting a cigar into his young employee's vagina. The inquiry also hinged on the material evidence of a semen stain on one of Lewinsky's dresses, an item of clothing that she had been persuaded to keep uncleaned by Linda Tripp, her more senior colleague who, on the advice of her literary agent, had secretly recorded her friendly conversations with the troubled intern. It is a sure sign that there is something rotten at the heart of the republic when it is a public servant's literary agent who offers patriotic and moral advice.

In a famous essay on 'Old Bloomsbury', Virginia Woolf described how one day in 1907 at an otherwise polite literary party in London the author Lytton Strachey pointed to a blemish on her sister's dress and asked, 'Semen?' For Woolf, that breezy interrogative inaugurated a new era in human relations: 'All barriers of reticence and reserve went down.' The hushed repression of the Victorian era gave way, all of a sudden, to a new frankness in human attitudes to sexuality. If we leap forward from Old Bloomsbury to late 1990s America – a leap that takes us almost the whole length of the twentieth century – we find a similar moment of revelation taking place in the glare of the world's news media. This was the cum shot that was heard around the world, reported on, analysed, discussed, interrogated and pored over by pundits and civilians alike. Whether this blizzard of attention inaugurated a new era of frankness and maturity in human sexual relations remains, however, a matter of some doubt.

⇱↑⇲

My first experience of pornography was site specific and deeply analogue. It took place on the Mount, an expanse of unkempt woodland and meadow that stretched down to the riverbank on the western edge of the town where I grew up, sometime around 1990 or 1991, when I was 11. It was here, beside a stream, nestled amid thick nettles and brambles, poorly hidden within the root ball of a tree, that my friends and I discovered a stash of porn mags. Hidden in the thicket from the prying eyes of passing dog walkers, we unstuck the pages of *Knave*, *Hustler*, *Escort* and *Penthouse* and pored over the images within.

These being top-shelf magazines available from your local newsagent or petrol station, the images contained no erect penises and no penetration, but the cornucopia of naked flesh and dreamy, far-away expressions of simulated arousal were deeply thrilling to our pre-adolescent sensibilities. The porn stash cast a lurid glow over our behaviour when we were in the coppice by the streambed. Our voices went up an octave; we made nonsensical jokes; we giggled incessantly; we threw sticks at each other. Then, after a few minutes in that strange vortex, we fled back to our bikes and raced around the fields. I think we returned to the coppice on at least four or five occasions, and then one day when we parted the bushes and climbed into the streambed, the stash was gone.

I preface this tale of youthful discovery – one that I suspect will be familiar, in its broad outlines, to many readers – with a description of the place where I grew up, because the experience was so indelibly tied to that place. The collection of magazines had formed into a matted clump as a result of being stored in the damp recesses of a tree's roots. The images we gawped at were flecked with bits of mud; there were tiny leaves stuck to the glossy paper. The experience has stuck in my memory precisely because of these local particularities.

Surely no one remembers their first experience of internet pornography in this way. Online porn is less firmly placed, less site specific. It emanates from the non-space of the digital cloud and pours forth as an infinite stream of content, a glowing sequence of portals that come to life at the click of a mouse. It can be consumed in the privacy of your own home via the same device that you use to talk to your friends, share pictures of your children, do the weekly shopping and read the daily newspaper. It also tends to be much more hardcore, much more punishingly mechanical and extreme than the glossy images of the top-shelf mags of yesteryear. The material itself comes neatly labelled and arranged for ease of use. Online porn is classified according to a taxonomy of such fine-grained precision as to make an eighteenth-century botanist weep with joy. From 'amateur', 'anal' and 'Asian' to 'swallow', 'squirt' and 'solo', there's a clearly defined category for every imaginable kink. These are the metadata of desire. There was no such specialisation in *Knave* and *Escort*. There were naked women in various locations – I think I can remember a fire station and a mechanic's garage – in a range of maybe twelve different poses. Sometimes they wore high-heeled shoes, sometimes they didn't.

I don't want to get all misty-eyed about the lost aura of analogue culture, the special glow that emanated from obscure or illicit cultural artefacts in an era before they were made instantly available for home delivery at the click of a mouse. There's too much nostalgia sloshing around in our culture as it is, without me adding my fondness for the mingled textures of glossy magazine paper and wet leaves to the mix. What's more intriguing – and potentially more illuminating of the distance travelled between the early 1990s and the present day – is the question of what online pornography, and the general condition of digital super-abundance, have done to our culture's capacity for shock. It seems that the conditions for obscenity and outrage were different in the 1990s with its pre-digital culture of video stores, print magazines, cable TV and celluloid cinema.

Perhaps the most telling example of the changing times is the decline of the Hollywood erotic thriller, which after its heyday in the early 1990s was rendered obsolete by internet pornography. The days when popular films would seek to entice viewers with the promise of bared breasts and steamy sex scenes have long since passed. Open your laptop and within seconds you're lost in an abstract flesh-scape of pounding members and pummelled holes, all of it oriented towards the most reductively male gaze. Log on to Netflix or Amazon, however, and the flesh-scape has shrunk considerably. Even *Fifty Shades of Grey* (2015), that supposedly edgy BDSM-fantasy flick, which originated with a self-published novel that made it big via Amazon's algorithms, comes with an R rating and is tame in the extreme. The flimsy narrative scenarios of classic 1970s porn have long been a thing of the past, but so are the fantasy locations and sartorial adornments of early 1990s softcore, which at the time seemed pretty hardcore.

The word 'obscene' is derived from the Greek term *ob skene*, meaning 'off-stage', which was where acts of violence usually took place in classical Greek drama. Obscenity occurs when something that should be off-stage is brought on stage, where it can be seen in its full reality, under the lights and before the crowd. Along similar lines, the anthropologist Mary Douglas defined dirt as 'matter out of place'. Douglas was thinking about the primordial social divisions between the sacred and the profane, the clean and the unclean. 'Where there is dirt there is system,' she slyly stated. The dirty and the clean need one another in order to mean anything. But Douglas's definition can just as easily apply to dirty books, as to unclean animals or social practices. Obscenity is cultural matter out of place, stuff that is brought from off-stage to on. This is how 1990s shock art worked – by transposing obscene materials from one part of the culture to another, from the porn mag to the art gallery, from the tabloid page to the canvas, from one aisle of the video store to another.

But for that to be possible, disparate cultural materials have to share the same general space. There must be clearly defined onstage and backstage areas, a recognisable set of categories that define what is sayable and not. Sometime in the early 2000s, the landscape of the obscene seems to have changed. The availability of obscene material has grown exponentially online, not just in the form of hardcore pornography, but also all manner of grotesque spectacles, from Isis beheading videos to torture-porn cinema to viral video nasties like 'two girls one cup', a coprophilic and emetophilic fantasia. What in the 1990s seemed extreme and shocking now seems, in retrospect, positively Ruritanian in comparison with the everyday horrors of the twenty-first century. The internet has turned out to be a giant, double-edged scythe. With one sweep of its blade it creates silos, specialisations, minute taxonomies, niche identities, segregated worlds and echo chambers; and with the return sweep, the sweep of cost-free dissemination and instant feedback, it disrupts those same boundaries, collapsing the near and the far, the familiar and the foreign, the clean and the dirty. Whether they were aware of it or not, the moral arbiters who denounced the work of Mapplethorpe, Koons, Ofili and all the rest were objecting to finding matter out of place. They wanted to keep the familiar boundaries of the world intact, a task that would become increasingly difficult in the hyper-accelerated digital culture of the twenty-first century.

10

Lonely Planet

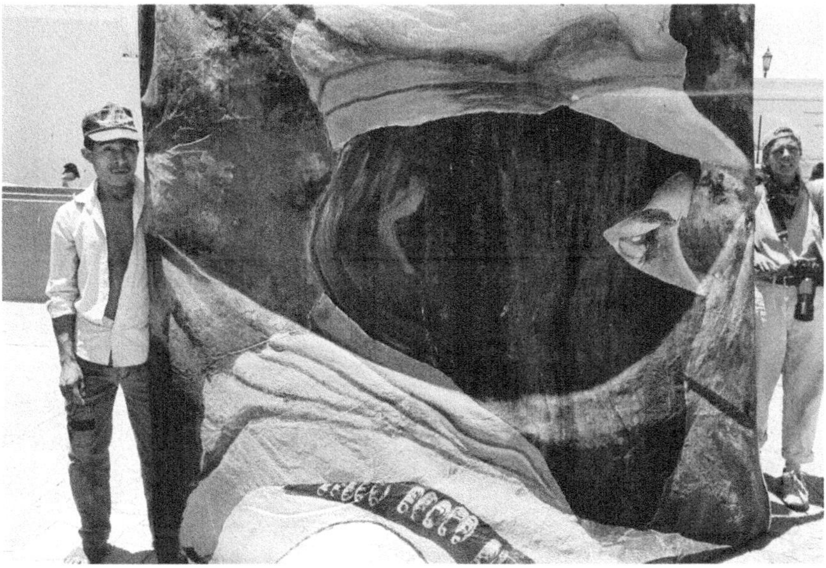

ACROSS ASIA on the Cheap: A Complete Guide to Making the Overland Trip began life in 1973 as a sheaf of mimeographed pages stapled together into a pocket-sized booklet, which was passed around by hand in the counter-cultural enclaves of Sydney, Australia. The guide helped readers navigate the hippy trail that led from Europe through Turkey, Iran and Afghanistan, down into the Indian subcontinent, across Southeast Asia, and eventually to Australia. In addition to the standard information about hostels and ferry times, *Across Asia on the Cheap* included more recherché details such as where to score the best drugs and how to pick up odd jobs along the way. The text was bashed out on a borrowed typewriter and accompanied by hand-drawn maps to secluded beaches and far-flung temples. This was a new kind of travel guide, a kind of anti-Baedeker, which offered an alternative to the sedate tours of cultural treasures and comfortable hotels that had been favoured by Western tourists since the nineteenth century.

The guide was compiled by Tony and Maureen Wheeler, a married couple from England and Northern Ireland, who were themselves fresh off the hippy trail. At first, the Wheelers thought the guide might help them earn enough money to fund an extra year of travel before they returned home to find real jobs. They converted the scrappy samizdat version into an initial run of 1,500 printed books. When those quickly sold out, they printed up another 3,500, this time with a glossy cover and journalistic endorsements on the flyleaf. In 1974, they published a second volume, *The Lonely Planet Guide to South-East Asia on a Shoestring*, named after a misheard Joe Cocker lyric about a space traveller who spies a 'lovely planet' and decides to stay. In the eyes of many Westerners at the time, Southeast Asia was the equivalent of outer space, a part of the world still haunted by memories of the Viet Cong and Indonesia's repressive Sukarno regime.

Without really thinking about it – or at least, that's how they would tell the story after they had become fabulously successful – the Wheelers were helping to invent a new kind of tourism, maybe even a new way of seeing the world. The Lonely Planet guides were aimed at young, adventurous, cosmopolitan travellers from the developed world who were keen to get off the beaten path and into the 'untouched' regions of the earth. Users were encouraged to think of themselves as travellers rather than tourists, part of a global community of seekers after experience and enjoyment, who were more attuned to the ways of life they encountered than traditional holidaymakers would be. By the 1990s, Lonely Planet had become a global publishing brand, with 350 titles in print and annual sales of over $40 million. The Wheelers' success is a classic tale of Bobo capitalism, which converted the hippy experience of the 1960s into the edgy but commercialised sub-culture of the 1990s.

In Alex Garland's 1996 novel, *The Beach*, the dream has turned sour. With their Lonely Planet guides in hand, the backpacker hordes have spread across Southeast Asia more like a deadly virus than a benign caravanserai of wide-eyed travellers. Garland's novel grafted an airport paperback-style thriller plot on to the hippy traveller setting of Thailand's 'banana pancake trail', the string of cheap hostels and beach resorts that catered to this new wave of budget travellers in the 1980s and '90s. *The Beach* became a massive bestseller and was made into a terrible film by Danny Boyle, who somehow managed to make backpacking through the tropics seem less exciting than life as a heroin addict in 1980s Scotland. The novel is narrated by Richard, a British traveller who wakes up one morning in a Bangkok hostel to find a hand-scrawled map pinned to the dead body of a raddled old hippy who has taken his own life. It is a scene ripped from the pages of Robert Louis Stevenson's *Treasure Island* and transplanted to the Khaosan Road; the map even has an 'X' to mark the spot of the hidden treasure. In this case, though, the treasure is not a glittering pile of doubloons, but a hidden community of travellers and the state of perpetual bliss their lifestyle promises. Along with a French couple he meets at the hostel, Richard makes the perilous journey across the choppy straights of the Andaman Sea, sneaks past the armed gangsters who guard the marijuana fields that take up half the island, leaps from the towering waterfall that marks the boundary of the beach, and then discovers the secret community of like-minded souls – shang-ri-la, utopia, paradise!

But there is no paradise without trouble, no utopia without its dystopian flipside. A whole novel about sitting on a beach and smoking dope all day would be about as interesting as sitting on a beach and smoking dope all day. The narrative thrills come in the form of run-ins with the local drug smugglers, deadly shark attacks, tensions between the founding fathers of the community and the callow newbies, and the rising levels of psychosis and paranoia that come from sitting around on a beach and smoking dope all day. But the real malaise that besets the islanders is historical, rather than a matter of predators and politics. The golden age of the hippy trail is long past. The last of the world's undiscovered paradises are steadily being hooked up to the global network of long-haul airflights and budget tourism. The last great illusion of the twentieth century, the fantasy that travel is a way to transform the self, is on life support.

The scariest thing about Garland's paradisal beach community is that it has no purpose other than leisure. After the thrill of discovery subsides and he is inducted into the ways of the community, Richard experiences an eerie sense of disappointment: 'It's silly really. I think I was expecting an ideology or something. A purpose.' Once their morning fishing and gardening duties are completed, members of the community lounge on the beach all day smoking dope and taking turns on the Nintendo Game Boy. When Richard stalks the drug dealers on the far side of the island, he imagines himself in a Vietnam War movie. The beach dwellers are a multinational community drawn exclusively from the developed nations of the world, without a single Thai or Asian member. They might be physically located on a tropical island in the South China Sea, but they are sealed within a bubble of Western culture and affluence. Have they really 'travelled' at all?

The Beach plays on the fear that gnawed at the consciences of the more self-aware global travellers of the 1990s: that backpackers were merely the advanced guard of the tourism industry. The backpackers' quest for 'otherness' – new experiences, foreign cultures, a brief encounter with third-world poverty – mirrors global capitalism's unquenchable thirst for new markets and consumers. Backpackers are the nimble, resourceful, adventurous pioneers who pave the way for the larger tour operators and global franchises to move in. Today, there is a Starbucks in Koh Samui.

↖↑↗

In the 1990s 'globalisation' became a global buzzword, uttered by journalists, politicians, CEOs, academics and protestors alike in order to convey their sense of living in a newly interconnected world. If you plug the word into Google's Ngram viewer, a data visualisation tool that tracks the frequency of search terms in the world's largest digital corpus of printed documents, you get a line on a graph that crawls along the x-axis for nearly 200 years, during which the term was barely used at all, until the mid-1980s, at which point it leaps into the air like a salmon in search of its spawning grounds, reaches a peak around 2001, then tapers off as the graph reaches the present. According to Google's databanks, the 1990s were the age of globalisation – or at least the age in which we became self-conscious about globalisation, to the extent that we invented a new term for the fact that the planet was becoming less and less lonely.

Strictly speaking, the process of globalisation began at least as far back as the fifteenth century CE, when Christopher Columbus and Vasco da Gama inaugurated the age of European colonialism. Some scholars push that date further back still to the Chinese Song Dynasty and the Mongol invasions that stretched as far as Eastern Europe. More immediately, though, the concern with all things global in the 1990s stemmed from the rapid growth in the second half of the twentieth century of a vast new transport and communications infrastructure that encircled the globe. Long-haul air travel, shipping containers and super tankers, radio and television, satellite communications, the internet and mobile phones: it was the increased flow of people, goods and information that sparked the sense of living in a single global system. The concepts of near and far, familiar and foreign, local and global had been transformed within the space of living memory.

It was only at a relatively late stage in human history, in 1967, when NASA released images from its ATS satellite, that we finally got to see what our planet looked like from space. Earlier satellite images had shown parts of the earth's curvature, but never before had our little green world been shown as a single orb suspended in the heavens. NASA's decision to release the image was prompted in part by a campaign by Stewart Brand, who would later go on to found the WELL, one of the first internet discussion boards, and become one of the leading Silicon Valley sages. One night in 1966 on the roof of his San Francisco Mission District apartment, Brand dropped some acid and mused on the potentially transformative impact of seeing the earth from space. When the acid wore off, he printed up thousands of lapel badges with a simple question emblazoned upon them, 'Why haven't we seen the whole earth yet?' When the image was released the following year, Brand put it on the cover of the first issue of his *Whole Earth Catalogue*, a vast compendium of 'tools' that helped to spark the communal living experiments of the 1970s and encouraged readers to think of the planet as a single living system that should be managed and conserved as such.

The explosion of the term 'globalisation' in the 1990s performed a similar function to the image of the earth seen from space in the 1960s. It was a way of seeing the whole earth, a linguistic tool for nudging ourselves towards an understanding of the bigger picture. Globalisation could refer to all manner of different things, from neoliberal macroeconomics to mass migration, and from the rise of the internet to the increasing ease with which one could find a decent sushi restaurant in a mid-sized provincial city. The tone of the debate might be analytical or declamatory, enthused or appalled. As is often the case with journalistic buzzwords, it was an extremely imprecise term, which often conveyed a vague impression of speed and connectivity, rather than concrete social facts. Taken as a whole, though, the debate about globalisation in the 1990s was considerably less star-struck and wide-eyed than Brand's 1960s vision of Spaceship Earth. More often than not, the new imperative to see the world as a whole induced a sense of complexity rather than clarity, a struggle to find a stable pattern in the otherwise turbulent flows of matter and information that coursed around the world.

The signature artist of the age of globalisation was Andreas Gursky, whose vast photographic prints captured this sense of a strange new order emerging from global connectivity. At the start of the 1990s, Gursky was mounting his first exhibitions in provincial German galleries; by the end of the decade he was a global art star. In 2011, his 1999 image *Rhein II*, which captures the straight lines of an unprepossessing section of the river under a dull grey sky, became the most expensive photographic print ever sold at auction. Gursky's images captured the inhuman scale of mankind's planetary civilisation at the end of the second millennium CE, the ant-heap agglomeration of people, buildings and infrastructure that lay scattered across the face of the earth. A container port in Salerno; a rave in Amsterdam; a Siemens factory in Karlsruhe; the Escher-like switchbacks of a desert motorway in Bahrain; the curvilinear forms of a Sao Paulo housing project. They were designed to make your head spin at the weird orderliness that emerged out of the teeming diversity of human behaviour. Gursky often shot his images from an elevated position and a wide-angle perspective, as though the viewer was hovering in mid-air above the Tokyo Stock Exchange or a Pyongyang political rally. This was an alien's eye view of mankind that was to be discovered not from outer space, as Stewart Brand had expected, but closer to the earth's surface – through the lens of a camera and in the pixellated interface of a computer screen.

↖↑↗

The politics of globalisation were driven by a growing alphabet soup of transnational organisations – GATT, WTO, OECD, IMF, NAFTA, EU, etc. – that set the legal and economic conditions for global trade and mobility. Some of these institutions were founded earlier in the century and some were newly created, but they all gained a heightened prominence in the 1990s in debates about the rights and wrongs of the emerging system of global capitalism. In 1995, for instance, GATT, or the General Agreement on Tariffs and Trade, was rebooted as WTO, or the World Trade Organization, a seemingly dull piece of acronymical reshuffling that had wide-ranging consequences. GATT was originally ratified in 1947 by twenty-three nations in order to reduce trade barriers and stimulate economic growth in the aftermath of the Second World War. Around the same time, the International Monetary Fund and World Bank were formed, the former to create a worldwide system of exchange rates and monetary stabilisation, the latter to fund reconstruction and development projects. These were the institutions that managed global trade for much of the Cold War period. In the 1970s and '80s, however, after the US left the Bretton Woods system that pegged global currencies to the gold standard, and with the declining political and economic influence of the Soviet Union, a new set of institutions was required. In 1995, after eight years of negotiations as part of the 'Uruguay Round' of talks (oh to be a fly on the wall during those thrilling exchanges), the new WTO rules were ratified by 123 countries, a number that increased to 164 in subsequent years, or 84 per cent of the world's nation states.

In concert with the IMF and the World Bank, the WTO helped to enshrine the neoliberal free-market system around the world. The loans and debt restructuring services that they provided to developing nations came on the condition that those countries opened their domestic markets to foreign competition, privatised state assets, shrunk social welfare programmes as a percentage of GDP and avoided deficit spending in favour of fiscal austerity. The terms of the original GATT treaty had stated its aim to reduce barriers to free trade 'on a reciprocal and advantageous basis' for all nations, but one of the chief architects of globalisation in the 1990s, Joseph Stiglitz, former chairman of the Council of Economic Advisors to the Clinton administration, would later acknowledge that the terms of the new deal tended to favour American and European economic interests. Smaller nations were encouraged to end protectionist practices, while the US and Europe retained their large agricultural subsidies. Liberalised financial markets favoured powerful Western investment funds and increased volatility in developing world markets. Multinational corporations engaged in officially sanctioned forms of bio-piracy by securing patents on crop seeds that had been at the heart of subsistence agriculture for generations. In theory, a rising tide lifts all boats; but in reality, if there are a couple of super tankers in the water, the smallest craft will be smashed to bits by the hulls of the mighty.

The new global framework for trade was accompanied by new and enhanced regional free trade areas. On 1 January 1994 the North American Free Trade Agreement came into effect, subsuming the 420 million inhabitants of the US,

Mexico and Canada in the world's largest free trade area. Bill Clinton once referred to globalisation as 'the economic equivalent of a force of nature, like wind or water'. According to this view, the growing interconnection of the world's economic, social and cultural systems was the inevitable product of technological changes that had unfolded over centuries. To try to hold back the forces of history would be as futile as the ancient English King Cnut's attempt to stop the waves of the North Sea lapping at the shore of his kingdom. The aim of centrist politicians like Clinton was, in another of his upbeat phrases, to 'put a human face' on globalisation. Neoliberal economics should be accompanied by environmental protections, labour rights and investments in social goods such as education and healthcare, in order to ensure that all members of the global family benefited. And yet Clinton still had to rely on Republican votes in Congress to get NAFTA ratified as law. A large section of his own party distrusted the fuzzy humanist rhetoric, objecting instead to the erosion of labour rights and the potential for large manufacturing corporations to move production south of the border to capitalise on cheaper labour costs.

In 1992 the Maastricht Treaty brought the EU into being, forging closer political and economic ties between the twelve member countries of the European Economic Community. Unlike the down-and-dirty trade deal of NAFTA, the EU was a much more ambitious, high-flown project, at the heart of which was a world historical vision of lasting peace achieved through ever closer economic, legal and cultural ties between the nations of a once war-torn European continent. The Maastricht Treaty paved the way for a single European currency, a European central bank, tighter military co-operation between member states, a single European market without tariffs or barriers to trade, freedom of movement for citizens between member nations, and a plan for expansion to the east and south to incorporate former Soviet satellites such as Poland, Hungary and Yugoslavia. In keeping with these high ideals, the EU increasingly adopted the trappings of statehood, including a flag and anthem to go with the jumble of executive, deliberative and legislative branches.

At the centre of all the pomp and verbiage was a giant free trade zone that encompassed most of the European landmass. In this respect, the EU was an expression of the post-political, managerialist approach to governance that had its heyday in the 1990s. The technical rules of the single market, which limited the amount of deficit spending member states could engage in, were overseen by the European Commission and Parliament from Brussels. Single market technocracy was meant to trump the vagaries of local, which of course meant national, politics. The Italians referred to this as *il vincolo esterno*, or the external bind on their own spendthrift politicians. To some it represented a beneficial form of collective discipline; to others, a dangerous new step in the depoliticisation of politics and the corrosion of national sovereignty.

When the politics of European integration were put to electorates in the 1990s, they were often met with decidedly lukewarm interest. Referenda were held in Ireland, France and Denmark in order to seek popular consent for the Maastricht Treaty. In Ireland, the vote passed easily, but in France it scraped by with what came to be known as the *petit oui*, when 50.7 per cent of a low turnout voted in favour. In Denmark when the first vote was a narrow *ingen* (no), the government negotiated a series of opt-outs to the treaty and instructed the voters to get it right a second time, which they did with 56 per cent in favour. In most member states, opposition to the EU as an institution, rather than the specifics of its free-market policies, was a fringe concern, the preserve of insalubrious far-right nationalists and single-issue wingnuts. In Britain, the Referendum Party, funded by Sir Jimmy Goldsmith, stood forty-two candidates at the 1997 election and failed to win any seats. It would take until 2016, or a mere twenty-one years later, for what was seen in the 1990s as the quixotic campaign of an eccentric millionaire to become a political reality when David Cameron called – and lost – the referendum on EU membership that opened the way for Brexit. Political scientists refer to the time span required for fringe ideas to migrate to the mainstream of political discourse as the 'Overton Window', after the founder of the theory. In 1992, when Britain's then prime minister, John Major, declared victory over the anti-European 'bastards' on the right wing of his party, little did he know that the Overton Window would shift so dramatically in such a short period time.

In spite of the upbeat political messaging and the fuzzy humanist talk, to most civilian observers in the 1990s the politics of globalisation seemed very distant from their everyday concerns. Trade negotiations and inter-governmental co-operation pacts were hammered out in air-conditioned hotels by heads of state and teams of besuited technocrats. The new layer of global institutions that guided the impossibly complex flows of money, goods and people around the world hovered in an abstract, invisible space somewhere beyond the day-to-day concerns of individual citizens. The British philosopher John Gray argued that, in spite of its seemingly technocratic neutrality, globalisation was in fact a utopian project inspired by the nineteenth-century vision of a perfect world market. Buried deep in the bland policy documents issued by the WTO, IMF, the World Bank and many of the world's most prosperous nations was a highly abstract vision of global markets as information processing systems and human beings as purely rational agents. According to this vision, *homo economicus* was the same in all regions of the world, irrespective of geographical, cultural, historical and ethnic differences. Given sufficient access to information and free rein to buy and sell as he or she chooses, this rational economic agent will act in its own self-interest and, via the harmonising influence of the market, ensure the interests of society as a whole. Gray decried this as a fantasy cooked up in university seminar rooms and Washington think tanks, an egghead's perspective that smothered the reality of individual lives enmeshed in the intractable webs of culture and history.

↖↑↗

It was as a cultural force that globalisation was most immediately felt in most people's lives. Even before the worldwide spread of the internet, multinational conglomerates created a global entertainment culture in which you could rent a VHS copy of *Bridget Jones's Diary* in the bazaar in Peshawar, eat a Big Mac in downtown Nairobi and speak to a call centre operative in Bangalore who, in order to ease the flow of information, might claim to be named Chandler or Phoebe after a character in *Friends*.

In its most optimistic moments, the popular culture of globalisation celebrated ethnic diversity, cultural hybridity, social and geographic mobility and, perhaps above all else, youthfulness. This upbeat mood was to the fore in a spate of smart, warm-hearted, gently critical movies that dealt with the experience of post-colonial migration. Mira Nair's 1991 *Mississippi Masala* depicted an interracial romance between Denzel Washington's Demetrius and Sarita Choudhury's Mina, the daughter of Indian immigrant parents who have made their way to Mississippi via England after being driven out of Uganda by Idi Amin's murderous dictatorship. As Mina says to Demetrius when they first get together, 'I'm masala mix,' the product of multiple places and cultures. 'Hot and spicy,' replies the equally luscious Denzel. The couple face opposition both from Mina's conservative Indian parents and Demetrius's struggling African American family. The film suggests that their ability to move beyond their suspicious, history-haunted elders is bound up with their youthful facility for cultural sampling. As they stroll on a Gulf Coast beach at sunset, Demetrius muses, 'race – or as they say nowadays, tradition – is passed down like recipes, and the trick is you've got to know what to eat and what to leave on your plate'. At the end of the film, they light out for the territories – or at least for Los Angeles in Demetrius's truck – to make a new life for themselves on their own terms.

The culinary motif was also to the fore in Damien O'Donnell's 1999 *East is East*, written by Ayub Khan Din, about a mixed race British-Pakistani family, which dealt with heavyweight issues of forced marriage, domestic abuse and racist neighbours egged on by Conservative politicians, all with a light comedic touch. The central refrain of the film is the response of 'half a cup', by George, the abusive patriarch, whenever his wife puts the kettle on, as though this is as much integration with British life as he's prepared to stomach. As with *Mississippi Masala*, the hybrid identities of the younger generation show the way forward. The kids sneak out to nightclubs in the middle of night, snog white girls in the back alleys, play football in the street, and even, in the case of the eldest brother, escape across the canal to Manchester with its high-end boutiques and whiff of cosmopolitanism and sexual freedom. The suggestion is that, with their shared cultures of music, art, fashion and football, the kids will be all right.

Many of these films took their cues from the social realism of Ken Loach and Mike Leigh but mixed it up with the strain of youthful ribaldry that was on display in Hanif Kureishi's script for *My Beautiful Launderette* (1985) and his 1990 novel *The Buddha of Suburbia*. As the ingenue Salim says in *Launderette*, 'much good can come of fucking'. The moderate success of these films paved the way for the smash hit that was *Bend it Like Beckham* (2002), a post-colonial comedy about the struggle of a Sikh girl from Southall with her conservative parents over whether she should be allowed to break with tradition and play on a women's football team, which made over $100 million at the global box office. *Bend it Like Beckham* was an expression of upbeat multiculturalism which capitalised on the growing popularity of the EPL in America and around the world. It also drew on the superstar aura of 'Posh and Becks', or Victoria and David Beckham, the former Spice Girl and the footballer son of an Essex taxi driver who once made a tabloid splash by wearing a sarong on a Balinese beach holiday. Underneath the fizzy montages and dance pop soundtrack was a message about the values of hybrid identity and cultural sampling that could have been taken from a post-colonial literary theory seminar. Jasminder – or Jess to her friends – bends cultures and soccer balls with ease.

This kind of glossy multiculturalism became a semi-official part of centre-left politics. In a famous speech in April 2001, Robin Cook, the New Labour foreign secretary who would later resign over the Iraq War, sought to recast Britain as a 'young country' that was at ease with – even positively revelled in – the tapestry of cultures and ethnicities that had been formed in the wake of decolonisation. In a much-quoted line, Cook celebrated the fact that chicken tikka masala was now one of Britain's national dishes, the hybrid product of the South Asian love of spice and John Bull's demand for gravy with his meat. Tellingly, Cook didn't just praise cultural hybridity as proof that people from different backgrounds could find ways to live together in relative peace, but also as a strategic advantage for British businesses in the age of globalisation. Cook highlighted London's status as a hyper-connected, multicultural global metropolis, citing the example of a high-profile national airline that had recently relocated to the city in order to capitalise on its position as an international air hub and the range of languages spoken by its immigrant population. Cook's speech drew attention to the same neighbourhood in which *Bend it Like Beckham* was set – the Sikh communities of Southall and Wembley that are in the flightpath of Heathrow.

In her 1991 book, *The Global City*, geographer Saskia Sassen analysed the new prominence of the global metropolis in the world economy. Global metropolises didn't just include the capitals of wealthy industrialised nations like London, Paris and Tokyo but also the buzzing urban centres of the 'global South', such as Buenos Aires, Shanghai, Jakarta, Lagos and Mumbai. Key sectors and neighbourhoods of these cities were intricately wired into the global economy, home to highly specialised businesses that provided niche services in finance and banking, media and broadcasting, accountancy, law, medicine, governance, logistics and other rarefied zones of the 'weightless' service sector. Global metropolises were often home to the regional offices of multinational corporations and their multilingual and multiethnic staff, sites of extreme cultural, linguistic and ethnic diversity as well as intensifiers of economic inequality. The white-collar service industry professional and the migrant labourer cleaning the office might brush against one another in the subway as they left or arrived at work, but they were divided by economic and spatial divisions built into the city's infrastructure. What Sassen and others showed was that while the new global order was creating new connections around the world, it was also recalibrating the relationships between urban and rural places, the up-to-date and the left behind; it was creating new kinds of inequality, new sites of conflict. All the buzzy talk about global prosperity and frictionless trade in the 1990s was accompanied by a newly harsh political vocabulary on immigration.

This was also the age of 'bogus asylum seekers' and 'Fortress Europe'. The free movement of capital and goods was accompanied by a sharpened focus on border control and human migration.

The great visual poet of the flight path was the Hong Kong filmmaker Wong Kar-Wai. With his string of global arthouse successes, *Chungking Express*, *Happy Together*, *In the Mood for Love* and *2046*, Wong and cinematographer Christopher Doyle created a series of bleary, smeary tone poems about romantic longing and geographical displacement that ranged from Kowloon to Tierra del Feugo. Much of Wong's work was concerned with the culture and politics of a very specific part of the world – Hong Kong, Taiwan and the regional superpower of China. But the mood of melancholy euphoria that he conjured in his super-stylised films about hyper-mobility and missed connections clearly spoke to audiences in all corners of the world. Sofia Coppola adopted much of this mood for *Lost in Translation* (2003), which explored the sense of estrangement and distance experienced by two Americans in Tokyo. In this case, the dislocation was filtered through Scarlett Johansson's Charlotte, a Yale philosophy graduate at a loose end, and Bill Murray's Bob Harris, a self-loathing movie star making a quick buck shilling for a Japanese whiskey company.

Wong's films offered a view of globalisation that wasn't tethered to a Western-centric outlook. They took evident glee in making offbeat connections between different parts of the world: a Tierra del Fuego lighthouse and a noodle stall in a Taipei night market; or a cramped apartment in the Chungking tower block in Hong Kong and the sun-kissed beaches of Southern California. This sense of mapping the world from a different perspective, of charting alternative lines of flight, was most apparent in *Happy Together*, the story of Ho Po-Wing and Lai Yiu-Fai, a pair of gay Chinese lovers who embark on a kind of extended gap year in South America. 'We left Hong Kong to start over,' states Fau in a voice-over that accompanies the opening black and white shots of their road trip to Iguazú Falls; but the couple soon become stalled by lack of money and the weight of the pasts they were trying to escape. As with so much of Wong's work, narrative events are less important than the atmosphere of woozy sensuality that he conjures. Gauzy black and white sequences of an Argentinian highway; super-saturated colour footage of the churning torrents of the Iguazú Falls; slow motion sequences in Buenos Aires tango clubs; and tight angle shots of Fai and Po-Wing's lovemaking are all designed to immerse the viewer in the immediacy of the present moment. But in Wong's filmmaking the inevitable corollary of that sensuous pleasure in travel and new experience is a simultaneous yearning for home. There is an extraordinary shot in *Happy Together* of an upside-down Hong Kong skyline, as though seen from the other side of the earth. It is both thrilling and fearful, suggests Wong, to be uprooted from one's home.

Wong Kar-Wai was one of several Hong Kong filmmakers who became worldwide stars in the 1990s. The Hong Kong film industry boomed in the late 1980s and '90s before the East Asian financial crisis of 1997 and pirate DVD sales burst the bubble. At the same time, Hollywood, that great engine of American soft cultural power, was opening itself up to new stylistic influences from the Far East. Quentin Tarantino and Robert Rodriguez both cited the influence of Ringo Lam and Tsui Hark's hyper-stylised action thrillers on their own early, breakout work. John Woo, the director of Hong Kong classics such as *A Better Tomorrow* and *The Killer*, both of which found large cult audiences in the West via VHS sales, made the shift to Hollywood in the mid-1990s with *Broken Arrow* and *Face/Off*. Perhaps the most influential contribution to the sinification of the Hollywood action movie was made by Yuen Woo-Ping, the veteran director of Jackie Chan kung fu flicks such as *Snake in the Eagle's Shadow* (1978) and *Drunken Master* (1978), who was hired as the action coordinator first for *The Matrix* (1999) and then for Ang Lee's *Crouching Tiger, Hidden Dragon* (2000).

The Hong Kong action style was pulpy, fast, hyperbolic and tongue in cheek. Wide-eyed Western film critics quickly ran out of synonyms for the 'balletic' and 'kinetic' action sequences that came to define the genre. Olivier Assayas's 1996 *Irma Vep* makes fun of an ageing French cineaste's chagrin that the Nouvelle Vague style of Alain Delon and Catherine Deneuve has been overtaken by this even newer kind of warp-speed global pulp cinema. Maggie Cheung, the Hong Kong star imported to add a touch of glamour to a French movie production, says she enjoys John Woo's 'balletic' style but not the 'nombril'-gazing approach of the French. And it wasn't just the French auteurs who were struggling to keep up. The Hong Kong martial arts style was nimbler and swifter than the lumbering juggernauts embodied in the bulky forms of Arnold Schwarzenegger and Sylvester Stallone in the 1980s. In the refined form of *The Matrix*'s bullet time and *Crouching Tiger*'s gliding magical swordfights, Woo-Ping helped to update the visual style of the Hollywood action movie for the new era of global networking and weightless information exchange. These films were precursors to the Jason Bourne films of the early 2000s, in which Matt Damon became the ultimate global backpacker, equipped with fake passports, Israeli martial arts skills and multiple languages that enabled him to shuttle around the global network and evade the shadowy Treadstone agency. Bourne even goes off grid in Goa at the end of the first instalment, a feat that neither Arnie nor Sly could have hoped to accomplish. Those lumbering hulks of the late atomic age would have stuck out like undercover cops at a Full Moon party on Anjuna Beach.

But the cinema of globalisation wasn't just a celebration of mobility and weightlessness and cultural hybridity. Several filmmakers sought to capture the sharp edges of the complex networks that connected people around the world in unexpected and often uncomfortable ways. Alejandro González Iñárritu's *Amores perros* (2000) centred on a car crash that brought the otherwise separate lives of three residents of Mexico City into violent contact: a young kid trying to escape poverty via the underground world of illegal dogfighting, a glamorous Spanish model and media personality, and a former left-wing guerrilla who lives on the streets and makes a living as a contract killer. Steven Soderbergh's *Traffic* (2000) traced the invisible drug trafficking networks that connected a US Congressman's daughter in suburban Washington DC with a downtrodden cop in Tijuana, Mexico.

Critics referred to these films as a new form of 'hyperlink cinema', which projected the infinite connectivity of the internet on to real world situations. They also shared a common visual style and set of narrative conventions: frequent use of shaky handheld camera, a bright or saturated colour palette, non-linear narratives that jumped back and forth in time, and the central metaphors of the network and the crash as exemplars of life in the global system. In its worst moments, such as the scene in Iñárritu's *21 Grams* (2003) in which Sean Penn mansplains chaos theory to Naomi Watts, or the colossal banality of Paul Haggis's Oscar-winning paean to American multiculturalism, *Crash* (2004), the genre tended towards kitsch pomposity of the 'everything's connected' variety. But at its best, such as *Amores perros* and *In This World* (2002) or Fernando Meirelles and Kátia Lund's favela epic *City of God* (2002), it could be a powerful reminder of the uneven nature of economic globalisation. Each of these films pointed to the existence of what the Marxist geographer Mike Davis called the 'planet of slums' that was by the end of the 1990s home to a billion people. In Rio de Janeiro or Cairo or Jakarta or Lagos, the plate-glass towers and air-conditioned malls of the global metropolis were ringed by ramshackle warrens of concrete blocks, corrugated iron roofs, recycled wood and plastic structures that housed the urban underclass. Their inhabitants' experiences were defined not by freedom of movement and the pleasures of cultural diversity, but by poverty, crime and deprivation. They too were citizens of the world.

⇖⇑⇗

Opposition to economic globalisation drew its inspiration from events in Latin America, perhaps the only remaining part of the world in which the revolutionary politics of the mid-twentieth century continued to have any real purchase. On 1 January 1994, the day on which NAFTA came into effect, the Zapatista Army of National Liberation (EZLN), a guerrilla force assembled from the Mayan peoples of Mesoamerica and a handful of Mexican activists and intellectuals, stormed four towns in the remote and mountainous southern state of Chiapas, from where they issued proclamations against the treaty and demanded constitutional recognition of indigenous rights. The Zapatistas denounced NAFTA as the last nail in the coffin of Mayan civilisation. The treaty would open the floodgates to American and Canadian agri-business, they argued, and undermine what was left of indigenous land rights and subsistence agriculture.

At first glance, the Zapatistas looked like a familiar proposition – men with guns emerging from the jungle to fight the government in the name of revolutionary principles drawn from Marx and Mao. In reality, though, they were a new kind of hybrid organisation, one that combined left-wing guerrilla tactics with what their spokesman, Subcomandante Marcos, called a 'scandalously Indian' structure. Instead of being led by a revolutionary vanguard – an inner core of true believers who spurred the rank and file onwards – the Zapatistas were a decentralised organisation, in which the voices of the Mayan peasantry were filtered upwards from local councils to the Clandestine Indigenous Revolutionary Committee, which in turn issued its pronouncements via an anonymous spokesman. Marcos, the be-masked, pipe-smoking, former university lecturer from Mexico City who addressed the world's media, was merely the final conduit in a channel that gave voice to the dispossessed people of Chiapas.

Marcos himself seemed like a figure out of revolutionary myth, a masked avenger from a 1920s film serial, a Zorro *de nos jours*, who only ever appeared in public clad in a black balaclava, often on horseback and with a rifle slung over his shoulder. In press conferences, he quoted poetry and told comic fables as well as issuing demands for constitutional protections for indigenous rights. His voluminous writings, which circulated on internet chat rooms and in paperback collections in Europe and America, eschewed leaden pronouncements about the historical dialectic in favour of punchy critiques of global capitalism. In addition to political tracts such as 'I Shit on All Revolutionary Vanguards' and 'World War 4', in which he cast neoliberal economics as the next planetary threat after nuclear apocalypse and world war, he wrote children's stories, poems, even a detective novel.

The first phase of the Zapatista uprising lasted for twelve days. Initially, the EZLN stormed and held six towns and several ranches throughout the region but were driven back into the jungle by the superior numbers of the Mexican Army. On 12 January, however, mass demonstrations in Mexico City prompted the government to negotiate a ceasefire and deal with the Zapatistas as a legitimate force in the region. While small-scale military engagements continued for several years, the Zapatistas were able to shift their focus from armed insurrection to community building and grassroots organisation. In interviews, Marcos repeatedly claimed that the EZLN was not a normal guerrilla movement 'because its proposal is to cease being an army'. Chiapas became a hub for anti-globalisation protestors from around the world. Caravans of activists from Europe and North America made their way to San Cristóbal de las Casas, the pretty colonial town that was the seat of the uprising and host of the Encuentro for Humanity and Against Neoliberalism conference in 1996. Many of these same activists would later help to organise the anti-WTO protests that took place in Seattle and Genoa at the end of the decade, and which constituted the largest and most visible mobilisation against free-market globalisation of the era. Part of the genius of the Zapatista movement was the way in which it wired a struggle for indigenous rights in the remote forests of southern Mexico into the world's political and media systems. In the language of the time, it made the local global.

Rafael Sebastián Guillén Vicente was born in Tampico in 1957 to a moderately prosperous middle-class family. His parents were former schoolteachers, who ran a small furniture store. At his Jesuit high school, he excelled in history and literature but was captivated by the exploits of Fidel, Che and the Cuban revolution that was unfolding just across the Gulf of Mexico. In his twenties, he moved to Mexico City to get his PhD and worked as a philosophy lecturer in the capital for several years. Sometime in the mid-1980s, perhaps out of disaffection with the life of a bourgeois intellectual, perhaps in order to flee the authorities who were monitoring his activities among Mexico City's leftist radicals, Vicente quit his academic post and headed for the jungles of Chiapas.

After this the details of his biography become cloudy, but the legend comes into sharper focus. As the story goes, Vicente, filled with revolutionary zeal and a somewhat doctrinaire adherence to Marxist principles, announced to the Mayan peasants that he intended to lead them in a proletarian uprising against the Mexican state in order to seize the means of production and declare indigenous ownership of the land. The Mayans, unmoved by his oratory, stared blankly back at the transplanted urban intellectual. They weren't 'workers' and nobody could 'own' the land, they said; the earth was not a commodity that could be bought and sold, but the living heart of the community and the dwelling place of the gods. The Mayans held a different view of globalisation. The world was already – had always been – a single planetary network, woven together not by international law and telecommunications but by the sacred relationships between humans and the natural world. It was only after the European colonisers had arrived that the world had been divided from itself.

In the Zapatista mythology, it was from this confrontation between Marxist theory and indigenous folk wisdom that the EZLN's new form of political organisation grew. The first words that Marcos spoke when he faced the media in San Cristóbal de las Casas after the EZLN had successfully captured the town from the Mexican government were: 'Through me speaks the will of the Zapatista National Liberation Army.' In interviews, Marcos often referred to his black balaclava as a mirror, in which marginalised peoples around the world could recognise their own struggles:

> Marcos is gay in San Francisco, black in South Africa, an Asian in Europe, a Chicano in San Ysidro, an anarchist in Spain, a Palestinian in Israel, a Mayan Indian in the street of San Cristobal, a Jew in Germany, a Gypsy in Poland, a Mohawk in Quebec, a pacifist in Bosnia, a single woman on the Metro at 10pm, a peasant without land, a gang member in the slums, an unemployed worker, an unhappy student and, of course, a Zapatista in the mountains.

It was the paradoxical glamour of Marcos's anonymous identity, the combination of facelessness and charisma, that made the Zapatistas into a worldwide cause célèbre. The very idea – the meme, if you like – of a masked guerrilla who channelled the unheard voices of the world's dispossessed resonated with the early internet age, in which DJs, hackers, chaos theorists and techno-futurists of all stripes celebrated the immersion of the self within complex systems and planetary networks. It was in large part due to Marcos's self-cancelling charisma that a regional dispute in the remote forests of Mexico was converted into a mass media phenomenon and the inspiration for protests around the world.

Received opinion casts the 1990s as a largely apolitical era, a time of relative affluence and political stability during which popular culture was defined by ironic self-awareness and heedless hedonism. As with most cliches, there is some truth in this observation, but it is far from the whole picture. The era of neoliberal globalisation sparked a worldwide protest movement that focused on the biennial meetings of the WTO and G8 summits, much-publicised gatherings of the bureaucrats and heads of state who held the levers of the world economic system. If globalisation was a highly abstract process, which unfolded in the rarefied domains of the world financial system and multilateral trade agreements, then meetings of this sort provided a public face and a local target for opposition.

The anti-globalisation movement was not a single organisation with a permanent bureaucracy and membership. Instead, it was a 'movement of movements', a loose coalition of activist groups from around the world which gathered at strategic locations to debate, organise and demonstrate. The crowd of 75,000 people who marched in protest at the WTO in Seattle in the autumn of 1999 was drawn from church groups, trade unions, student organisations, environmentalists, indigenous rights activists and anti-capitalists of various stripes. It included representatives of New Zealand's Maori tribes, the Gandhian State Farmers' Association of Karnataka, India and the Canadian Postal Workers' Union. Anti-globalisation activists used the very technologies of globalisation – internet discussion boards, email, mobile phones and cheap airfares – in order to assemble in large numbers before the world's television cameras at the specific location in which global economic policy was being made. There was often a carnivalesque atmosphere to proceedings. In among the crowd were marching bands, sound systems, puppet shows and street theatre performers. The aim was to create a counter-spectacle to the WTO or G8 meeting and to project an alternative vision of what humanity was capable of, a different way of being together in the world that was a riposte to the atomised, acquisitive, self-interested logic of global consumer capitalism.

In Seattle and two years later at the next major anti-WTO protest in Genoa, media attention was disproportionately directed towards the Black Bloc, a small group of black-clad, mask-wearing protestors who eschewed the peaceable tactics of the majority in favour of direct action against the symbols of global capitalism. In Seattle, this involved smashing up Starbucks, Gap and Old Navy storefronts and engaging in pitched battles with riot police. The Black Bloc were inspired by the Italian autonomist movement, which rejected bureaucratic structures and mass membership in favour of anarchist self-organisation and highly confrontational direct action. The Seattle Police Department responded to the violence with military-style tactics, using tear gas and rubber bullets not only against the Black Bloc but also against otherwise peaceful protestors. Washington State Governor Gary Locke called in the National Guard and instigated martial law. This ensured that the protests were headline news all around the world and were reported on through a thick fog of tear gas smoke and moral outrage. Some leaders of NGOs and protest groups bemoaned the fact that the details of their critiques of free-market globalisation were lost in the scandal. Others argued that, without the ruckus, the anti-globalisation message would not have been heard at all.

Only a few weeks after the 'Battle in Seattle', Naomi Klein's *No Logo* was published. Whether it was a matter of luck or judgement, or some inscrutable mixture of the two, we will never know, but Klein's book was perfectly timed to package anti-globalisation politics for a wider audience. Within a couple of years, *No Logo* had been translated into thirty languages and sold more than a million copies worldwide, which is quite a feat for a radical critique of 'brand bullies' such as Pepsico, Starbucks and Nike, which, claimed Klein, used hip and supposedly iconoclastic marketing strategies ('anti-branding') to draw attention away from their role in exploiting foreign workers and contributing to environmental degradation. *No Logo* covered similar territory to Douglas Coupland's *Generation X*, but in this case its energy was directed towards resistance and activism rather than numb resignation. Part of the book's appeal was that it drew a clear line between young people's first-hand experiences of corporate cynicism, the everyday awareness that everything from coffee to fashion to entertainment comes wrapped in a finely calibrated web of hip cultural associations, and the otherwise invisible relationships of exploitation and inequality that accompanied the new global economic system. *No Logo* also joined the dots between the various small-scale and localised protest movements that had sprung up in opposition to the global free trade system, from British Reclaim the Streets to the French 'altermondialisation' movement to Canadian Adbusters. In this respect, *No Logo* was a kind of *Lonely Planet* guide to anti-globalisation politics.

Ultimately, the movement proved to be relatively short lived. As the global 'War on Terror' ramped up after 9/11, activist energies were redirected towards the anti-war movement, which in 2003 saw some of the largest street demonstrations in history. Things move fast in the global network society, and the ability of both governments and protest movements to keep up with events is often stretched beyond capacity. The 'movement of movements' that assembled in Seattle in 1999, Genoa in 2001 and Warsaw in 2004 prided itself on its 'horizontalist' approach. This was a non-hierarchical, leaderless structure that practised what scholars call 'prefigurative politics' – that is, its own organisation was intended to prefigure the new world that it wanted to bring into existence. In the case of the anti-globalisation movement, this meant a form of direct democracy in which all voices received equal weight in collective decision making, a process similar to the one practised by the Zapatistas in the jungles of Chiapas. On the streets of Seattle and Genoa, activist groups of various religious and political leanings from all around the world co-ordinated their actions via cell phone communications and a series of pre-arranged hand signals that would later be adopted by the Occupy Wall Street movement after the financial crash of 2008.

This was touted as a new kind of organisation for the flexible, mobile, hyper-accelerated world of the network society. The aim of the movement was not to reject globalisation as a whole. In fact, many activists were suspicious of the term 'anti-globalisation' as it suggested isolationism, enhanced border protections, even a return to the nation state as the ultimate source of political and social organisation. One of the pithiest slogans to emerge from the movement was the desire for 'a world in which many worlds fit'. It was a campaign for multiplicity and sustainability in a global system that was all too easily dominated by giant corporations and powerful nation states. And yet the question remained as to how such a movement could have a lasting impact in the absence of those stubbornly persistent Old World political forces – strong leadership and durable organisation.

11

Crash

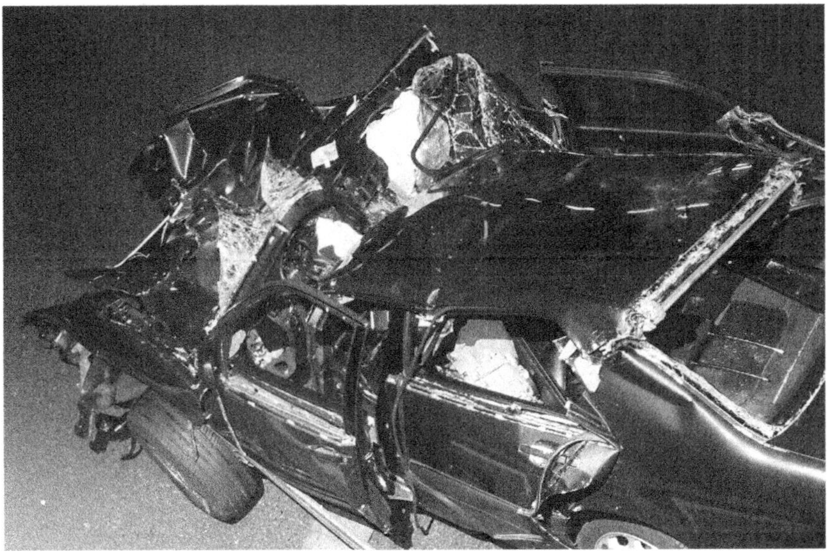

IN BOTH life and death, Lady Diana Spencer straddled multiple dimensions of time. The car crash in the Pont de l'Alma tunnel in Paris that caused her death played out at the level of microseconds: the synaptic twitch, the alcohol-delayed muscle response of her driver, the moment of impact. The facts of the matter were fixed in this moment. All that followed – the palace's slow response, the great outpouring of public grief, the saturation coverage in the global media – was triggered by the infinitesimally complex sequence of events that unfurled in the tunnel as the car spun out of control and its occupants were crushed by the deadly force of metal colliding with concrete colliding with flesh. Everything else was pure response, action and speech trailing in the wake of a sublime event that was frozen in an irretrievable past.

Most of Diana's life had been lived in the glare of the paparazzi's flash bulbs – the eternal now of the camera's gaze and the voracious curiosity of the celebrity-obsessed public. The pack of photographers who had been pursuing her car since it left the Hotel Ritz arrived at the scene of the crash before the emergency services. According to eyewitnesses, they took pictures of the carnage before they offered assistance. When the first ambulance arrived, the paramedics had to shoulder their way through the media scrum in order to get to the wounded. French police arrested several paparazzi at the crash site and confiscated their cameras, but images of the dying princess encased in crushed metal still made it into magazines in France and Hong Kong.

Diana was pronounced dead at around 4 a.m. after receiving treatment at the Pitié-Salpêtrière Hospital. The morning papers reported that Diana was merely injured, but by mid-morning the news had made its way around the world via television and radio bulletins, internet news sites and rolling twenty-four-hour cable TV coverage, with its strange mixture of dead time and momentary bursts of new information. For several days, all other events faded from notice. This was the only story, the all-consuming spectacle. And yet, in reality, nothing had changed since shortly after midnight on Sunday morning of 31 August. Diana, her lover, Dodi Al-Fayed, and their driver, Henri Paul, were dead. Her bodyguard, Trevor Rees-Jones, survived.

Diana was a unique celebrity icon whose appeal encompassed both the modern obsession with the lives of the rich and famous and the ancient glamour of the monarchy. In interviews and photo calls, she cast herself as the warm, humanitarian alternative to the damp squibs and cold fish of the Royal Family. The causes she championed told the story of the late twentieth century: working as a UN ambassador in the landmine-strewn warzones of Bosnia and Angola; shaking hands with an HIV/AIDS patients in St Thomas's

Hospital in London; even her friendships with eccentric celebrities like Elton John made her seem more attuned to the spirit of the age than her haunted tree of a husband, Prince Charles. But Diana was not just a celebrity, not just a face in the spotlight; and she wasn't just famous for something so commonplace as having an exceptional talent or contributing to world affairs. The context for her vast fame, the backdrop that enabled the princess to shine with a greater lustre than even the best known of her fellow superstars, was the deep historical time of monarchy itself, the ancient order of the British crown that claims divine, rather than merely secular, authority. Her peers were not only Marilyn Monroe and Jackie Onassis, but also Marie Antoinette and Anne Boleyn, maybe even Bluebeard's wife and Sleeping Beauty.

History is a distant presence in most people's lives. We watch it on TV and read about it in books, but we spend most of our lives absorbed in the mundane concerns of the here and now. And yet, from time to time, events cut through the noise of everyday life and history imposes itself on our consciousness. Pearl Harbor, VE Day, the assassination of JFK, the Apollo moon landing, the fall of the Berlin Wall, 9/11: these are all moments on which many of us can look back and say, 'I remember where I was that day.' The death of Diana, Princess of Wales, was another such event. This, however, was neither an act of war, nor a political assassination, nor or a pioneering feat of exploration, but the death of the world's most photographed woman in a world increasingly defined by images.

↖↑↗

The crash in the Pont de l'Alma tunnel was the climactic scene of the soap opera that had been playing out in the House of Windsor since Diana's marriage to the Prince of Wales in 1981. This was the spectacular season finale that drove up viewing figures to barely imaginable heights – up from 1 billion worldwide television viewers for the wedding to roughly 2.5 billion for the funeral – and seemed to have been scripted by J.G. Ballard, the visionary novelist of the celebrity car crash and the hyper-mediated death drive.

In the beginning, when Charles and Diana were driven to be married in Westminster Cathedral in a red-velvet-lined postillion landau that could barely hold the 25m-long train of her dress, palace insiders and royal correspondents believed that the new princess would be a boon to the British monarchy. According to the logic of the court, this virginal daughter of the British aristocracy was a modernising figure who would help an institution that was hundreds of years old stay relevant to its subjects' lives in the age of mass media and tabloid journalism. In a sense, they were right. Charles quickly discovered that his dim star power was eclipsed by the adulation Diana received whenever the couple processed through the streets of the former colonies or distant provinces they visited on royal tours. Diana was the conduit between monarchy and modern celebrity culture, a blonde fairy-tale princess; even the Archbishop of Canterbury colluded in the Disneyfied fantasy when he referred to Diana on her wedding day as 'the stuff of which fairy tales are made'. But if the Royal Family was trying to become more demotic, part of the general churn of news stories about politicians, actors, musicians and sport stars who were 'in the media' due to their talent, luck or notoriety, then they would also be owed less of the old currency in which monarchy was traditionally paid: deference and respect.

The pressure started to build right from the start. The fairy-tale romance of the princess and the wedding and the coach and the crowds was merely a surface display, a dance of mechanical figurines, that was powered by a hidden mechanism of enormous complexity and rigour. Where to sit, where to stand, how to address the various ranks of the family, how to deal with the vast palace staff: this was a world of protocol with few opportunities for privacy or intimacy. All members of the Royal Household were bent out of shape by the cogs and gears of its machinery, but for the 20-year-old princess, herself the product of a broken aristocratic home, the alienation of palace life was extreme. She later told her biographer that on the night before her wedding she felt like a 'lamb to the slaughter'.

The trouble was compounded by the presence of Camilla Parker Bowles, Charles's supposedly ex-lover with whom he continued to spend a suspicious amount of time at weekend shooting parties and balls. Today, the details of the Wales's failed marriage are well known: his distance and haughtiness; her loneliness and desperation; his refusal to bend his will or alter his routine to accommodate her desires; her bulimia and self-harm; their infidelities (Diana also sought affection elsewhere when it became clear that the marriage would be an empty shell); their competition for the limelight; their attempts to control the media narrative in their own favour. Life in the clockwork depths of the palace was scrutinised from the outside with ferocious, almost demented zeal by the press. Throughout their marriage, a group – what is the collective noun for press photographers? A swarm? An infestation? A plague? – of journalists were camped at the palace gates or stalked the perimeters of their country estates with their telephoto lenses at the ready to capture any moment of marital awkwardness. Charles and Diana's travails coincided with a new culture of tabloid journalism that was driven by the competitive and iconoclastic ethos of the 1980s. Fleet Street tabloids were happy to build up and then tear down celebrity icons, even – or perhaps especially – royal ones, on the sole condition that the stories drove up sales and gave their papers an advantage in an increasingly amoral marketplace.

From the late 1980s onwards, there was a steady stream of negative news stories about the Wales's marital problems, but the truly bumper year for royal scandal was 1992, or what the queen ill-advisedly called her *annus horribilis*. In a sign that the British tabloid press could still produce moments of comic genius, as well as rank hypocrisy and moral depravity, *The Sun* ran with the headline, 'One's Bum Year'. Throughout 1992, the Royal Family was seemingly never out of the headlines, and seemingly always for the wrong reasons. There were topless photos of Sarah Ferguson, Duchess of York and wife of Prince Andrew, having her toes sucked by a Texan billionaire on a Moroccan beach. There were pictures of a solitary Diana on an official tour of the Taj Mahal, quite obviously estranged from her absent husband. *The Sun* published the transcript of secret recordings made in 1989 of a telephone conversation between Diana and James Gilbey, her then lover, in which she referred to marriage to Charles as 'torture' and proclaimed her ambition to eclipse the Windsors in fame and adulation. Notoriously, Gilbey repeatedly called Diana his 'Squidgy', which of course became the semi-official name for the ensuing brouhaha at the palace – 'Squidgygate'. Hot on the heels of *l'affaire Squidgy*, as the French might have called it, came another royal sex scandal, this time featuring Charles and his lover. 'Camillagate' involved another secret recording of an intimate conversation between the star-crossed lovers in which the future king of England expressed his fondest wish to serve as his beloved's tampon.

By the end of the year, three royal couples had separated – Princess Anne from Captain Mark Philips, Prince Andrew from Fergie, and, the Big Kahuna, Prince Charles, the future king of England, from Diana Spencer. If that wasn't enough to take the shine off the queen's *annus*, then the fire that broke out at Windsor Castle in November 1992 most certainly was. Public support for the monarchy reached its lowest point since the Roundheads were in charge when it was announced that the state would have to foot the £60 million bill for the repairs because Her Majesty had neglected to take out an insurance policy on her priceless abode.

One of the most striking features of the bad royal press of 1992 was that the most scandalous revelations were made by Diana herself. In June of that year, *The Sunday Times* began its serialisation of Andrew Morton's biography, *Diana: Her True Story*, which was written with the full, albeit clandestine, co-operation of the Princess of Wales. Morton's book outlines Diana's unhappy childhood, her alienation within the palace, her bulimia and suicide attempts, Charles's infidelity (though not her own), the stifling froideur of a family raised on the Victorian ideals of duty and emotional suppression, the Queen Mother's gaslighting (she dismissed Diana's complaints as the overwrought imagination of a 'silly girl'), and the general misery of life chez Windsor. It was, of course, a highly strategic form of self-revelation, in which multiple transactions were taking place, multiple agendas being pursued. Diana wanted to tell her side of the story, play on the public's affections and, in doing so, win more control over her life in the depths of the palace machine. The scandal that the book caused had precisely that effect, prompting the queen to agree to Diana and Charles's separation as a damage-limitation exercise.

But the process of giving the interviews for the book, mainly via an intermediary so as to avoid detection by palace spies, also seems to have provided Diana with genuine spiritual succour. In the preface to the twenty-fifth anniversary edition, Morton relates how in those interviews Diana would unburden herself of her story in great uninterrupted flights of confession. Of course, Morton has his own agenda to pursue. And yet, in spite of the inevitable framework of cynicism and propaganda in which all royal press is conducted, Diana's collaboration with Morton seems to have taken place at the invisible tidal point where public performance shades into the most intimate zones of the self. For Diana, it seems to have been part PR strategy, part moral absolution.

The revelations contained in *Diana: Her True Story* sparked a media war between the opposed camps of the prince and princess – what came to be known as the 'War of the Waleses'. Charles hit back with his own authorised biography, written by loyal establishment man Jonathan Dimbleby. The book was accompanied by a two-and-a-half-hour-long television documentary, replete with flattering scenes of the kilt-wearing prince besporting himself with his young sons in a sun-dappled glen on his Balmoral estate, during which he offered his views on everything from public policy to religion to the future of the monarchy. But the Walter Scott scenography was undercut by Charles's admission, under the very gentlest of Dimbledonic questioning, of his affair with Camilla and his evident unease in discussing such matters in front of the cameras.

In response, Diana went one better with a much more fluent confessional interview with Martin Bashir on the BBC the following year. As with the collaboration with Morton, this interview was also prepared in secret: a camera crew was quietly smuggled into Kensington Palace on a Sunday evening after the staff had been dismissed; the queen and Sir Marmaduke Hussey, the director general of the BBC, were both kept out of the loop until the morning of the broadcast for fear that they might pull the plug. The headline quote from the interview was the now infamous line, 'Well, there were three of us in this marriage, so it was a bit crowded'; but the more telling statement was Diana's rejoinder to the continual infantilisation she suffered at the hands of her husband and her in-laws: 'I don't think I've been given any credit for growth. And my goodness, I've had to grow.'

The statement of personal growth was the true currency of the new style of confessional celebrity interview that emerged in the 1990s. The queen of the confessional mode was of course Oprah Winfrey, who came into her regal pomp in the 1990s with the most-watched talk show on American television and who was well on her way to becoming the richest Black woman in history. Oprah sold many commodities via a media empire that expanded to include her TV chat show, book club, magazine, television network and production company. She sold beauty products, lifestyle advice, novels, cars, even American presidents (her endorsement of Obama in 2008 is credited with adding roughly a million votes to his tally), but the most alluring and least tangible commodity of all was absolution. Oprah was revivalist preacher, shrink and lifestyle coach rolled into one, a secularised televangelist who would hold hands with her guests and weep as they spilled their guts on live television. And, what's more, Oprah's tears could be counted on as the real thing because she was a survivor too, the victim of teenage sexual abuse who had dragged herself up from rural poverty to the commanding heights of the US media establishment by sheer force of character.

It was on *The Oprah Winfrey Show* that Sarah Ferguson, formerly the Duchess of York, confessed in 1996 to selling access to her husband, the duke, and thus began her journey back towards the sunny uplands of moral grace and renewed celebrity status. It was also on *The Oprah Winfrey Show* that Ellen DeGeneres, the TV sitcom star and soon-to-be chat show host in her own right, came out as gay, a major event in the 'Don't Ask, Don't Tell' climate of 1990s America. Oprah was the go-to confessional – and high-profile career rehabilitation machine – for doping athletes, staff harassing TV presenters, dwindling Hollywood actors and members of the British royal household for many years to come.

Back in the 1960s, Marshall McLuhan famously cast the cool and handsome John F. Kennedy as the ideal presidential candidate for the TV era, in contrast to his opponent, Richard Nixon, whose overheated verbal style better suited him to the radio age. The new mode of confessional self-presentation that was Oprah's stock in trade, and which was used so effectively by Diana against her husband and his family, was the product of a media landscape that had shifted dramatically since those first televised presidential debates. By the 1990s, viewers could access hundreds of cable and satellite channels from all around the world, not just the handful of network broadcasters that carried major events like the Kennedy–Nixon debate in 1960. News updates were drip fed into the public consciousness via rolling twenty-four-hour news channels, as well as via the edited packages broadcast on the lunchtime and evening news bulletins. Paparazzi photographers used enormously powerful telephoto lenses that could capture a grainy image of a figure in a palace window at a distance of more than a mile. Helicopter camera crews could broadcast live footage as they pursued O.J. Simpson's white Ford Bronco as he fled the scene of his wife's murder on a Los Angeles freeway. With each new update from the lives of Michael Jackson, River Phoenix, Kurt Cobain, Anna Nicole Smith, Prince and countless other lesser lights, tales of haunted and hunted celebrities proliferated at an alarming rate in the new media age of the 1990s.

Websites and online discussion boards were starting to buzz with the chatter of celebrity gossip and speculation. One of the first successful attempts at streaming video on the web came in 1995 when the homemade sex tape produced by Tommy Lee and Pamela Anderson, the Mötley Crüe bassist and *Baywatch* nymphette, was stolen by a disgruntled workman at their Hollywood Hills mansion and broadcast for all to see. The Pam and Tommy sex tape wasn't only responsible for an early surge in internet use as punters were drawn online in the hopes of seeing their Saturday afternoon *Baywatch* viewing fantasies come true, but also helped to spark the massive proliferation of amateur (or in this case perhaps semi-professional) porn footage online, by no means all of it made or shared with the consent of the people captured on film. As media technology changes, so do our expectations about where the boundaries between public and private, self and other, should be drawn. Our assumptions about what we have a right to know about public figures shifts. The limits of what we allow ourselves to desire are extended. In the midst of the media frenzy surrounding Charles and Diana's failing marriage in 1992, Lord McGregor, the head of the UK's Press Complaints Commission, accused journalists of 'dabbling their fingers in the stuff of other people's souls'.

In her book *The Drama of Celebrity*, the literary historian Sharon Marcus shows how modern celebrity culture has always relied on a three-way exchange between the star, the media and the public. At the beginning of the nineteenth century, Lord Byron embarked upon a dance with the pamphleteers and critics on one side of him and the heaving bosoms of the reading public on the other. A century later, Sara Bernhardt cut a similar caper with the press and her adoring fans on either side of her. In each case, the glamour of celebrity, the *je ne sais quoi* of star power, could only have been possible with the collaboration of each member of this deeply complicit trio. But in the always-on mediascape of the 1990s, the traditional roles of star, media and audience were being scrambled up and blended together in unfamiliar ways.

A new style of chatsploitation TV talk show took the confessional mode pioneered by Oprah and added extra dimensions of kitsch and depravity. Ricki Lake and Jerry Springer dispensed with glamorous stars altogether and instead made heroes and villains of members of the general public. Under the guise of lifestyle coaching and televised group therapy, volunteers had their extra-marital affairs, illicit love children, perverse fetishes and all-round human weirdness – 'I slept with 251 Men in Ten Hours'; 'I Cut Off My Manhood' – pored over by a live studio audience. This wasn't celebrity in the traditional sense so much as a fleeting kind of notoriety achieved by offering oneself up for the judgement of the crowd; more like a televised version of the circus sideshow tradition, the old weird America in ill-fitting jeans on afternoon television. Some guests 'grew' from the experience, finding peace and reconciliation; others welcomed the jeers and resisted the solicitations of the host, embracing their role as scapegoats and sinners. And yet the volunteers continued to line up to receive the boos or hurrahs of the audience. In a sense, you might even say that the audience was consuming itself, or at least parts of itself, outlandish allegorical representations of their most vulnerable places and their most deeply suppressed urges, as they watched the baby daddies and love rats and secret Klansmen achieve forgiveness or damnation.

Without a doubt, though, the most consequential new media format of the era was reality television, which hit its stride at the start of the millennium with the massive success of *Big Brother* in the UK and *Survivor* in the US. Like chatsploitation, reality TV made stars out of ordinary people, at least for the duration of the show. In this case, the pretext for the audience's voyeurism was social experiment rather than group therapy. *Big Brother* sold itself as a serious (-ish) experiment in modern surveillance culture, a self-reflexive investigation into human behaviour in the age of mass celebrity and rapidly proliferating CCTV. The premise was as follows: what might happen if you were to enclose eleven regular Joes and Janes in a purpose-built house, set them weekly challenges, stage a weekly telephone vote to decide which of the housemates should be evicted, grant the final contestant a significant cash prize, and then record the contestants' every movement with dozens of cameras positioned throughout the house? Which otherwise hidden facets of human nature might be revealed? What anthropological insights might emerge? That was the premise, but in reality the scientific trappings were quickly discarded in favour of the real business of unfettered voyeurism and consequence-free judgement.

If *Big Brother* took its cue from George Orwell's totalitarian dystopia, *1984*, then *Survivor* looked further back in literary history to *Robinson Crusoe* for its social experiment. In this case, sixteen contestants were 'stranded' on an island off the coast of Borneo with nothing but their inborn wit and a moderately sized television production crew to ensure their survival. The contestants had to compete in weekly challenges of their physical and mental strength in order to win fresh supplies and exemption from that week's public vote, all in the hope of being the last man or woman standing and claiming the million dollars in prize money. In the petri dish world of the show, the contestants became human specimens as well as mayfly celebrities.

In subsequent years, reality TV became one of the most popular and certainly the most profitable format on television, spawning a whole range of sub-genres and franchises – talent shows such *Top Chef*, *Top Model*, *Pop Idol*, *Dancing with Former Daytime TV Hosts*, *Armenia's Got Talent*; docusoaps such as *Airport*, *Driver's School* and *The Choir*; and scripted reality shows such as *The Real Hausfraus of Lower Saxony*. And, of course, lest we forget, the reality TV phenomenon also gave us *The Apprentice*, which debuted in America in 2004 and was produced by the same team as *Survivor*. Not only did *The Apprentice* convert the corporate boardroom into a mass media entertainment spectacle, but it also helped to propel Donald Trump from his mid-1990s doldrums as a clapped-out real estate mogul to his 2016 triumph as president of the United States. If new media was causing celebrity culture to fragment into a seemingly endless array of niche channels and micro celebs, then Trump became one of the few stars of sufficiently grotesque size to register on all channels and capture all eyeballs.

One of the reasons for the financial success of reality TV was that it was easily templated. Reality shows were high-concept formats – sixteen young people locked in a panopticon; pitch your talent to a panel of dead-eyed industry insiders; flatter a narcissist in exchange for a corporate career – that could be remade in new locations around the world with new contestants. *Big Brother* and *Survivor* were both franchises imported from Europe, *Big Brother* from the Netherlands and *Survivor* from Sweden, where *Expedition Robinson*, a more sober and high-minded version had aired in 1997. Reality shows were also catnip to senior executives as they were much cheaper to produce than traditional drama or documentary shows. In the guise of 'scripted reality' or 'docusoap' formats, production companies could dispense with whole sections of their crews, in particular writers and set designers. Most of the stars were non-professionals who were willing to work for a pittance in the hope of striking it rich by winning the contest or, failing that, signing a side deal as a singer, actor, product endorser or novelty nightclub act.

Reality TV was in fact born out of a labour dispute. In 1988, Fox Studios began work on what would become one of the longest-running reality shows, *Cops*, a mixture of docusoap and true crime show that sent film crews out on patrol with a different American police department each season. *Cops* received the greenlight from studio executives because filming of the network's drama shows was on hold due to a twenty-two-week-long writers' strike over pay and conditions. *Cops* proved to be a sneaky way of bypassing the strike and a long-term money spinner which combined low overhead costs with almost unlimited footage of high-stakes, real-life crime scenarios.

The patron saint of reality TV wasn't Donald Trump but rather Andy Warhol, who didn't just predict that in the future everyone would be famous for fifteen minutes, but also showed exactly how that would happen in the form of his DIY celebrity 'Factory' in New York, where he used the mass media technologies of film, tape recorders and silk screen printing to make celebrities of the everyday Joes and Janes of the New York underground. Reality TV was Warholian in both of these senses – the way it made celebrities out of random members of the public and the way it revealed the very mechanisms by which fame was created. *Big Brother*, *Pop Idol*, *America's Next Top Model*: these were all shows about the process of celebrity formation, as much as they were about particular singers and models. Everyone can be a star, they proclaimed, but only so long as we all recognise that being a star is a function of the media system itself, rather than an inherent property of the individual. Reality TV was thus ironic to its very core, maybe even tragicomic, in the way in which it bestowed the laurels of celebrity just at the point that it revealed their fundamental emptiness.

↖↑↗

Diana's death was the media event of the century. One historian has estimated that it produced more magazine and newspaper coverage than any other event in history, an accolade it will surely retain given the subsequent decline of the print media in the digital age. When the news of the crash was first announced both the BBC and ITV, Britain's two main national broadcasters, interrupted their scheduled programming and switched to twenty-four-hour, cable-news-style rolling coverage, a rare event in those pre-9/11 days. BBC radio imposed a blanket policy across all of its stations of playing only downtempo and mournful tunes. In the case of BBC Radio One, the corporation's flagship pop station, this meant that its usual chart offerings were replaced by infrequently heard ambient classics by Ryuichi Sakamoto, Sabres of Paradise and Giorgio Moroder. The crash was a kind of event horizon in the media system, a happening of such all-consuming significance that all channels were filled with its strange signal. On the Monday after the news broke, *The Sun* newspaper sold a million extra copies to customers hungry for yet more coverage.

The funeral itself was watched by an estimated 2.5 billion viewers worldwide. That puts it in the same bracket as a summer Olympics opening ceremony or the FIFA World Cup final, the point where modern celebrity edges into the territory previously reserved for angels and gods. On the day of the funeral, vigils were held in all corners of the globe, from the candlelit processions in LA and San Francisco to the gatherings of anti-landmine campaigners in Bosnia to the South Sea islands, where an official wake was held by the Tongan Royal Family. In the more upmarket sections of the press, articles described the unprecedented global reach of the event, as though Diana's death, tragic though it was, also furnished a brief glimpse of the invisible ties that bound the global village together as a single community.

After the initial news had broken, the focus of the coverage shifted from the event itself to various parties' responses to the event. Just as reality TV scrambled the traditional roles in the celebrity system, Diana's death triggered a frenzy of emotion and judgement during which the paparazzi, the palace and the public each took their turn in the spotlight. On the face of things, reality TV is the polar opposite of the monarchy – it is based on social experiment, rather than organic tradition; it runs on naked ambition, rather than an ethic of duty and service; it displays a high degree self-awareness about the mechanisms of modern celebrity, rather than the monarchical fantasy of heredity, or the atavistic notion that distinction is bred in the blood, rather than conferred by the camera. But over the course of the preceding two decades, as the Royal Family had become more and more a part of general celebrity culture, the less those distinctions held. The constant press surveillance, the retinues of PR consultants, the vying against each other for the limelight, the competition for the affections of a capricious and judgemental public, even the strange pointlessness of the 'work' the royals performed as part of their official duties: all of this suggested that the British monarchy had finally collapsed into its opposite: *Big Brother*, Windsor Edition.

When they received the news, the Royal Family was on holiday at Balmoral. After issuing a solemn press release, that is where they remained, even as large crowds of mourners gathered on the Mall and signed condolence books outside Buckingham Palace. With her divorce from Charles, Diana had been stripped of her title as Her Royal Highness and divested of her official position within the institution. In keeping with this state of affairs, the queen treated the death as an essentially personal matter. Notoriously, even while flags on official buildings around the world were lowered out of respect, the Royal Standard was not flown at half-mast at Buckingham Palace. The strict observance of protocol maintained that the standard should only fly when the queen was in residence, which she was not. Newspaper reports and television news interviews gave voice to a rising tide of resentment at the chilly and distant royals. Of course, no one could directly see the queen and her family's actual response; no one could really gauge the authenticity of their private feelings as they sat with their grief; but the signals they sent were deemed inadequate to the occasion.

As Diana had already proved in the preceding years, authentic emotion and strategic public messaging need not be mutually exclusive. This was a lesson that Tony Blair had learned, even if the palace had not. On the Sunday morning directly after the crash, Blair gave a brief press conference on his way to church in his Sedgefield constituency in the north-east of England. His words set the tone for much of what would follow in the week leading up to the funeral. Diana was, in Blair's pre-scripted words, the 'people's princess'. He added: 'I feel like everyone else in this country today, utterly devastated … We are today a nation, in Britain, in a state of shock, in mourning, in grief.' Everyone seemed to agree that Blair, fresh from a landslide election victory and backed by a slick communications team, performed well in the moment. His aura was burnished as he spoke words appropriate to the occasion. But his invocation of the 'people's princess' was a novel phrase at the time, a populist touch that has since become a standard part of the political lexicon on both the left and the right of the spectrum. Blair's statement was issued on an occasion that was as close to apolitical as any can be for an elected politician: the recognition of the death of a public figure. And yet in its invocation of the will of the people as though it were a homogenous thing beyond the control of politicians and the press, something given rather than made, he used a populist strategy that would only become more appealing to politicians in years to come.

As the royals kept their distance, an extraordinary outpouring of public grief was taking place throughout the country. It would be wrong to dismiss this great, gaseous cloud of sentiment as entirely the product of the media; the droplets began to gather and form into a fine mist as soon as the news broke and people started to make their way into the streets surrounding Buckingham Palace. But when the television cameras arrived and the crowd itself became the story, then the mist became a cloud, which then became a weather system, which then became an entire climate of feeling that settled over large swathes of the national consciousness and sent gusts eddying out into the wider currents of the global media system. With its constant coverage, one-tone commentary, and frequent vox pop interviews of members of the public who gathered on the Mall, the media created a vast feedback loop that generated wave after wave of mimetic grief. The Mall was the scene of the biggest rave of the decade, only this time the individual members of the crowd gave themselves over to the ecstasy of collective mourning, rather than hedonism.

The images were instantly 'iconic' in a more literal sense than that in which the term is generally used. Children laying hand-drawn cards at the palace gates. Couples consoling one another. Grown men weeping. Tourists, office workers, families up from the provinces by train, the young, the old, the halt and the lame, all paying their respects to a lady whose way of life was almost impossibly different from their own, yet somehow seemed comprehensible to them, an object of grief and sympathy, 'relatable'. The crowds brought with them a vast collection of votive offerings – cards, photographs, homemade posters, toys, letters, balloons, and a sea of flowers piled against the gates of Kensington Palace and spilling out into the street, a tidal wave of kitsch folk art.

The funeral at Westminster Abbey on Saturday, 6 September, a week after the three deaths in the tunnel in Paris, was the climax of the public mourning, the ceremonial rite that broke the fever and dispersed the cloud. The ceremony was a hybrid affair, part official state occasion, part celebrity spectacle. Tens of thousands of silent watchers lined the streets as the coffin was drawn through central London. Princes William and Harry, then aged 15 and 12, followed on foot behind the cortège with their father, their uncle and their grandfather, as a single bell tolled. Guests at the abbey included workers from Diana's favoured charities alongside heads of state from around the world and Hollywood stars. In his eulogy, Charles Spencer, Diana's brother, echoed the public mood when he observed that his sister possessed a 'particular brand of royal magic' that exceeded the common or garden variety bestowed by the crown. He also denounced the paparazzi and cast Diana, named for the ancient Roman goddess of the hunt, as the 'most hunted woman in the world'. His speech, broadcast around the world and projected on giant screens in St James's Park for the gathered crowd, raised a spontaneous ripple of applause which began in the street and was then taken up by the congregation inside the abbey.

The mood was sustained by Elton John's performance of 'Candle in the Wind', a song originally written to commemorate the death of Marilyn Monroe, another mythical blonde caught in the trap of fame's penetrating gaze, but now applied to his dead friend. When it was released as a single shortly after the funeral, 'Candle in the Wind' spent five weeks at number one in the British charts and was a massive global hit. Some estimates make it the second highest-selling single of all time, after Bing Crosby's 'White Christmas'. It has a much better claim to have captured – or maybe that should be *to have created* – the zeitgeist of the late 1990s, at least in terms of raw numbers, than any Britpop or grunge or dance anthem has.

↖↑↗

Why did so many people feel so deeply about the death of Diana Spencer?

Many observers noticed how the scenes had a vaguely religious air. Hilary Mantel described Diana as an archetypal figure of 'conjugal and maternal love', a symbol of idealised femininity removed from the late twentieth-century world of rational calculation and material self-interest. When she died, that part of her which existed in the mythic dimension came to the fore, rather than the celebrity cover girl who holidayed on friends' yachts in the Mediterranean and attended Paris Fashion Week. Her death seems to have released an untapped reservoir of emotion that lay beneath the surface of everyday life – feelings of love, grief, loss, victimhood, the desire for recognition, the need to be held, the hankering for what my grandmother used to call 'a really good cry'. The cards and letters that accompanied the sea of flowers at the palace gates evinced a sense that Diana's travails were a reflection of their authors' own struggles in life. To them, Diana was both distant and close at hand, both strange and familiar.

Ultimately, the motivations of the hundreds of thousands of people who gathered on the Mall could never be reduced to a single cause. Was this a new kind of religious devotion for a secular age? A yearning for solidarity in an era of competitive individualism? A perverse desire for control, the urge of the fans finally to possess the object of their devotion in the moment of her death? Or maybe it was the expression of a desire to enter into history itself, to bathe in a kind of significance that could never apply to one's own poor, unremembered life? The crowd will always remain something of a mystery both to itself and to those who seek to comprehend its psychology.

But what about those of us who felt nothing? For the doubters, the cynics, the critical thinkers, the disengaged and the merely nonplussed, it was a strange time indeed. Coverage of the event was almost entirely uniform in tone and perspective. Dissenting voices were very few and far between. Christopher Hitchens took to the airwaves on both sides of the Atlantic to offer critical commentary on Diana's empty humanitarianism, which he argued perpetuated injustice by attending only to its symptoms rather than its causes, and launch barbs against the sickly uniformity of the coverage. He called Britain a temporary 'one-party state' in its semi-official insistence on public conformity. The feminist publisher Carmen Callil went one better in comparing the public mourning to the Nuremberg rallies. Another commentator coined the term 'floral fascism'.

For most people unequipped with Hitchens's rhetorical gifts and brass neck, it seemed churlish to speak out, but many felt uncomfortable at the ease with which their fellow citizens allowed themselves to be drawn into the spectacle. The contagion seemed viral somehow, as though the crowds had been taken over by an alien force. Diana's death was a subtly polarising event, especially in Britain where the monarchy is part of the fabric of the nation, rather than just a quaint tourist attraction or juicy media narrative. Unlike many divisive public events, in this case the polarisation took place at the level of feeling, rather than thought. It was not so much a question of whether you were monarchist or republican, or whether you were for or against the characters involved in the palace drama, but instead of the extent to which you allowed yourself to be swept up in the hyper-mediated feeling of public grief.

It is now almost a cliché to depict Diana's death as a seminal moment in recent British history, the point at which the nation pivoted decisively away from the old codes of deference and stiff-upper-lippery towards the more inclusive, emotionally unbuttoned mode of public discourse we have today. This is the official line conveyed by Stephen Frears's 2006 film *The Queen*, a highly effective piece of heritage cinema, which conveys the tension between the old and new establishments, or between the taciturn crown and the emotionally fluent, media-literate world of Tony Blair and his phalanx of spin doctors. But while Frears's film marks the point of departure from the old way of feeling, it does not look forward to what was lurking just beyond the horizon of 1997. In many ways, the public response to Diana's death prefigured the soon-to-be-born world of social media, and the viral contagion of judgement, shame, anger, vainglory, paranoia, etc. that can so quickly spread through the interconnected, online world. The vast sea of tributes laid at the Buckingham Palace gates and along the Mall would today take the form of likes and messages on an official Facebook or Instagram page. The sheer scale of the tributes invokes the same sense of the mathematical sublime that accompanies viral videos online: 56 million hits, 102 million followers, etc.

One of the most disquieting features of that week was the sense of fragmented reality that the public response engendered. Those who were inside the bubble were, for a short while at least, in a different dimension from those on the outside. They were inside the spectacle. From their perspective, it wasn't even a spectacle at all. What they cared about was the reality that was playing out within this dimension: the death, the grief, the mourning. For those of us on the outside, all we could see were the nuts and bolts of the machinery that produced the spectacle – the cameras, the commentators, the press agents, the willing dupes who wanted to be absorbed in the collective hallucination. Looking back from today, the public mourning of Diana's death looks like the first big filter bubble of the coming digital era.

12

Prizes for All

IT IS impossible to tell the exact point in the 1990s when Western popular culture reached peak irony. Unlike Virginia Woolf, who famously claimed that 'on or about 1910 human nature changed', we cannot state with any certainty the moment when humankind in the affluent West finally decided that it had had enough of the self-referential, ironic, vaguely postmodern and increasingly cynical style in art, literature, film and television. No doubt it was a gradual change, a creeping sense of emptiness amid the knowing laughs and the *de haut en bas* shrugs. Some claim that the events of 9/11 were the final nail in the coffin of the pomo-ironic style, the moment of deadly impact when something indubitably real burst everyone's bubbles. But the rot had set in long before that. As early as 1993 David Foster Wallace, the bandana-wearing genius of the post-postmodern scene, had looked forward to a time when 'some weird bunch of anti-rebels will have the childish gall actually to endorse single-entendre principles'.

The questions that face the intrepid cultural historian as he delves into the archives of this distant and alien epoch are these. Where did the high-ironic style of the 1990s, which ranged so broadly across the arts and popular culture, from *The Simpsons* to Quentin Tarantino, and from *Seinfeld* to post-structuralist literary theory, come from? What was its purpose? And why did it run out of steam? After all, irony isn't good or bad by definition. Just look at Socrates, who in Plato's dialogues used irony to defeat specious arguments, or Oscar Wilde, who used it on the West End stage to satirise Victorian social mores. Irony can be a weapon of satire and critique, but it can also become a kind of crutch, an endlessly knowing and world-weary stance that excuses the user from ever actually taking a stance.

Strictly speaking, irony is a rhetorical device in which the speaker says something but means the opposite. Stanley Kubrick was being ironic in *Dr. Strangelove* when he had Peter Sellers utter the immortal line, 'No fighting in the war room!' But irony can mean much more than a conscious rhetorical strategy. Situations can be ironic. Events too. Irony resides in the gap between expectation and outcome, the often cruel and humorous disparity between intention and effect, or maxim and action. Much of the ironic mode in 1990s popular culture grew out of a heightened awareness of this kind of situational irony. Indie bands appearing on corporate magazine covers; Conservative politicians and defenders of 'family values' caught in the act with a lover; climate activists who flew on gas-guzzling jets to international conferences; radical artists whose main source of income were government grants. Irony was both a rhetorical device (a kind of knowing wink) and a state of being in the world (a kind of inevitable moral corruption endemic to life at the end of the twentieth century). But even if we agree on this broad definition of how irony works, we have to draw a line somewhere. When Alanis Morissette sang, 'It's like rain on your wedding day / It's a free ride when you've already paid … And isn't it ironic?' she was really just singing about mild disappointment.

⇖⇑⇗

As with so many other aspects of the 1990s, the high-ironic style had its provenance in the 1960s, the decade which saw the final exhaustion of artistic Modernism and the defeat of the worldwide student revolutions. Modernism encompassed a huge range of artistic styles and movements that stretched roughly from Charles Baudelaire in the mid-nineteenth century to The Who in the mid-1960s and included everything from Monet's water lilies to Gertrude Stein's experimental prose to Le Corbusier's *ville radieuse*. What united this otherwise disparate set of styles and approaches was an underlying belief in artistic progress. Modernists could be radical or reactionary in their politics, but they all believed that innovation in the arts opened up new frontiers of human expression and made possible new ways of living in the world. This was a different view of history from the nineteenth-century liberal belief in the gradual march of progress. Rather than seeing history as an arc of self-sustaining improvement, Modernist artists saw it as a series of revolutions and counter-revolutions, breakthroughs and retreats, that were, at least in part, driven by the arts themselves. Modernist art was a way of keeping pace with – and appropriating some of the demonic energies of – the revolutions in science, technology, urbanisation, warfare and politics that transformed everyday life over the course of the twentieth century.

Sometime around the latter third of the century that sense of forward momentum in the arts dissipated. The great Modernist project seemed to run out of steam. Modernism itself became a form of tradition, rather than the radical new thing. Eliot, Pound and Stein were taught on school and university curricula. Picasso, Mondrian and Duchamp were displayed in the world's most prestigious museums. Urban vistas were increasingly crowded with the rectilinear forms of Le Corbusier, Van der Rohe and their many imitators. The explosion of mass media in the mid-twentieth century also took the wind out of Modernism's sails. The higher calling of art as a vehicle for personal and social transformation was drowned out by the mass media's universal call to entertainment. The vast and hungry engine of popular culture proved highly capable of absorbing Modernism's best tricks and most radical styles without any of its high-flown claims to historical significance and revolutionary progress. Avant-garde movements still existed in the later twentieth century, but more often than not in their own rarefied enclaves, from where they had less impact on the culture at large. Gone were the days when Stravinsky's *Rite of Spring* could empty a concert hall or Luigi Russolo's futuristic noise machines could provoke a fist fight between radicals and traditionalists.

So, what comes after Modernism? There is no intrinsic reason why the next catch-all cultural movement should be 'Postmodernism'. Classicism was followed by Romanticism, not by Post-Classicism. The Baroque transmuted into the Rococo without recourse to a prefix of any kind. But with postmodernism, the sense of coming after the long-drawn-out event of Modernism was the whole point; the sense of belatedness, of cultural energies running out of steam, was conveyed via that all-important 'post'. The term was popularised by the architecture critics Robert Venturi, Denise Scott Brown and Steven Izenour in their 1972 book *Learning from Las Vegas*. For Venturi and company, Las Vegas pointed the way forward from the stale formulae of the high Modernist style in architecture, the instantly recognisable and increasingly bland parade of straight lines and tasteful geometries that could be found in most world cities. They praised Las Vegas for its lavish and self-conscious artificiality; for its hodgepodge mixture of styles borrowed from different historical eras; for its rejection of the myth of creative originality in favour of quotations and allusions; and for its privileging of hedonism and enjoyment over moral seriousness and profundity. Postmodernism was the way forward from Modernism, but only in the sense that it jettisoned the ideas of both 'way' and 'forward'.

The term quickly slipped its moorings and floated free of the specific use to which it was put in architectural criticism. It became a much grander – and much more nebulous – concept that was used to describe the cultural conditions of late twentieth-century life. In 1979 the sociologist Jean-François Lyotard defined the 'postmodern condition' as 'incredulity towards metanarratives', or a dwindling of belief in all-encompassing systems of meaning, such as socialism, Freudian psychology, historical progress, the march of science or monotheistic religion. Writing in 1985, the literary critic Fredric Jameson defined postmodernism as 'the cultural logic of late capitalism'. For Jameson, postmodernism was not just a particular style of architecture, nor even a group of artistic movements, but an entire 'cultural logic' that arose with the shift to a globalised information economy. Its characteristic modes were nostalgia, pastiche, irony and a generalised sense of historical weightlessness; it could be found everywhere from Andy Warhol's silkscreen paintings to the historical novels of E.L. Doctorow to cyberpunk movies like *Bladerunner*. At its best, postmodern culture was an ironic commentary on the absence of any alternative to the global capitalist system. At its worst, it was 'speech in a dead language', a giant karaoke bar, in which writers, artists and filmmakers crooned the words to songs written by other, better singers in the past.

By the 1990s, postmodernism was itself experienced by most at second, third or fourth hand. Like 'globalisation', 'postmodernism' became one of the words of the day, stretched beyond its original context and emptied of any precise meaning. It cropped up in newspaper opinion pages, on TV talk shows and in popular film and television series. In *Heat*, Michael Mann's 1995 crime thriller, Al Pacino's grizzled LA detective launches a tirade against his ex-wife's 'dead-tech, postmodernistic bullshit house', which is a neat way of conveying Pacino's old-school values but not much in the way of architecture criticism. My grandfather once used the term at the Sunday lunch table to refer to anyone who didn't believe in God. When, relishing the opportunity to use the new lingo I had picked up during my first year studying literature at university, I replied that religion was only one of the 'metanarratives' discarded by postmodernism and compared late twentieth-century capitalism to a state of schizophrenia, he scoffed so vigorously that he spilt sherry down his regimental tie.

Surveying the panoply of mass media available at the end of the twentieth century, the historian Eric Hobsbawm observed that 'never had it been harder to avoid aesthetic experience'. This was one of the central paradoxes of postmodernism. On the one hand, there was more culture and entertainment than ever before. Everyday life in the mass media age was a constant bombardment of visual and verbal stimuli in the form of television, cinema, radio, books, newspapers, magazines and advertisements. But on the other hand, so much of that culture was trash, and almost all of it was produced for more or less cynical commercial reasons. The high Modernist idea that art could be a lever for moving the world was drowned out by the babble of light entertainment. Even the postmodernist idea that ironic self-awareness could be used to draw attention to the constructed nature of all experience in a media saturated world had lost its novelty and become something of a cliché.

As Naomi Klein pointed out in *No Logo*, a book that was part of the shift away from the resigned ironic mode at the end of the decade, consumer capitalism increasingly came wrapped in a bowdlerised version of the post-1960s counter-cultural ethos: creative destruction, individual style and charisma, anti-establishment posturing, a studied casualness, but all in an easily digestible style ready for purchase, rather than as a challenge to received opinions and ways of life. The 1990s were a great age of faux-radical advertising: Martin Luther King was featured in a Gap advert; Gandhi in one for Microsoft. If you tuned into MTV circa 1995 you could enjoy the highly ironic spectacle of William Burroughs selling trainers for Nike. In the advert, the sallow face of the great Beat author appears on a flickering TV screen in an urban park. 'The purpose of technology is not to confuse the brain, but to serve the body,' he utters from beneath his trademark fedora hat, as the screen flickers with an onslaught of blurry footage of people of all races and abilities playing sports of various kinds. If any refugees from the counterculture still doubted the capacity of capitalism to co-opt oppositional energies, then surely the myth died as soon as Burroughs opened his mouth.

The kind of mildly critical irony that flourished in 1990s popular culture – *Seinfeld*'s 'no hugging, no learning' rule, or Jean Baudrillard's ironic provocation in *The Gulf War Did Not Take Place*, or even Kurt Cobain appearing on the cover of *Rolling Stone* magazine wearing a t-shirt bearing the slogan 'Corporate Magazines Still Suck' – was a response to this polluted mediascape. Ironic self-awareness was a kind of intellectual armour for a world in which all the best styles had been used up, all culture was a product and marketing had been elevated to the status of an artform.

But all too often it could also function as a kind of excuse. In 1995, Brian Eno, one of the great pioneers of the pop music avant-garde in the 1970s and 1980s, wrote in his diary that he had turned down a commission to compose the soundtrack to a Hollywood film. 'If I were a little less snobbish,' he reflected, 'I'd have been cleverly ironic about it all and just take the money.' In many cases, irony was a cod-intellectual smokescreen for dubious pleasures. It was under the cover of ironic self-awareness that all manner of previously tasteless activities were rehabilitated. In the UK, 'lads mags' like *Loaded* and *FHM* rehabilitated the top-shelf soft-porn magazine under the cover of a mildly ironic post-feminism. In America by the end of the decade, slacker culture was morphing into the new cult of the 'hipster', made up of predominantly white middle-class bohemians, usually employed in the cultural industries, who adopted red-neck fashions such as trucker hats and cheap beer as a homage to the blue-collar culture of the 1960s and '70s, the era before union membership declined and footloose global capitalism moved production offshore. The ironic re-appropriation of everything from pole dancing to greyhound racing jettisoned the undertone of political critique in favour of world-weary hedonism.

↖↑↗

None of which is to say that postmodern irony wasn't fun or didn't produce moments of pop cultural genius. One of the crowning achievements of the 1990s ironic mode was *The Simpsons*, which began life in 1987 as a short cartoon insert on *The Tracey Ullman Show* and went on to become the longest-running scripted programme in American television history. Matt Groening, the show's creator, was a graduate of the Evergreen State College in Olympia, Washington, the same hip college town that gave birth to Nirvana and the Seattle grunge scene. Like Nirvana, Groening took the off-kilter, anti-corporate sensibility of alternative rock into the mainstream; in this case, into the lion's den of Rupert Murdoch's Fox TV network. The result was a show that made gentle-but-pointed fun of capitalist cynicism and cultural vacuity in a weekly primetime slot.

The genius of *The Simpsons* lies in the tension between its limited frame and its almost infinite range of reference. Every episode is set in Springfield, features the Simpson family and a handful of other regular characters and is preceded by the same antic credit sequence in which the family rushes home from work or school to the couch in front of the television. But even within this tight frame, almost anything can happen. The credit sequence is subtly different in each of the show's more than 700 episodes to date. Lisa always plays a different riff on her saxophone; the exact manner of the family's arrival on the couch is always a surprise. The show's writers incorporate a vast range of cultural allusions: Bill Gates, Werner Herzog, Elizabeth Taylor, Tito Puente, Sonic Youth, Britney Spears, Thomas Pynchon, etc. Into this ceaseless churn are fed the issues of the day, from the birth of the internet to political corruption and from environmental pollution to Pop Art. In spite of its taste for the miscellaneous, the show has become iconic in the true sense reserved for only a handful of genuinely global cultural figures: Mickey Mouse, Charlie Chaplin, the Beatles, Bart, Lisa, Homer and Marge.

The Simpsons also encapsulates one of the central tensions within postmodern culture – that between irony and sincerity, or between Bart's all-knowing cynicism and Lisa's will to believe. Bart Simpson is many things – a 10-year-old American boy, a Krusty the Clown fan, a regular in Mrs Krabappel's after-school detention period. But he is also the living embodiment of the Dionysian urge in postmodern culture. Bart has no fixed values beyond a certain will to playfulness and enjoyment. He is a master of all social and cultural codes. He is charming and amoral. He lives in a perpetual present, cut loose from the burdens of history and responsibility. Lisa, by contrast, is a sincere realist, who knows her place within American history, reveres its civic republican values and has a powerful thirst for self-improvement and education. There is not a cynical bone in her squishy yellow body.

The tension between irony and sincerity ran like a fraying thread through much of 1990s popular culture. No doubt Springfield has its seamier side, and perhaps Otto, the school bus driver, would know where to score some dope, but the connection between *The Simpsons* and *Trainspotting*, Danny Boyle's 1996 indie blockbuster about heroin addiction in 1980s Edinburgh, might not be immediately apparent to most viewers. And yet, the famous 'Choose life' speech that opens and closes Boyle's film is as thrilling an example of the high-ironic style as you're likely to find. 'Choose life ... choose a job ... choose a career ... choose a family ... choose a big fucking television ... choose washing machines, cars, compact disc players and electrical tin openers ...' intones Mark Renton as he and his mates are chased by the fuzz after a shoplifting spree on Princes Street. But this paean to consumer culture is sharply undercut by the accompanying images of petty theft and Renton jabbing a needle into his vein in a warmly lit smack den. The gap between expectation and outcome, maxim and action, is writ large right from scene one.

Renton and his pals can easily see through the empty rhetoric of consumer society. Buying a big fucking television won't make them happy, but heroin will, at least for a while. Their refuge from consumerist anomie is not the kind of knowing irony that Danny Boyle conveys with the staging of the opening scene, but instead something that most viewers will never experience for themselves: the warm embrace of heroin. This is the ultimate form of sincerity. 'Who needs reasons when you've got heroin,' muses Renton at the climax of the opening scene. Trainspotting was one of several works in the 1990s to make a connection between addiction and consumer culture, including Darren Aronofsky's film *Requiem for a Dream*, Elizabeth Wurtzel's memoir *Prozac Nation*, Helen Fielding's *Bridget Jones's Diary*, even Nick Hornby's novel about obsessive record collectors, *High Fidelity*. These works all make the case that addiction, whether it be to prescription drugs, heroin or daytime soap operas, is one of the few things that unites the otherwise atomised members of consumer society.

Irvine Welsh's 1993 novel, the source material for Boyle's film, was a product of an underground literary sensibility inspired by William Burroughs and the Beats, Jean Genet's existential tales of the criminal underworld and Richard Allen's skinhead novels of the 1970s. Delivered in unadorned Scots dialect, *Trainspotting* was a disruptive force in the otherwise sedate literary world. But even the unreconstructed hard nuts in Welsh's novel are prone to nostalgia for the good old days. Sick Boy bemoans the deadening effects of watching football on television compared to the authentic experience of freezing your balls off in the stands with a skinful of lager in your belly: 'It's like shagging wi a durex oan. Safe fuckin sex, safe fucking fitba, safe fuckin everything.' In both its book and movie versions, *Trainspotting* echoed much of the retro culture of the 1990s – post-*Goodfellas* gangster films, the fashion for 1970s sportswear, Britpop, Gen X, 'French Touch' disco-influenced house music – in looking wistfully back to a prior era of popular culture before gentrification and mainstream co-optation. More often than not, retro culture was nostalgic not for an imagined golden age before consumerist alienation, but for earlier eras in which the responses to alienation were more intense and full-blooded – the spittle-flecked days of punk, the pre-AIDS disco era, the unreconstructed machismo of the golden age of gangsterism, or, in the case of Sick Boy, the Sean Connery-era James Bond, with his Savile Row glamour and nakedly predatory desire.

↖↑↗

The past can be a burden, but it can also be a resource. In some of its best moments, 1990s popular culture delved into the vast archives of twentieth-century mass media unburdened by any sense of belatedness and managed to craft something new from what it found. In the late 1980s and early 1990s cheap electronic samplers helped to spawn the golden age of hip hop. In the 1970s, in the very earliest days of the genre, DJs would cross fade between two copies of the same record to extend a single beat for five, ten, even twenty minutes at a time as the backdrop for a rapper to showcase his skills. But with the democratisation of sampling technology, artists like Public Enemy, N.W.A., De La Soul and A Tribe Called Quest could weave together dozens of snippets of sampled sound into their own sonic tapestries. Sampling converted the discarded culture of the recent past into a treasure trove of raw material that could be collaged, remixed, cut and pasted into new forms; the defunct sounds of the past were relaunched into a second, artificial life in the electronic and digital media of the present. For artists like Public Enemy, who famously sampled Malcolm X's 'Fire and Fury' speech on 'Bring The Noise' ('too Black, too strong'), sampling was a kind of hands-on cultural politics, which passed on the radical Black tradition to a new generation in a new form.

One of the most sampled records in history is The Winstons' 1969 track, 'Amen, Brother', a six-second snippet of which was used on records by hip hop artists like Afrika Bambaataa, N.W.A. and 2 Live Crew in the late 1980s and then became the foundation for an entire new musical genre in the 1990s, drum and bass. But The Winstons received no royalties from the prolific career that their record enjoyed after its first release. Sampling blurred the line between love and theft. Hip hop artists saw sampling as an act of homage and a creative re-animation of forgotten fragments. Lawyers and record companies increasingly saw it as copyright infringement. In 1989 The Turtles, a long-forgotten 1960s soul band, brought a lawsuit against De La Soul for illegally sampling their 1969 track 'You Showed Me' on the album *3 Feet High and Rising*. The parties settled out of court for $1.7 million, but the case was the first of several brought against high-profile hip hop acts and ushered the free-for-all era of cultural plunder to a close. When the Beastie Boys recorded *Paul's Boutique* in the same year, an album built entirely from samples taken from 105 different records, their record company paid $250,000 in licensing fees to artists ranging from the Eagles and Curtis Mayfield to Funk Factory and Alphonse Mouzon.

Today, sampling is a ubiquitous part of popular culture. Vast amounts of cultural material have been digitised, converted into zeros and ones that can be streamed on a laptop and chopped into whatever form we choose. Social media and cheap editing software have turned all users into potential producers. Memes, GIFs, fanfiction, user-generated content, links and threads, tweets, likes and shares: the culture of sampling and remixing has only accelerated with the growth of the internet. In the age of what the media critic Henry Jenkins calls 'convergence culture', or the incorporation of film, television and the written word within the universal medium of the internet, large corporations actively encourage fans to remix their intellectual property in order to encourage franchise loyalty and consumer engagement. When cut and paste is everywhere, it loses some of its radical edge.

But before the arrival of broadband and video streaming in the early 2000s, sampling culture was still rooted in analogue archives, still had the capacity to surprise and alarm. When Wu-Tang Clan turned up at the Hit Factory to record their first album in 1993, RZA brought with him a collection of his favourite Hong Kong martial arts movies on VHS. From these four tapes, plus a cache of old soul records, Wu-Tang Clan built one of the all-time great hip hop records, a fully realised alternative world composed from snippets of movie dialogue, soul riffs, crunchy breakbeats, little interludes of verité-style street talk, New York mafia lore and legend, blasts of kung fu mysticism and esoteric mutterings. Wu-Tang Clan went far out to get real; or, as RZA put it, 'The only thing I rely on is the truth, so therefore I rely on nothing.' Their genius lay in their ability to create rhythm and flow out of the fragmentation and disorder of life in the projects on Staten Island in the post-Civil Rights era. Wu-Tang Clan and the host of other producers, such as DJ Shadow, Massive Attack, Tricky and Portishead, who mixed sonic collage and breakbeat atmospherics, weren't necessarily trying to resolve the impasses of postmodernism, but with their dedication to building new worlds from recycled materials they injected a certain vitality and meaning into a culture that all too often wore its cynicism as a badge of honour.

Perhaps the most successful cut-and-paste artist of the 1990s was Quentin Tarantino, who didn't use a sampler and turntables, but instead built an entire cinematic universe out of allusions to the cult movies he watched while working as a video-store clerk in the 1980s. *Reservoir Dogs*, *True Romance* (directed by Tony Scott from a Tarantino script) and *Pulp Fiction* were indie blockbusters that launched a fleet of imitators, most of which deployed the master's signature style of hip dialogue and stylised ultra-violence to significantly less charming effect (see, for example, Guy Ritchie's entire, lamentable oeuvre). *Pulp Fiction* was the first independent movie to gross more than $200 million at the box office, a monster success that consolidated Harvey Weinstein's status as the new Hollywood powerbroker who presided over the fertile mid-budget territory between the indie underground and the blockbuster spectacle that was home to prestige fare such Jane Campion's *The Piano* and Anthony Minghella's *The English Patient*.

Tarantino's early films were idealised versions of the cult genre movies of the past, whole-cloth cinematic universes built from fragments of gangster flicks, classic noir, Blaxploitation, Hong Kong martial arts, Hollywood New Wave and French New Wave. The scripts shimmered with self-awareness. The characters talked like they were in a movie. The apotheosis of the style was the famous scene in *Pulp Fiction* where Vincent Vega and Mia Wallace danced in a lavishly appointed movie-themed diner, a scene that recalls both Travolta's performance in *Saturday Night Fever* and the famous dance scene in Jean-Luc

Godard's *Bande à part*. Here was a movie scene set on a simulated movie set in which the two principal characters, both of whom were, for complicated reasons within the plot, performing fake versions of themselves for the other's assumed benefit, danced in a manner that alluded to some of the most famous dance scenes of movie history. The layers of ironic self-awareness were multiple and the potential for the scene to go down like a pompous lead balloon was clear; and yet, the effect that Tarantino was aiming for was one of grace and flow. Like Wu-Tang Clan, DJ Shadow, Daft Punk and all the other cut-and-paste artists of the 1990s, when the trick went well it could be sublime. It created the sense of dancing in the strange, timeless space of media itself, an eternal now of light and colour and form somewhere beyond the reach of history.

And yet, in his early work, before the sterile, mannered excesses of *Kill Bill* and *Inglourious Basterds*, Tarantino still had one foot planted in the real world of workaday Los Angeles, a landscape of movie theatres and strip malls and highways and suburban tract homes that existed beyond more storied neighbourhoods like Beverly Hills. When Vince and Mia's blind date takes a turn for the worse after Mia mistakenly snorts a line from Vince's heroin stash, he whisks her to the home of one of his dealers to receive an adrenaline shot. After the giddy artificiality of the diner, Lance's home is thoroughly mundane: a modest bungalow cluttered with cheap furniture. It could be the setting for a Robert Altman movie or some low budget indie drama. Tarantino's love of self-referential world building grew out of his life in just such a lower middle-class suburban neighbourhood. The giddy streams of cult movie allusions and the heightened sense of artificiality grow out of a fan's desire to cross over into the frame, to enter the world of the movie itself.

↖↑↗

For David Foster Wallace irony was more than a rhetorical trope or an awkward situation; instead, irony was the central theme of the late twentieth century, the expression of a deep-seated existential malaise at the heart of everyday life. What began as a cultural defence mechanism, a way of shielding the soul from the corrosive effects of junk culture and political cynicism, had hardened over time into a self-defeating armature that locked the individual into his or her own fear of being conned, rather than filtering out the world's corruption. 'We are shown how to fashion masks of ennui and jaded irony at a young age where the face is fictile enough to assume the shape of whatever it wears', he wrote in *Infinite Jest*, his cult 1996 novel, which performed the rare and impressive feat of being both 1,079 pages long with 388 endnotes and becoming an international bestseller. In the late 1990s and early 2000s, Wallace became an intellectual icon whose work was rapturously reviewed in the press and pored over at academic conferences, and which garnered a dedicated fan following online.

Especially among his most dedicated admirers, Wallace was revered for both his intellect and morality, a rare combination in the postmodern literary world where smartness is often associated with the cynical debunking of society's values and institutions. Wallace grew up in the American mid-west and was the child of academics, his father a philosophy professor and his mother a lecturer in English literature. At the dinner table his dad would read passages from *Moby Dick* while his mum quizzed the children on recondite grammar rules. In his mid-twenties, he suffered a nervous breakdown and dropped out of the Philosophy PhD programme at Harvard. As in the cases of Allen Ginsberg and Sylvia Plath, a stretch in the asylum added lustre to the myth of literary genius. The casually mythic persona was further embellished by his habitually scruffy appearance and trademark bandana (which he required both to mop up nervous sweat and 'because I'm kinda afraid my head's gonna explode', as he put it.) Wallace's novels and essays weave together a vast range of references in dizzying feats of intellectual pyrotechnics: Wittgenstein, mathematical set theory, polymer chemistry, the postmodern fiction of John Barth, Donald Barthelme and Thomas Pynchon, Hedy Lamarr movies, daytime soap operas, hip hop, 1970s soft rock. He was the pure product of intellectual hothousing in the Ivy League and large amounts of time spent goofing off in front of the TV. Or as Zadie Smith once put it: 'He's so modern he's in a different space-time continuum from the rest of us.'

Infinite Jest is set in the Boston metropolitan area in a semi-dystopian near future, shortly after the US, Mexico and Canada have joined together to form ONAN, or the Organization of North American Nations. Their president, Johnny Gentle, is a vapid third-party candidate, a former B-movie actor and lounge singer who is part Ralph Nader, part Bing Crosby. One of his chief concerns is how to deal with 'The Great Concavity' (or 'The Great Convexity' in Canadian parlance), a vast toxic dump in the north-eastern US that has spawned various mutant species of woodland fauna and where time itself seems to have decelerated due to the unforeseen side effects of an experimental nuclear fusion process. In the non-toxic regions of ONAN, life has been transformed by super-advanced digital media – or, as Wallace puts it,

'InterLace TelEntertainment, 932/1664 R.I.S.C. power-TPs w/ or w/out console, Pink2, post-Primestar D.S.S. dissemination, menus and icons, pixel-free InterNet Fax' – which furnishes users with an unimaginable range of audio-visual entertainment and the ability to work exclusively from home and thus avoid all social contact.

Wallace offers a gonzo version of the popular internet futurology that was so common in the 1990s. But while most internet boosters envisioned the technological enhancements that would arrive in the near future, Wallace was more concerned with the spiritually corrosive effects of a world of total entertainment – domestic self-confinement, near universal narcissism, and the further encroachment of commerce into the very fabric of what we once quaintly termed 'reality'. This is a future world in which even the neutral and supposedly objective nature of time itself has been colonised by corporate sponsorship. The plot takes place not in the near future of, say, 2009 or 2022 but in *The Year of the Depend Adult Undergarment* and *The Year of the Trial-Size Dove Bar*. The corporate calendar isn't just funny, it's also sad and poignant. The calendar is sponsored not by glamorous big-ticket items such as high-performance automobiles or expensive watches but by cheap sanitary products designed to mask the vulnerabilities of the human body, the stinks and seepages that bring us all down to earth. Like Swift and Voltaire before him, Wallace's satire had a large dose of sadness in it, a melancholy awareness of humankind's mortal nature mixed in with the righteous gusts of laughter.

Wallace's surrogate in *Infinite Jest* is Hal Incandenza, a cripplingly self-aware teenaged tennis prodigy and son of James Incandenza, a one-time optics postdoctoral researcher turned avant-garde filmmaker who accidentally invents the ultimate form of home entertainment. 'The Entertainment', as it is known to all, is a video experience so intensely pleasurable, so profoundly immersive, so imaginatively transporting, that its viewers lose all desire to engage in any activity other than watching The Entertainment; they become transfixed by its ecstasy-inducing dance of colour and light, and eventually die from exhaustion and malnourishment. Riven with regret, James kills himself by rigging a special device that enables him to insert his head into a microwave oven and turn on the heat; his individual suicide serves as a metaphor for the cultural suicide of an American nation addicted to shallow entertainment and TV dinners.

As in *The Simpsons*, *Trainspotting*, *Pulp Fiction* and much else besides, *Infinite Jest* is pitched in the ambivalent zone between irony and sincerity. The science fiction trappings and the extended comic riffs on the absurdity of life in a high-tech, postmodern consumer society are offset by a heartfelt, even sentimental recognition of the basic human need for connection and spiritual succour. In spite of his everyday mask of knowing irony, Hal:

> privately theorizes that what passes for hip cynical transcendence of sentiment is really some kind of fear of being really human, since to be really human (at least as he conceptualizes it) is probably to be unavoidably sentimental and naïve and goo-prone and generally pathetic.

Hal is a believer who hides behind the mask of an ironist. And yet, even in this depiction of Hal's sincerity, Wallace is playing a double game. Hal's innermost thoughts are framed by the authorial voice with a heavy layer of ... yes, you guessed it ... self-aware irony. Hal's reflections on human nature are expressed in the argot of a TV-addicted teenager, rather than the stately prose of a moral philosophical treatise. His theory of moral sentiments is sincere and ironic at the same time.

The battle between sincerity and irony, universals and particulars, high-flown philosophical statements and pop cultural glossolalia was at the heart of Wallace's project in *Infinite Jest*. His aim was to produce a work that was absolutely steeped in the cultural conditions that generated the hip ironical mask and also somehow managed to overcome those conditions to generate authentic feeling. This torch was taken up by a loose group of young literary authors at the turn of the millennium, including Zadie Smith, who broke through in 2000 with *White Teeth*, and Dave Eggers, whose memoir *A Heartbreaking Work of Staggering Genius* became a bestseller in the same year. On the back on his newfound fame, Eggers founded *The Believer* in 2003, a literary magazine devoted to what would come to be known as the 'New Sincerity' in culture and the arts. These writers had all come of age in the post-modern era. They were well versed in critical theory, could deconstruct the systems of power and oppression that went hand in hand with the march of civilisation, were as immersed in hip hop and gangster movies as they were in the works of Dostoevsky and De Beauvoir. And yet they still had a hunger for moral seriousness and an abiding attachment to the liberal humanist ideals of prior literary ages.

In the 1990s, it was becoming increasingly difficult to tell the difference between a book and any other mid-price consumer durable. Book publishing was dominated by a handful of giant conglomerates – Random House, Penguin, HarperCollins, Simon and Schuster – that had grown to bloated size via a series of mergers and acquisitions in the 1980s and 1990s. The introduction of digital computers streamlined inventory and distribution, with companies now able to monitor consumer preferences in minute detail. Marketing departments at publishing houses grew in size and power. Large chain bookstores started to resemble high-end gift shops where one could purchase stationery, calendars, stuffed toys and small pieces of furniture, as well as browsing the latest prize-winning literary fiction. In 1995, the first book was sold at Amazon.com, which was based out of Seattle, Washington, but could be accessed from anywhere in the world, so long as you had a computer and a modem. In a 1997 letter to shareholders, Jeff Bezos stated that his aim was to unlock the potential of the internet as a platform for book sales and for Amazon to become an 'enduring franchise'. Little did the shareholders know that within twenty years their boss would be announcing his ambitions to colonise space. Who said books don't have an impact on the real world?

The mood of many literary types in the mid-1990s was one of low-key resignation to an increasingly marginal status within the great churn of electronic and digital culture. Media gurus had been predicting the decline of reading in the electronic age since the 1960s, but the launch of the internet triggered a heightened sense that the days of serious novelists rubbing shoulders with film stars and politicians on TV chat shows – and, more importantly, being respected voices in the public sphere – were coming to an end. The American critic Sven Birkerts voiced the mournful mood with his 1995 book *The Gutenberg Elegies*, in which he made what would become an increasingly familiar and oft-repeated plea for the continued importance of reading highbrow literature in a post-literate age.

One of the few boom areas of the literary world in the 1990s was the increase in popularity of reading groups, spurred in large part by the launch of Oprah's Book Club in 1995. Oprah performed a noble service in exposing her very large audience to canonical works of literature – Morrison, Faulkner, Dickens, Tolstoy, etc. – but the format of the book club tended to encourage empathetic responses to these works, rather than informed literary judgement and analysis. Literature was 'relatable' insofar as it was absorbed into the confessional culture of the TV talk show. Famously, Jonathan Franzen, the highbrow literary novelist and mentor to Wallace, was dumped by Oprah after he expressed his ambivalence that his 2001 novel, *The Corrections*, had been selected for the book club. Many of Oprah's choices might in fact have been 'schmaltzy' and 'one-dimensional', as Franzen claimed, but the Ivy League-educated white male novelist did not enjoy the best PR optics as the spat played out in the media. As literary contretemps go, it was a far cry from catty barbs hurled by Dorothy Parker and Truman Capote at the cocktail parties of yore.

Infinite Jest was never likely to be selected for Oprah's Book Club. Journalists referred to the book's length and difficulty so frequently that it became one of Wallace's many bugbears. His book wasn't simply *Infinite Jest*; instead, it was the *thousand-pages-long-with-hundreds-of-footnotes-Infinite-Jest*. But references to the book's gargantuan size (it sat unread upon many a bookshelf alongside that other rarely finished work of the 1990s, Stephen Hawking's *A Brief History of Time*) weren't just expressions of a dumbed-down, know-nothing culture, but also registered a genuine insight into the book's ambition. *Infinite Jest* was a self-consciously big book. It was an ambitious young man's attempt to create a new form that could somehow encapsulate the sublime complexity of life in the super-saturated high-tech media environment at the end of the second millennium CE in the world's wealthiest, most powerful and, in many ways, especially in view of its commitment to individual liberty and hedonistic self-satisfaction to the exclusion of almost all other social and moral commitments, strangest societies in the history of the world.

The vast scale of the thing was the whole point. *Infinite Jest* was designed to outstrip the reader's capacity to absorb its narrative in a comfortable fashion, as they would most other works of literary fiction published at the time. The narrative was slow. The characters were non-naturalistic, hyper-self-conscious and engaged in various kinds of extreme and self-defeating behaviour. The flow of the story was constantly interrupted by endnotes, some of which were twenty pages long and contained their own endnotes. The notes related information of dubious relevance to the central plot – annotated bibliographies of James Incandenza's little-known experimental films, say, or detailed explications of the transfinite mathematics that underpin the game of tennis. When his editor asked Wallace to trim the notes, he shot back a lengthy missive explaining the importance of the notes to the work as a whole. His aim was to 'mimic the information-flood and data-triage I expect'd be an even bigger part of US life 15 years hence'.

The question for Wallace was how to live well – and how to write great works of soul-redeeming literature – under such conditions. The most viable answer that he can muster in the information dense pages of *Infinite Jest* is: play. Play not in the sense of casual amusement and idle distraction, but serious, committed, self-transcending play, play that achieves a state of ecstatic flow wherein the petty concerns of the ego melt away into a pure consciousness of the game as an end in itself. In *Infinite Jest*, the semi-monastic commitment to play takes place in two institutions that, while occupying radically different ends of the social spectrum, are mirror images of one another. These are the elite Enfield Tennis Academy, where Hal Incandenza and his friends train in the hopes of making good on the astronomically small odds that they will make it as tennis pros; the other is Ennet House, a halfway house and addiction rehabilitation centre, where Don Gately and various other desperate characters undergo the hard spiritual labour of weening themselves from their addictions and carving out a viable way of life in a cruel and uncaring society. On the one hand, privilege, wealth and a commitment to sporting and intellectual excellence; on the other, deprivation, damage and the search for redemption. But in both cases the inmates of the asylum are in search of a state of grace, a freedom from the burdens of the ego, a self-transcending state of play. The problem is telling the difference between real and fake ecstasy, the good clean self-transcendence of the perfect volley or a great day's writing – Wallace would often write in day-long bouts of inspiration when he 'couldn't feel my ass in the chair' – as opposed to the self-annihilation of drink and drugs and television and cynical irony and base calculation that enclose the ego in a false sense of sufficiency.

Infinite Jest is one of several 1990s works that are set in self-enclosed worlds in which a small group of like-minded adepts dedicate themselves to rarefied forms of play. In *Fight Club*, Brad Pitt and Edward Norton retreat into a secretive netherworld of basement clubs and disused warehouses in order to purify their souls through the ancient sport of bare-knuckle boxing. In *Generation X*, Andy, Claire and Dag retreat to the desert to cleanse their souls via the ancient art of storytelling. In *The Matrix*, Neo and the gang retreat to the pure white space of the construct where they prepare for the coming revolution, a process that looks suspiciously like playing videogames.

Even *Friends*, one of the most successful sitcoms of the era, is set in the bland vanilla worlds of the apartments and the coffee shop where Phoebe, Chandler, Ross, Monica, Rachel and Joey dedicate themselves to the serious business of being friends and having a good time. *Friends* existed at the outer fringes of the Gen X slacker-verse. The characters were quirky, beatific, unhampered by restrictive gender roles (no one cared that the girls were just as sexually promiscuous as the boys) and generally relaxed about wealth and careers. Their principal assets were their quirky personae. Their upbeat eccentricity worked like a magical charm that made life a blast, whether you were an out-of-work actor or a corporate analyst, a masseuse or a palaeontologist. What the show shared with spikier works like *Fight Club* and *The Matrix* was the belief that the cynicism and irony of life at the end of the twentieth century could be redeemed by a serious commitment to having a good time with friends.

↖↑↗

Even the briefest of forays into the online world of David Foster Wallace fandom is enough to confirm that the author's status as a post-postmodern sage has only increased since his suicide in 2008. There are discussion boards devoted to unpacking the arcane references threaded throughout his oeuvre. Fansites collect personal recollections of the great author and testimonies of his impact on people's lives, such as 'Why Lawyers Love DFW' and 'We Must Feel the Sadness in Our Lives – Long-Time Howling Fantods Reader Allison Bonnell Remembers'. There is a growing body of *Infinite Jest* fanfiction, in which enthusiastic imitators struggle to re-create the heavily endnoted fractal extravaganza of Wallace's style. There are also numerous denunciations of Wallace's abusive relationships with women, particularly his harassment of Mary Carr, a fellow writer whom Wallace stalked for several years. There is plenty of outrage at the fact that he sometimes had one-night stands with the star-struck young women who showed up at his readings after *Infinite Jest* hit the big time. *Infinite Jest* is now the fodder for ironic memes about the reading habits of bad Gen X dates.

For the true Wallace fan, however, it would seem that analysing quotes on a website cannot adequately convey the profundity of their attachment to the words of the master. For those to whom Wallace really spoke, those for whom his meta-ironical, hyper-self-aware paeans to human truth and goodness genuinely cut to the quick, the only really appropriate medium in which to display one's devotion is that of the tattoo. The everlasting wound of his words upon the flesh is all that will do. Judging by the numerous Instagram feeds and curated online collections of Wallace-themed tattoos, the most popular is the simple statement, 'This is water', which was the title of the commencement address he delivered to the graduating class at Kenyon College in 2005. In classic Wallace style, the speech was a highly self-aware deconstruction of the conventions of the college commencement address – a short, uplifting oration to a highly educated audience in the confines of an elite academic institution usually delivered by a politician, business leader or cultural figure – which nevertheless managed to rehabilitate the simple moral message expected of such a performance. Or as Wallace put it, 'banal platitudes have a life-or-death importance'.

It seems only fitting that Wallace's star should continue to rise after his suicide, even if he is mocked by Millennials as the worst kind of Gen X bore. His techno-prognostications were sometimes comically misconceived – we do not, in fact, live in a world of Interlace Cartridges and 'pixel-free InterNet Fax' – but his analysis of the spiritual conditions of life in the digital age were prescient. The crippling self-awareness, the irony edging into cynicism, the egocentrism and culture industry enabled narcissism, the anxious hunger for connection that is channelled into all manner of dubious and sterile forms: these were all signs of things to come that Wallace wove into the near future world of *Infinite Jest*.

As it turns out, the irony-sincerity agon didn't simply disappear with the end of the 1990s. Instead, it went nuclear, spreading like a particularly virulent case of Japanese knotweed through the online world. On the one hand, the newly turbulent political climate of the early twenty-first century, a world shaken into new forms by 9/11, the 2008 financial crash, the climate crisis, Occupy Wall Street, #MeToo, Black Lives Matter, Brexit, Trump and all the rest of it, has injected a renewed sense of earnestness into politics and culture. Looking back from the 2020s, the heedless hedonism of the 1990s can seem rather brittle and self-absorbed, its ironic postures somewhat 'problematic' in the language of today's critical discourse. New strains of cultural politics insist not only on equality of representation but also authenticity of representation. Identity is no longer a postmodern game, a performance, a ruse, an epiphenomenon, but an essence, a non-fungible possession, something to fight for.

On the other hand, ironic distance and self-awareness are hard baked into digital culture. The 1990s might be seen as an inflection point after which cynical irony would no longer be the preserve of the progressive left. The cultural critic Angela Nagle has pointed out how the alt-right and neo-reaction movements that came to prominence in the 2010s adopted the hip ironic style for their own purposes. Alt-right provocateurs struck Nietzschean poses and declared the relativity of all values at the same that they rehabilitated offensive stereotypes and political authoritarianism. In the very online worlds of social media, every word and gesture seem to reverberate with multiple dimensions of irony. Every statement is curated, every post targeted; every utterance is in search of likes, every viral video the possible occasion for a book deal. With the further expansion of the technological means of human expression, the possibility of sincere utterance, of 'single-entendre principles', as Wallace put it, seems further away – and perhaps more necessary – than ever.

13

Irrational Exuberance

THE CULTURAL symbols of 1980s capitalism are pretty well fixed in the popular imagination: pinstripe suits worn with red braces, Filofaxes and brick-like mobile phones, the pulsing electro pop of Frankie Goes to Hollywood's 'Relax' and Gordon Gekko's mantra of 'greed is good'. As yet, no such iconography exists for the long economic boom of the 1990s, which began around 1992–93 after a recession in the early years of the decade and roared away until the dot-com crash of 2000. But if you were looking for a symbol of the boom years, you'd be hard pressed to find a better one than the Hummer SUV.

The High Mobility Multipurpose Wheeled Vehicle – or the 'Humvee' as it was dubbed by US military personnel – was a beefed-up version of the classic Jeep that had been the mainstay of US military logistics in the Second World War, Korea and Vietnam. The Humvee was essentially a Jeep on steroids – bigger, heavier, more angular, more forbidding. It was first deployed in 1989 during Operation Just Cause against Panama's drug-smuggling military strongman, Manuel Noriega, and then used extensively in the First Gulf War. The Humvee was the rugged, ground-based accompaniment to the high-tech airpower of the F-117 stealth bomber and laser-guided missile systems that projected American force around the world in the post-Cold War era.

The public campaign to persuade the manufacturer AM General to produce a civilian model of the Humvee was led by that renowned tribune of the people Arnold Schwarzenegger. In the late 1980s, when he took up the cause of the Humvee, Arnie was still a muscle-bound action hero and Austro-American symbol of power and violence, who was yet to adopt the softer, free-market environmentalist stance that helped him to become the Republican Governor of California in 2003. When the first civilian Humvees rolled off the production line in 1992, vehicles number one and two were delivered straight to Arnie's home in acknowledgement of his campaign.

The Hummer hit the streets of America just as the internet was going public and the new digital economy was sparking into life. Like the internet, the Hummer was a piece of military technology repurposed for civilian use. It was also giant, ostentatious, possessed of a strength entirely in excess of the tasks for which it was actually used, and looked like something out of a science fiction film – an interplanetary assault vehicle designed to withstand Xenomorph attack. Throughout the 1990s, Hummer sales grew as Americans' stock portfolios and mutual fund investments climbed to previously unimaginable heights on the frothy surge of the financial markets. The Hummer was the inverse expression of the new weightless economy that fuelled the boom: a literal ton of precision-engineered steel in exchange for a metaphorical ton of abstract symbols dancing through the flickering relays of the digital economy.

The Hummer was also a Neocon's wet dream. The fact that it got a mere 10 miles to the gallon only made it more appealing to a certain kind of American consumer. Fuel economy was for liberal arts professors. The Humvee was a flame-grilled whopper of a gas guzzler, which came with a built-in aura of confrontation and anti-PC braggadocio. In the 1996 film *The Rock*, Sean Connery pilots a stolen Hummer through downtown San Francisco in a frenetic, white-knuckle bid to escape from Nicholas Cage's FBI agent, who gives pursuit in a yellow Ferrari. The sight of a Humvee smashing through historic Haight-Ashbury, spiritual home of 1960s counterculture and epicentre of the 1990s digital revolution, was a cultural symbol with all of the nuance and subtlety one might expect of a Michael Bay movie. Although, it should be noted that, at an average speed of 70mph, Connery's rogue former Special Forces agent with a grudge against the US government would only be able to keep going for a couple of hours before having to stop to refuel.

Both the rise and fall of the mighty Hummer were symbolic of the 1990s boom times. In 1998, just as the tech stock bubble was nearing its peak, General Motors acquired the Hummer brand and released the H2 and H3, smaller, less aggressively angular, but still impractically giant and gas-thirsty vehicles, to go with the military-styled H1. Sales were strong and this now iconic machine became a regular sight on America's highways. But after the financial crash of 2008, during which GM had to be bailed out to the tune of $51 billion by the US government, the Hummer became a symbol of the American auto industry's decadence. As America and the world entered a new period of economic austerity and environmental anxiety, production of the Hummer was shelved and dealerships closed down. If you want to buy a Humvee today, you'll have to look to the second-hand market, where they are bought and sold like memorabilia from a long-lost historical era.

↖↑↗

In the 1990s, even serious economists were prepared to entertain the possibility that high-tech modern capitalism was on the verge of breaking free from the laws of economic gravity that had been in operation for centuries. Buoyed by the highest rates of growth in decades and swept up in the techno-futurist excitement of the digital revolution, pundits began to talk of a 'New Economy' that would generate prosperity and peace in the long term, rather than just over the course of the next cycle of boom and bust. In 1997, *Wired* magazine, a publication not famed for its immunity to hype, ran a series of articles predicting a 'long boom' over the next two decades that would be driven by digital networking and massive productivity gains. 'We're facing twenty-five years of prosperity, freedom, and a better environment for the whole world. You got a problem with that?', boomed its headline writers. But even technocrats like Alan Greenspan, chair of the US Federal Reserve, gave serious consideration to the notion that the American economy was undergoing a tectonic shift for the better. Pointing to a prolonged cycle of high growth and cheap credit without the expected rise in inflation, Greenspan mused in a speech to economists at the University of California, Berkeley, whether 'there has been a profound and fundamental alteration in the way our economy works'. Even the sober technocrats were a little giddy during the boom times.

The theory of the New Economy was based on a series of premises that cast the 1990s as a moment of rupture with prior economic history. The first of these premises stated that technological change would drive up productivity exponentially – a kind of Moore's Law effect for the American worker. This did not mean that the average working stiff would suddenly become a Stakhanovite superman, urging his body or mind to new feats of productivity out of sheer devotion to the free-market system, but rather that new technologies would make his current levels of effort equate to ever higher degrees of economic value. As new technologies were adopted in ever more rarefied niches of the economy – not just spreadsheets for office workers, but also teleconferencing and email, digitised accountancy and legal services, robotised manufacturing processes, and all manner of specialised uses for digital networking – more value per hour of human labour could be extracted.

The same kind of levelling up would be applied to the products of human labour, as well as the human labourers themselves. Digital networking would solve the long-standing problem of inventory, or the fact that non-perishable physical stock – pallets loaded with tins of tomatoes or *Star Wars* toys or toilet brushes – would often languish in warehouses or on store shelves for extended periods of time, waiting to be purchased and consumed. During this time, the capital invested in creating those products lay idle, simply treading water while the rest of the economy continued its liquid course. Digital networking would enable the real-time flow of information from stores to warehouses to production facilities and thus facilitate 'just-in-time' delivery of stock to consumers. Products would languish no more; liberated from the inertia of the supply chain, they would be released into a constant dance of exchange and consumption, their abstract financial value no longer constrained by lags in the system.

There was much talk in the press of a 'Third Industrial Revolution' that was being driven by digital networking and the new information economy. The digital computer – or more accurately the *networked* digital computer, since stand-alone computers had been in operation for decades – would be to the twenty-first century what the steam engine had been to the nineteenth and the Fordist production line to the twentieth, a defining technology that reshaped the structure of society as a whole.

Tech gurus also pointed to the fact that the pace of change itself seemed to be accelerating as the new millennium approached. The self-reinforcing nature of technological progress – the virtuous feedback loop wherein technological advancement and scientific know-how seemed to speed up the processes of invention and discovery itself – was another key premise in the theory of the New Economy. In the twenty-first century, humankind would not have to wait so long between technological revolutions. Rather than waiting more than a hundred years for the steam engine to be supplemented by the electric lightbulb – the kind of patience only realistically to be expected of staid Victorians, who found Charles Dickens's cliff-hangers sensational and thought they might be vaporised by travelling at 25mph by steam train – wired-up hyper-moderns could expect transformative new technologies every couple of decades. Soon the Fourth Industrial Revolution of artificial intelligence would be at hand and shortly thereafter the Fifth Industrial Revolution of nanotech would come online, the early stages of which could already be detected in the present. With this seemingly continuous surge of technological innovation, so the thinking went, the traditional business cycle would become obsolete. The regular pulse of boom and bust, or the melancholy fact that each rising wave of growth always contains the seeds of the next phase of slump, would no longer apply. The guarantee of continuous and self-reinforcing technological revolution would turn the wavy line of economic history into the smooth upward curve of the future.

↖↑↗

As one might expect, the economic high spirits of the 1990s were at their giddiest on Wall Street and in the globalised financial markets of London, Frankfurt, Tokyo and Hong Kong. Over the course of the 1980s and '90s, Wall Street enjoyed one of the longest bull markets in American financial history. Even the crash of 'Black Monday' on 10 October 1987, during which the Dow Jones Industrial Average lost a massive 22.6 per cent – still the largest single-day loss in its history, sending financial markets around the world into a nosedive – proved to be a temporary blip. Debate continues to this day as to the precise causes of Black Monday. Was it the announcement of a bigger than expected US trade deficit, or was it newly digitised insurance portfolios that exacerbated the sell-off? But what Black Monday made clear to everyone was, first, the tightly interwoven nature of the world's financial markets, as analysts watched in real time on television as the panic spread around the world, and, second, the resilience of those markets, especially in the US, as the enormous losses were quickly recouped.

In the collapse of Black Monday, the Dow plummeted from over 2,400 points to just over 1,700 in the space of twenty-four hours, but it quickly rebounded and continued its long, bullish upward cycle. In May 1991, it broke the 3,000-mark for the first time in its history. It took until February 1995 to break through the 4,000-mark, but then, like a sports car shifting through the gears, the Dow began to accelerate at a stunning pace, reaching 5,000 by February 1996, 6,000 by October 1996, 7,000 by February 1997 and then 8,000 shortly thereafter. It broke through the symbolic 10,000 mark in early 1999, well in time for the advent of the new millennium.

During the recession of the early 1990s, many American corporations 'streamlined' their operations by laying off employees and moving production capacity overseas. While this increased unemployment and dampened consumer activity, it nevertheless caused share prices to rise as companies increased their profitability. As the stock market boomed, pundits began to talk of a 'People's Market' to accompany the 'New Economy'. With the decline of final salary pension schemes and dwindling social insurance payouts, more and more American citizens were turning to mutual funds and stock portfolios as ways to save for retirement. Cable news channels such as Fox and MSNBC introduced a new style of financial journalism, which provided 'real-time' coverage of market fluctuations and hyped-up commentary based on the advice of charismatic experts. This was a new kind of market populism that cast the stock market not only as a repository of speculative investments but also as a barometer of the health and wealth of the nation.

In 1995, with the initial public share offerings of Netscape and AOL, two of America's fastest-growing internet companies, the dot-com bubble started to inflate. The rise of the Dow over the course of the 1990s was impressive, but the trajectories of tech stocks were, in the technical jargon of the industry, totally insane! In 1998, theGlobe.com, a social networking site created by a pair of Cornell University undergraduates, made the highest first-day gain in US stock market history, beginning trading at $9 per share and ending at $63, a barely comprehensible 606 per cent increase. The two college dropouts made an enormous pile of money and were feted in the financial press before their company was massacred in the NASDAQ bloodbath of 2000, when their share price fell from over $90 to a mere 10 cents.

As the bubble inflated, investors were happy to ignore the fact that companies like theGlobe.com didn't currently make a profit and gamble that they would in years to come. Of course, all stock prices are by nature speculative judgements about a company's prospects, bets on growth and profitability in future quarters. But this speculative dimension was accentuated in the case of dot-com stocks because no one could predict with any real assurance how the myriad technologies that underpinned that abstract, almost mythical entity known as 'the internet' would develop in the future, much less how those technologies would be converted into profitable businesses with secure revenue streams.

A case in point was AOL, or America Online, one of America's largest internet service providers in the mid-1990s, the moment when the general public started to log on. AOL offered customers access to a curated suite of websites for a fixed number of hours at a fixed monthly price. Its advantage was that it made the new and unfamiliar thing that was the internet seem manageable and familiar to everyday consumers. Its disadvantage was that its fixed price and limited-access models would quickly be superseded by open-ended search engines and unlimited time packages. It was also somewhat unfortunate that a disproportionate amount of its revenues were generated by customers who used the service for pornography and chat, rather than prestigious content such as the National Geographic and Smithsonian Institute websites that AOL made so much of in its promotional materials. AOL executives understood these disadvantages but were willing to make a bet that their company's size and familiarity would enable it to corner enough of the market before anyone really noticed.

AOL threw itself into a madcap race to 'get big fast', a motto that was coined a few years later by Jeff Bezos, whose plucky little start-up got bigger faster than any other company in history. AOL poured its cash resources into a campaign to sign up as many new customers as possible and recoup its costs sometime in the future when it was the dominant player in the market. In effect, AOL became a giant marketing operation with an internet company attached for good measure. At one point, shoppers received a free AOL installation disk with their supermarket-bought frozen steaks, a surefire way to win the affection of the American heartlands. What's more, these enormous expenditures on advertising were never entered on the company's annual balance sheet, but instead counted as 'deferred subscriber acquisition costs'. This was the point at which corporate Newspeak met barely legal accountancy practices, to the effect that to the inexpert investor the company's bottom line looked much healthier than it was in reality, as hundreds of millions of dollars of expenditure had simply been punted down the road. In January 2000, flush with stock market investors' cash, AOL purchased Time Warner, home to prestigious brands such as *Time* magazine and CNN, to become one the largest media conglomerates in the world. Shortly after the merger was completed in January 2001, the NASDAQ crashed, the company started to haemorrhage cash and within a few years had been broken up and cannibalised by corporate raiders. AOL got very big very fast; but then they got chopped into little pieces in the post-crash feeding frenzy.

Everything seemed to happen faster where the internet was concerned. The lifecycle of the average company accelerated in order to meet the competitive demands of the present and stake a claim on the future ahead of others. The most ambitious start-ups could go from incorporation to their first public stock offering in a mere eighteen months. While it took the corporate behemoths of the past decades to reach a market valuation of $1 billion, the hottest internet start-ups could make it in a single day's trading. This headlong dash to invest in tech stocks was driven partly by the optimistic sense that the future was being built right here, right now and partly by the anxious fear that someone else might get there first.

Many people at the time compared the dot-com explosion to the Californian gold rushes of the nineteenth and early twentieth centuries. In the 1990s, many a wide-eyed prospector liquidated their assets, moved to Silicon Valley and poured their lifesavings into the digital start-up concept that might just make them a billionaire before the age of 40. But unlike the gold rushes, there was no single and durable commodity at the centre of the boom, unless you count that highly abstract, relativistic thing, information, as a durable commodity. Vast quantities of personal savings, venture capital and investment funds coursed through the NASDAQ in search of the emergent forms of the digital economy. In the cases of Boo.com, which set out to become the biggest and hippest online fashion retailer, Webvan.com, which set out to corner the market in rapid online grocery deliveries (anything you want delivered to your door within thirty minutes), and Pets.com, which aspired to be the world's biggest online pet supplies retailer (and which had enough revenue to buy TV advertising space during the 2000 Superbowl), all of which went bust in the 2000 crash, those bets turned out to be spectacularly wrong.

It wasn't just tech companies that were operating at warp speed. Digital networking was also delivering an accelerationist jolt to the basic infrastructure of financial markets. It was in the 1960s that ticker-tape machines, descendants of the electric telegraph which received and printed out financial information, gave way to computerised stock market data on trading floors. Even after it had been posted on brightly lit screens on the floor of the bourse, this information still had to be relayed by telephone or 'runner' – literally, a junior employee who ran with the information – to investors. Beginning in the late 1980s, stock market figures were posted in real time on the internet, which cut some of the time lag out of the process and enabled investors to make trades from anywhere in the world without an intermediary. Short-term trading now became a matter of capitalisation on market fluctuations over the course of seconds and minutes, rather than hours or days. Market populists cast this as a sign of economic good health, the democratisation of investment and a source of greater transparency. But it also accentuated the volatility of financial markets, as large numbers of individual investors sought to ride the short-term dips and surges of the market. Before long, sophisticated software programs could measure market fluctuations at the level of nanoseconds and make automatic trades based on their technological advantage over other traders. A kind of computational arms race broke out between high-frequency trading companies – and the leaden-footed regulators who struggled to keep up with the new technology – to reach the fastest possible server and transmission speeds, and thus wring profit from ever more minute fluctuations in prices. The birth of 'automated high-frequency trading' in the 1990s inaugurated the age of post-human finance capital, the point at which machines began to replace the human capacities of guile and guts in making bets on the market.

Speculative energies were intensified in less glamorous, low-tech industries as well. The practice of replacing executive pay and bonuses with stock options became widespread in the 1990s. This meant that giant pay packets could be kept off the company's balance sheet, as they were not entered as outgoing costs; the effect was to make the company appear in ruder financial health than it otherwise would, which had the knock-on effect of increasing its share price, which of course was good for investors (and very good for the executives with multi-million-dollar stakes in the company), but not necessarily good for the underlying health of the company. The financialisation of CEO pay helped to create a system of perverse incentives which encouraged executives to seek short-term gains in share price, rather than looking after the long-term prospects of their companies. In retrospect, it seems fitting that the two biggest accounting frauds in American history were revealed in quick succession at the close of the 1990s – Enron in 2001 and WorldCom in 2002.

Traditionally, investors in the stock market spend large amounts of time studying the underlying strengths and weaknesses of the companies in which they plan to purchase a stake. Each bet on a stock equates to a judgement about the fundamental value of that company, or at least so says a slightly simplified version of what is known to economists as the 'rational market theory'. The theory states that, in spite of its temporary fluctuations, over the long run the stock market is an efficient mechanism for appraising the true value of things. Ultimately, the prices on the screens on the stock market floor are connected to the real conditions of the economy, which is to say actual factories and warehouses and stores and workers and consumers. Over time, good investments make money and bad ones don't; investors get rich or lose their fortunes and, in the process, the true value of things is discovered. Increasingly in the hyper-accelerated digital marketplace of the 1990s, however, share prices were decoupled from the underlying realities of revenues, profits, assets, debt, etc. Investors sought to gauge the momentum of prices, rather than assess the relationship between those prices and some kind of fundamental reality. Stock market investing become ever more like surfing, a matter of catching a rising swell, riding the surge and exiting safely before the wave crashed on the shore. Momentum investors assessed trend lines on a screen, surveyed the dance of symbols, rode the tides of zeros and ones. The problem, of course, was that many lost sight of the fact that the wave must eventually reach the shoreline and the tide must eventually turn.

A short walk from Wall Street brings you to the Bowery, which used to be one of Manhattan's toughest slum neighbourhoods and home to the infamous gangs of New York, but is now better known for its trendy coffee shops and gyms. The Bowery, or *Bouwerie*, as it was once known, is one of the oldest streets in America and a reminder of New York's original incarnation as New Amsterdam, a township founded on Lenape tribal lands by the venturesome scions of Dutch trading families in the late seventeenth century. The great stock market bubble that inflated on Wall Street in the 1990s resembled nothing so much as the speculative fervour of Tulip mania that had convulsed old

Amsterdam in 1637 when investors won and then lost thousands of guilders in the market for tulip plants, recently introduced from the Ottoman empire.

Stock market bubbles come and go, but the underlying psychology remains the same. Tulip mania, the South Sea Bubble, the railway manias of the nineteenth century, the Wall Street crash of 1929, the dot-com bust of the early 2000s: all were driven by the ancient human motor of greed and fear. What is most striking, according to the economist John Kenneth Galbraith, whose slim 1990 volume *A Short History of Financial Euphoria* analysed the economic history of financial manias, is the human capacity for forgetfulness. Galbraith pointed out a roughly twenty-year-long cycle of forgetting (around the length of a single generation), which caused investors to ignore the evidence of prior crashes and believe in their own special power to triumph over the inevitable laws of boom and bust. He referred to this process as a form of financial 'dementia', in which the investor class ceases to be able to access its collective memory banks and becomes absorbed in a deluded but rapturous awareness of the present moment. The bubble economy of the 1990s, like the bubble economies of the past, generated a similarly skewed perception of time and history. As the promise of the future loomed large, the lessons of the past shrank from view. The present became soft and delicate like the petals of a tulip. Everything was going to work out for the best this time.

↖↑↗

Beneath the dollars and cents, the pounds and pence, the euros and renminbi, beyond the stocks and shares, the bonds and securities, the credit default swaps and the collateralised debt agreements, behind the fancy logos and the men in suits, the spreadsheets and the pie charts, there is a single, intangible property that ensures the smooth running of the economy: trust. There has to be a certain amount of faith in the system for the system to work at all.

In order to bolster their faith, investors are apt to look to authority figures who seem to understand the arcane processes of the market. During the 1990s bull market, the authority in whom investors placed most faith was Alan Greenspan, chairman of the US Federal Reserve and, if you were to believe the glowing testimonies of journalists and politicians, the wizard behind the curtain of the American economy. In 1996, as the Dow began its historic surge, *Fortune* magazine, the in-house publication of the American investor class that was founded in the wake of the 1929 stock market crash, ran with the headline, 'In Greenspan We Trust', which none too subtly suggested that Greenspan's re-appointment as chairman of the Fed was of greater import than Clinton's election to a second term as president. In its review of America's top banker, *Fortune* promised that with Greenspan at the helm America would suffer 'no recession, no inflation, no voodoo'. It is a rare occurrence for a central banker to become a figure of popular mythology, but in 1990s America you could buy Alan Greenspan t-shirts and mugs. In the public imagination, Greenspan had become part eggheaded expert, part white wizard, the only man who could defeat the forces of economic voodoo.

Greenspan was also the only one of the world's central bankers ever to have played jazz clarinet alongside the bossa nova legend Stan Getz. In high school in New York in the 1930s, young Alan was a railway enthusiast who spent his evenings poring over train timetables, and a keen musician whose teacher once arranged for him to play in an impromptu ensemble alongside the young Getz. Before studying business at NYU, he spent a year at Julliard, the elite music conservatory. His head for statistics and macroeconomic theory won out in the end, but maybe the residual traces of Greenspan's musical enthusiasms – his taste for the loosely co-ordinated harmonies of jazz, a collective order that emerges from the spontaneity and flair of individual players – can be detected in his later commitment to economic laissez-faire.

Greenspan cited as his greatest intellectual influence neither Adam Smith nor Milton Friedman, the gods of classical free-market economic theory, but Ayn Rand, the Russian émigré novelist and philosopher, whose Manhattan salon he joined in the 1950s. Rand was the author of the bestselling novels *The Fountainhead* and *Atlas Shrugged*, and a proponent of the philosophy of objectivism, a form of capitalist libertarianism that abjures all forms of restraint upon individual agency. Objectivism was as much a rejection of mid-century conservatism, with its faith in family values, tradition and the authority of the state, as it was a rejection of post-war social democracy and the New Deal. At its heart, it was a philosophy of ethical individualism, which took calculating reason as the sole guide to right action. The only way to secure the rights of the individual, according to Rand, was via the purest form of free-market economics. All other systems bred dependency and unfreedom; they corroded the will. Rand's novels were pulpy celebrations of super-heroic businessmen and high-net-worth individuals who struggled against the constraints of herd morality and big government: Nietzsche in the boardroom.

It is impossible to trace Rand's influence in specific decisions Greenspan made as chairman of the Fed. His working week was occupied with discussions of interest rates and bond yields, quarterly reports from the auto-parts industry and the inter-bank lending market, rather than philosophical debates about free will and social responsibility. But operating behind these diurnal concerns was the libertarian-Randian belief that the market was a neutral domain for individual moral action; the belief that ultimate responsibility for market forces lay with individual investors and their own rational (or otherwise) choices. This thinking lay in the deep background of Greenspan's reluctance to intervene too aggressively in the market. To do so would be to undermine the agency and judgement of individuals, who deserved to be rewarded or punished for the choices they made.

In 1996, however, seeing the huge gains being made by the Dow and NASDAQ exchanges, and gauging the high-spirited mood among analysts and pundits, Greenspan sought to inject a dose of sobriety into the markets. The last thing he wanted to do was to mention the word 'bubble', which would have triggered an instant sell-off, and his laissez-faire instincts cautioned against direct intervention in the form of raised interest rates or margin requirements (the amount investors were allowed to borrow in order to buy stocks), both of which could be used to rein in speculative energies. Instead, in an after-dinner speech at the American Enterprise Institute, a right-wing think tank in Washington DC, Greenspan invited his audience to ponder the following question: 'How do we know when irrational exuberance has unduly inflated assets?'

The question was purely rhetorical, designed to nudge investors into more cautious habits, a polite suggestion that they reconsider the relationships between reality and desire, judgement and speculation, the present and the future. But as Greenspan well knew, this was a rhetorical question that would be reported in the financial pages of newspapers all over the world. The following morning, stock markets in Tokyo, Sydney, Hong Kong, Frankfurt and London all tumbled as investors interpreted Greenspan's speech as cause for gloom. But by the time markets opened in New York, several hours behind the rest of the world, the shock had diminished. The Dow and NASDAQ wobbled but rallied before the end of the day. The warning of America's head banker went unheeded and the high spirits – or the 'irrational exuberance' – continued. The wizard behind the curtain knew that the current conditions couldn't last for ever, but many of the inhabitants of Oz didn't want to listen.

↖↑↗

What does it feel like to be right at the frothy centre of a financial bubble? Most of us will never know, as our jobs and livelihoods are only distantly related to financial markets. Perhaps our pension plan or mutual fund investments enjoy a better-than-average couple of years. Or perhaps, if we are fortunate enough to own a home, we find that its market value has increased, while we were simply going about our days and nights with a roof over our heads. For most ordinary citizens, the economy is too abstract to feature much in our everyday thoughts; the stock market is simply a thing that is sometimes mentioned on the news. But for the venturesome spirits who were drawn to the high-tech industries clustered in Silicon Valley and Silicon Alley, the Manhattan outpost of the new digital economy, the bubble was palpably real, an almost visible sheen that clung to the sparkling new office spaces, the whirring server stacks and the youthful CEOs who came to work in shorts and sandals and parked their Porsches in the company lot. The bubble was why they were here. The power and wealth and faith in the future that it represented was the invisible force that stirred the frenzy of entrepreneurial activity that coursed through these hallowed zones of the American economy. Soon there were silicon outposts around the world – Silicon Glen in Scotland, Silicon Roundabout in London, Silicon Island in Japan, Silicon Peninsula in China.

Today, the term 'Silicon Valley' refers not so much to a specific place as to the values associated with a certain high-profile stratum of the tech industry – innovation, disruption, techno-solutionism, not paying taxes. It conjures images of Elon Musk launching his space rocket and Mark Zuckerberg facing Congress to explain his company's alleged role in enabling a Russian-backed electoral misinformation campaign. In reality, Silicon Valley is neither a single place nor does it have a single ideology. The place itself is comprised of a loose collection of towns, suburbs, malls and business parks that are dotted throughout the Santa Clara Valley to the south-east of San Francisco, where El Camino Real once threaded its way in the days of the first Spanish missionaries. If this is where the digital future arrived in the 1990s, then that future looked less like the cyberpunk visions of *Bladerunner* and *The Matrix*, and more like a spruced-up version of the suburban landscapes to be seen in films like *Bill and Ted's Excellent Adventure* and Kevin Smith's slacker comedy, *Mall Rats*. It is a place of low-rise mallscapes surrounded by twelve-lane highways and punctuated by high-rise 'downtown cores' whose glass and steel frames glint in the noonday sun.

The Silicon Valley tech industry was also comprised of a wide variety of companies with a range of different corporate cultures. Long-established players like Hewlett-Packard and Xerox were fairly traditional corporations with research-and-development centres in Palo Alto. Apple married Steve Jobs's anally retentive design ethos with hippy-ish ideals of employee well-being and human potential. The leviathan Microsoft blended Bill Gates and Paul Allen's original geek energy with an increasingly bureaucratic and competitive corporate culture. Then there was a host of smaller, nimbler start-ups – the e-commerce ventures, web media concepts and software companies – that raced to attract investors, develop products and work towards the holy grail of the stock market IPO. These smaller firms were often scrappy, shambolic, youthful and energetic, just as the Silicon Valley myth required them to be, but, in reality, very few of them ever floated on the stock market and even fewer became lasting businesses with multi-millionaire CEOs.

Hanging over it all was the promise of the kind of wealth and power that bordered on the magical. The industry fed itself on stories of garage start-ups that bloomed into billion-dollar companies in a matter of years; of 30-something billionaires who had dropped out of MIT with nothing more than a hot concept and some coding skills to their name. The accelerated pace of growth was driven by the new dynamics of the digital marketplace. Move fast, break things, get big quick and catch the updraft of the mysterious network effects and mathematical power laws that governed the digital economy and could transform fledgling companies into vast global concerns in record time.

The immediate goal for start-ups was the IPO bonanza but beyond that it was something like world domination. What were the biggest and most successful tech companies doing if not creating the infrastructure on which all of human life would be lived in the coming millennium? In the words of Josh Harris, whose company pseudo.com pioneered web TV in the mid-1990s, 'we are in the business of programming people's lives'. The Silicon Valley goldrush was about power as well as wealth. It wasn't just about making $100 million before your fortieth birthday (which Harris did until it was wiped out in the crash), but also about owning a stake in the future, having a hand in determining how people would communicate, work, shop, think and entertain themselves in the next phase of human history. It was about programming rather than being programmed, doing rather than being done to. During the dot-com boom there was a kind of casual Faustianism in the air. A series of deals were struck with the devil by a handful of young men in jeans and hoodies who had little experience of the world beyond their own computer screens.

For most people who worked in the tech industry, though, the great majority of software programmers, multimedia designers, engineers, lawyers, accountants and sales representatives, the pay-off was existential as much as financial. 'We work here, but we are cool,' was how the media critic Alan Liu summed up the ethos of corporate information work in his 2004 tome, *The Laws of Cool*. A certain hip cachet was attached to office work in the new information economy, especially for the software developers and coders who grappled with the building blocks of the digital world. Even if the hours were long and the work was sometimes gruelling, information workers were close to the machinery, intimate with the cool logic that operated in the background of the new reality that was being born. Even for non-coders, the sense of being in contact with the way the world worked now had a certain cachet, brought with it the sense of being at the forefront of things, at the bleeding edge.

Silicon Valley gave birth to a new style of corporate culture that mixed the Protestant work ethic with the 1960s ethos of self-realisation and personal authenticity. Tech firms were notable for their casualness and collegiality. Dress codes were relaxed so that executives and employees could come to work in the same casual apparel. The old markers of corporate hierarchy were put aside. A certain spontaneity and informality of speech was encouraged. Increasingly, office spaces were redesigned. Grayscale cubicles and corner offices were replaced with open-concept work zones, flexible and programmable space, brightly coloured walls and furniture, recreation rooms and outdoor contemplation areas. Corporate headquarters were recast as 'campuses', places for open-ended creativity and innovation, rather than the daily grind. Google's headquarters in Mountain View, California, which opened in the early 2000s, became the *beau ideal* of the new workplace, with its bright atria, gleaming frontages and cartoon-like statues dotted throughout the grounds. It was like going to work in a Pixar movie.

Down among the start-ups and the fledgling firms, workers shared in the sense of adventure and precarity that was hardwired into the industry. Everyone understood that there was a higher degree of risk involved in the tech industry, that companies could easily burn through their cash stocks without knowing where the next round of investment would come from, that bankruptcies were common, that jobs were temporary. But with the accelerated churn of companies, jobs, ideas and technologies, there came a certain sense of excitement. The precarity was part of the thrill. For the wannabe entrepreneurs and inventors who upped sticks, liquidated their assets, borrowed as much as they could from friends and family and poured their savings and labour into a fledgling internet business, work was a kind of adventure. It was a way of proving one's existential mettle and wrestling some kind of meaning from life. In this respect, Silicon Valley start-up culture shared some of the ethos of those other characteristically 1990s activities, adventure tourism, extreme sports and rave music. All were driven by the urge to experience more by travelling faster, a technologically enhanced attempt to live right on the cusp of the now. In reality, working eighty-hour weeks designing software and pitching to venture capitalists wasn't exactly like bungee jumping in New Zealand or partying in Ibiza; but the stories we tell ourselves often count for more than the actual details of what we're up to.

The irrational exuberance that Alan Greenspan sensed on Wall Street filtered down on to the dancefloors of the Manhattan and San Francisco nightclubs rented out by glitzy new tech companies. All market bubbles are driven by hype. The dot-com bubble was inflated by over-eager pundits, breathless analysts, gullible journalists, glib sales representatives and slick PR teams. At its height, internet companies poured millions of dollars into corporate entertainment in order to feed the buzz. No one seemed to be able to provide concrete evidence that these shindigs increased sales or attracted investment or even helped to retain staff, but they were part of the culture and to ask for evidence seemed churlish. Glitzy tech companies often hired out the Fillmore in downtown San Francisco, the legendary music venue that played host to 1960s luminaries such as Hendrix, the Doors and Jefferson Airplane. Software engineers and venture capitalists danced to Euro trance and discussed stock options where the flower children had once wigged out to psychedelic rock. But the question remained – were the dancers at the Fillmore driving up prices on the NASDAQ with their euphoric belief in the future? Or were they dancing to the tune of the weightless symbols that were skipping through the market's digital relays? In the middle of an asset bubble, how can you tell the dancer from the dance?

↖↑↗

The NASDAQ reached its peak at around 7,400 in March of 2000 and then plummeted to below 4,000 by the end of the year, a drop of 54 per cent. The losses continued into the following years, reaching a trough of 1,742 in September 2002, a decline of more than 70 per cent from its peak; it was not until 2017 that the NASDAQ regained the valuation it had reached at the top of the boom. Of course, that value existed only on paper, or at least in the form of the digital pulses registered in the automated relays of the NASDAQ's servers, but even notional values have real-world effects. In Silicon Valley there were mass layoffs as hundreds of companies went bankrupt. By the end of 2000, there were shortages of U-Haul rental trucks in the Bay Area as recently laid off tech workers packed up their belongings and moved back to where they had come from. Office and warehouse space through the Santa Clara Valley and in downtown Manhattan's high-tech cluster stood empty. The dot-com party scene of the late 1990s gave way to a brief fad for 'pink slip parties', as newly jobless coders and software engineers had one last hurrah on what was left of their companies' petty cash.

The dot-com crash was spectacular, but it was not an isolated phenomenon. By 2002 the Dow was down in the 8,000s after peaking at 11,722 in 1999. The irrational exuberance had spread throughout the financial markets and was not just contained within the tech sector. New Economy boosterism, overstated profits, media hype, flimflam accounting, deregulation and political inaction had all contributed to the speculative euphoria that gripped the system. As the 1990s shifted into the early 2000s, it started to dawn on investors that their hopes for the future were excessive, their euphoric enjoyment of the present misguided, and that the market was due for a large-scale correction.

As is inevitably the way with these things, some people made killings while many more got soaked. Some saw the crash coming and diversified their holdings or got out near the top of the market. In her history of the 1980s and 1990s bull market, Maggie Mahar points out that a large-scale insider sell-off began in 1999, before the real avalanche was triggered in March 2000. Some canny professionals sensed that the momentum of the bubble was shifting and made their own investments secure before the great mass of investors realised what was happening. This was not adjudged to have amounted to insider trading, but large investment firms looked to their own security before they let the world know what they believed was about to happen. Not everyone was so canny or cynical. Many company executives lost giant paper fortunes. Edward Lenk, the CEO of E-Toys, watched as his personal stake of over half a billion dollars dissolved in the crash, but at no point sought to sell up and bail out. As he later told a journalist, he was more committed to the ideal of building a company of lasting value than the fantasy of paper wealth. But it was individual investors who bore the brunt of the losses. Over $5 trillion of value was wiped out from individual stock portfolios. The dot-com crash laid waste to a whole host of flimsy business ideas, but it also shredded the retirement plans of many millions of private citizens.

As the bursting of the bubble conclusively proved, the internet would turn out to be a complete flop and the high-tech digital economy would be replaced in subsequent years by a boom in traditional handicrafts, organic farming collectives and handwritten inter-office communications. Of course it didn't. As we all know, the tech industry – that vast and amorphous term that encompasses everything from internet start-ups to online education platforms to nanotech to space exploration – would continue to grow in size and power over subsequent decades; it would also continue to exert a huge influence on how human beings understood themselves and their place in the world. With the advent of broadband in the early 2000s, the internet became the universal platform that analysts had predicted in the mid-1990s. The mystical dreams of power and wealth that hang in the air about Silicon Valley in the mid-1990s were eventually realised in the form of the 'Big Five' tech corporations – Google, Apple, Facebook, Amazon and Microsoft – which dominate the digital economy today. What the dot-com bubble did signify, though, was that in the 1990s there was an excess of money chasing a dearth of real and tangible value in the here and now. The bubble was an expression of overexcitement about a future that was yet to be built and which turned out differently than expected.

14

False Apocalypse

BOB BREMER was an unlikely prophet of doom. Bob was many things – a practically minded Texan, a gifted computer scientist who had worked at the RAND Corporation and IBM, a member of the team who created COBOL, one of the most widely used early programming languages – but he was not necessarily what you would expect of a modern-day Cassandra. Bob was a guy in a suit whose personal motto, expressed in the logical commands favoured by computer nerds the world over, was ((((DO SOMETHING) SMALL) USEFUL) NOW), which didn't exactly suggest a man given to apocalyptic pronouncements. But it was Bob Bremer who first alerted the world, or at least the readers of the Fall 1971 issue of the *Honeywell Computer Journal*, to the software glitch that would later come to be known as the 'millennium bug' and which precipitated a vast global effort to debug billions of lines of computer code in the lead-up to the year 2000 in order to avoid the potentially catastrophic consequences of a vast systems failure.

The problem stemmed from the seemingly banal fact that most software systems stored the year as two digits rather than four in order to save memory space. ((Computer scientists love parsimony.) (See Bob Bremer's motto above.)) The simple question that Bremer posed was, what would happen to this two-digit system at the turn of the millennium, or the precise point when 11.59.59.31.12.99 switched over to 12.00.00.01.01.00. Without two extra digits to indicate the shift from 1999 to 2000, would the world's software systems become confused, issue strange commands, crash, descend into paroxysms of self-doubt? Or would they simply carry on with their usual business of shuffling bits of information around and enabling the smooth functioning of the high-tech post-industrial information society that had come into being in the latter decades of the twentieth century? No one knew the answer to that, so Bremer urged the adoption of a four-digit date storage system as a new industry standard. In order to prevent a potentially large and disastrous event in the future, Bob did something small and useful in the present.

In the subsequent decades, many other computer scientists and business managers took their own small-scale, useful and immediate steps towards fixing the potential glitch. In 1984, Jerome and Marilyn Murray wrote *Computers in Crisis: How to Avert the Coming Worldwide Computer Systems Collapse*, which laid out the scale of the problem and suggested a series of measures that might help to remedy it. Marilyn had discovered the bug for herself when she was working as an insurance underwriter and tried to add a policy to her database that had an annuity in the year 2000. When she tried to enter the date, her computer spewed out a string of incomprehensible numbers and then crashed. What might happen, mused Marilyn, if this were to play out in all, or even just some, of the world's computers at exactly the same time? Faced with the potentially disastrous consequences of this scenario, she did what any career-oriented, computer literate professional would: she wrote a book and struck out for the conference circuit.

Little by little, progress was made. In 1987 the New York Stock Exchange, an organisation that was at the forefront of the digitisation of the world's financial markets, spent $29 million making its software millennium-bug-proof. The following year, the American National Standards Institute introduced the four-digit year code as the industry standard for all software products. And yet ANSI's standards were voluntary and only applied to new products. The countless lines of code buried within the 'legacy' systems that continued to run on computers throughout the world were unaffected. When they wrote their two-digit year codes back in the early days of the computer revolution, most software designers assumed that the programs they were working on would be obsolete and out of service long before the year 2000. But software does not progress in uniform stages. Buried in the sedimentary layers of old code that made up large parts of the world's computer systems was a glitch with the potential to cause cascading effects throughout the system as a whole.

While software programmers were taking small, useful and immediate measures to solve the problem, the world's digital infrastructure was growing at an astronomical rate that massively outpaced their efforts. By the 1990s, it was becoming clear that acting on the local level was inadequate to the scale of the challenge. Computers were everywhere. The millennium bug wasn't just a technical glitch, it was also a devilishly effective mechanism for making everybody aware of the otherwise overlooked presence of computers in almost all aspects of life at the end of the twentieth century. Computers were integral to the most basic functions of the economic and financial systems. In the event of a system-wide crash, ATMs would cease to work. Credit and debit card transactions would stop. This would trigger panic, as trust in the financial system evaporated. This in turn would trigger a run on the banks, as the public flocked to extract paper and metal currency in the absence of the weightless system of digital transactions. Welfare cheques, mortgage payments, business loans, payroll transfers: the very lifeblood of the economy would cease to flow. The panic in the streets would be further inflamed by cascading effects in other delicately calibrated social systems. Computer failures in A&E departments and ICUs could place patients at risk. The collapse of digitised security systems could leave prison doors swinging open and dangerous offenders roaming the streets. Air traffic control, satellite global positioning systems and nuclear missile systems all rely on digital code for their safe functioning. If the glitch went unfixed, what might life look like on the morning of 1 January 2000?

By the beginning of the 1990s, as the clock ticked toward the day of reckoning, the worldwide effort to debug software programs picked up pace. One of the first warnings to cut through from the nerd fringes to the political mainstream was Peter de Jager's 1993 article in *Computer World*, 'Doomsday 2000', a title cunningly designed to make the non-technically minded sit up and take notice. Buoyed by the success of his article, de Jager embarked on a new career as a leading Y2K consultant, speaking at industry conferences and advising governments. In 1996, the US Congress struck a Y2K investigative committee which issued a report warning of the potentially dire consequences of the glitch and urging large-scale collaboration between the federal government and the private sector in their efforts to fix it. On 4 February 1998, President Clinton signed Executive Order 13073 – Year 2000 Conversion, which laid out a series of policy measures and industry guidelines to ensure that 'no critical Federal program experiences disruption because of the Y2K program'. Government advisors and private sector consultants worked to protect key infrastructure including banks, financial markets, telecommunications, health, transport and power. Similar efforts were made in jurisdictions around the world. The OECD and EU developed their own guidelines and taskforces to ensure their members were Y2K ready. The estimated cost of this massive global effort was in the $600 billion range. Whatever else we might think about the great saga of the millennium bug, the amount of money expended upon it by governments and corporations should at least convince us that some very important people were taking it very seriously.

It was in 1996 when Congress took an interest that Y2K became a mass media phenomenon. This is when the issue cut through from the pages of *Computer World* and Congressional reports to mainstream news outlets and the culture at large. Y2K become the stuff of water cooler debates, urban legend, TV talk-show jokes and news maven one-upmanship ('Actually, I read that ballistic missile systems have manual fail-safe mechanisms that protect against digitally induced misfiring,' spluttered know-it-alls at dinner tables around the world). The coverage in the media ranged from the drily factual to the soberly sceptical to the gently speculative to the outright apocalyptic. At the more bug-eyed end of the spectrum, a sub-industry of Y2K survival guides played upon the peculiar mixture of fear and enjoyment that many people seemed to feel when contemplating the possible end of high-tech global civilisation. If most right-minded citizens dismissed the threat as far-fetched or at least trusted their governments to take the necessary steps to prevent its worst effects, there remained a significant section of the populace who weren't ready to let go of the enticing prospect of civilisational collapse just yet.

One of my personal favourites in the millennium bug freak-out sub-genre is a VHS documentary released in 1999 called *Y2K Family Survival Guide*, with Leonard Nimoy. As Philip Glass-style synth music swells in the background, the former Lieutenant Spock appears before stock footage of life in the global network society: the earth seen from space, telecommunications satellites, crowded Tokyo streets, oil wells in the Arabian desert, bits of digital code looming out of a Matrix-like background. Nimoy begins:

> Our island in space. Our home. Our civilisation. Our human innovations. How could the omission of two simple digits affect the destiny of humankind? Y2K: What does it mean? How will it affect you? Your family? Your community? Your nation? Our world?

There are many things to like about this techno-apocalyptic survival guide. There is Nimoy's Vulcan-like drawl, which makes him sound like a doomier version of Carl Sagan, the great science broadcaster of the 1970s and '80s. There is the uncannily regular rhythm of the sentence fragments – 'Our island in space. [Pause]. Our home. [Pause]. Our civilisation.' – and the mantra-like repetition of 'Y2K', as though Nimoy were a cult leader looking for acolytes rather than a celebrity documentary presenter. But, most of all, it is the combination of the sublime and the ridiculous that really appeals. In spite of the apocalyptic scene setting, the stakes are obviously quite low. Only a real dupe would fall for this schtick and start making preparations for the end of the world. The film has a similar air of knowing make-believe to *The Jerry Springer Show* or *Big Brother*. It's the end of the world as we know it, and we all feel fine.

↖↑↗

Y2K was a boon to prophets and doomsayers the world over, but especially in the US, with its long tradition of millenarian religion. Jerry Falwell, one of the leading figureheads of the Christian evangelical movement, cast the millennium bug as one of 'God's instruments to shake the nation, to humble this nation'. He advised his flock to stock up on canned food and guns and hunker down for the end times, when the sheep would be sorted from the goats and Christ's eternal reign on earth would bring about the end of merely human history. In spite of its banal technical aspect, the Y2K phenomenon was easily woven in with the most ancient of biblical prophecies. Noah Hutchings, a radio preacher from Oklahoma City and author of *Y2K = 666*, fulminated against internet surveillance as a tool of the Antichrist and a vehicle for Satan's coming reign on earth. But it wasn't just Christians who saw Y2K as a sign of the apocalypse. Fringe members of other denominations got in on the act, too. A messianic rabbi in Michigan warned his followers that the chaos of Y2K would lead to a totalitarian world government.

Christian millenarianism had been on the rise in the US at least since the 1980s when Ronald Reagan was president. Reagan was raised in his mother's Campbellite Baptist faith, with its unique mixture of evangelical pre-millennialism and Scottish Enlightenment philosophy. In office, Reagan made a number of apocalyptic statements, the best known of which was to a visiting Israeli diplomat: 'I turn back to your ancient prophets in the Old Testament and the signs foretelling Armageddon, and I find myself wondering if we're the generation that's going to see that come about.' In the last days of the Cold War, it was nuclear apocalypse that stoked millenarian fantasies; some prophets of doom even claimed to see the sign of the beast in the birthmark on Mikhail Gorbachev's forehead. But even after 1989, as the threat of nuclear war diminished, the feverish imaginations of the doomsayers found plenty to feast upon in George H.W. Bush's announcement that a 'new world order' was being born. To most viewers of the nightly news, this sounded like a speechwriter's well-crafted line delivered by a practised statesman. To the conspiracy theorists in the American hinterland, it sounded like a nefarious plot to form a totalitarian world government and re-establish Satan's dominion on earth. If anything, the conspiratorial-apocalyptic strain in American society was intensified and accelerated in the post-Cold War era. Without the evil empire of the Soviet Union on hand to soak up the psychic excesses of fear and paranoia, fringe groups were free to dream up new threats and even grander plots than those suggested by the stand-off between capitalism and communism.

There were all manner of ways to be a conspiracy nut in 1990s America, most of which fell within the following Venn diagram of craziness. First, there was the paranoiac suspicion of the federal government and, hovering somewhere above that, the United Nations, both of which were taken to be manifestations of a secret plot to establish a single world government. The televangelist Pat Robertson's bestselling 1991 book, *New World Order*, was one of the main vectors for this style of conspiratorial thinking. Robertson warned that the new world government would practise a form of liberal totalitarianism that was almost perfectly designed to get under the skin of American conservatives: legalising gay marriage, extending abortion rights, enacting gun law reform, providing social security for those in need. Right-wing libertarian paranoia overlapped with the ancient antisemitic fantasy of a secret cabal of Jewish financiers bent on world domination, which was re-imagined in the 1980s and 1990s in the form of ZOG, or the Zionist Occupied Government, which was planning to infiltrate global institutions in order to erase white Christian identity.

It was from this intellectual swamp that the right-wing militia movement grew. Militiamen stockpiled weapons and supplies in preparation for the final showdown with the Feds, the UN, ZOG and the devil himself. Mostly, they existed as a tiny minority far from the mainstream of American public life, off the grid in places like Montana, Idaho and other far-flung reaches of the Western frontier; but it was a growing movement and one that would periodically break through into mainstream consciousness, such as when the Gulf War veteran Timothy McVeigh bombed a federal building in Oklahoma City in 1995, killing 168 people. Islamic terrorism would dominate public consciousness throughout the later 1990s and early 2000s, but the conspiratorial fringes of the far right were quietly growing in prominence at the same time.

To these anti-government and antisemitic strains, Christian evangelicals added the visionary contents of the Book of Revelation, in which John of Patmos is whisked up to heaven in order to watch an exclusive preview screening of the blockbuster spectacle of the Apocalypse, complete with seven seals on seven scrolls, four horsemen, the death of a quarter of the world's population, the revelation of the names of the martyrs, a series of earthquakes, meteor strikes and plagues, the 144,000 elect who are to live forever in the Kingdom of Heaven upon Earth, the seven trumpets, and the apparition of the beast from the bottomless pit. Revelation is a numerological feast, a sumptuous banquet of signs and portents that, if you so wish, can be made to fit almost any evidence. For most of us who lived in some version of the real world, the Y2K phenomenon offered a once-in-a-lifetime opportunity to imagine, if only for a brief moment, the end of civilisation and the advent of a new year zero. For latterday fans of the Book of Revelation, that eventuality was always on the near horizon, palpably visible whenever any combination of the numbers 7, 666, or 144,000 could be descried on the TV news.

The great catalysing event for the millenarian-conspiratorial fringe in America was the Waco siege of 1993, when an apocalyptic Christian cult became embroiled in a prolonged armed stand-off with federal authorities. The Branch Davidian Church was an offshoot of the Shepherd's Rod Church which was itself an offshoot of the Seventh Day Adventist Church – a sect of a sect of a minor denomination which began its life as a sect. The Branch Davidians came right out of the marrow of the American prophetic tradition. They believed that in the End Times Christ would return to sit upon King David's throne and install his divine reign upon earth with the 144,000 elect who were beginning to assemble at the biblically named Mount Carmel in Texas. David Koresh, the group's charismatic leader, generated funds by selling unlicensed firearms at rural gun shows. This is where he picked up the far-right conspiracy theories that he wove in with the apocalyptic visions of the Book of Revelation. In preparation for the coming day of judgement, Koresh manipulated his acolytes into practising bigamy and offering their underaged daughters up as vessels for an apocalyptic breeding programme intended to raise a new biblical dynasty.

The siege began on 28 February 1993, when the Bureau of Alcohol, Tobacco and Firearms raided the compound after receiving a tip-off from an informant within the sect. The initial raid culminated in a firefight, which left eight cultists and six federal agents dead. This was followed by a prolonged stand-off, during which government forces surrounded the compound, blasted it with loud rock music, negotiated the release of the wounded and hoped for some kind of peaceful, non-apocalyptic resolution. During those fifty-one days, the Waco siege became an international news story. The compound was surrounded by an inner ring of federal agents and an outer ring of mobile broadcast teams, their trucks sprouting satellite dishes ready to transmit daily updates to news studios around the world. Koresh had predicted that Armageddon would arrive in 1995; nevertheless, he must still have been pleased when federal authorities stormed the compound on 19 April 1993, as this would only serve to confirm his prophecies about the demonic power of the state and provide him with the martyr's death he craved. On the final day of the siege the compound was consumed by fire. It remains unclear who set the fire – the Feds as a pretext to enter, or Koresh as an apocalyptic spectacle – and authorities recovered the bodies of fifty-nine adults and twenty-one children, many of them killed by gunshots. The prophecy, the conflagration, the invasion by government forces, the charismatic martyr, the mass media coverage: the Waco siege was a spectacular event that helped to propel a fringe ideology into the mainstream public awareness.

End Times fantasies were given a further boost with the publication in 1995 of Tim LaHaye and Jerry B. Jenkins's *Left Behind: A Novel of the Earth's Last Days*, which wove together the same strains of anti-government paranoia, religious prejudice and Christian millenarianism to bestselling effect. Written in a fast-paced thriller style – Dan Brown meets the Book of Revelation – *Left Behind* opens with the Rapture, when the elect are beamed directly up to heaven and the sinners are left to face the 'tribulation', or God's wrathful judgement of those who are left behind. The scenario is apocalyptic in the way that Y2K fantasies were: planes fall from the sky, nuclear war breaks out, civilisation lies in tatters. In this case, though, the struggle for survival is metaphysical in scope, a final cosmic battle of good against evil, rather than purely logistical. Nevertheless, the two sides take on familiar worldly forms. The Antichrist is embodied in the form of Nicolae Carpathia, the Director General of the United Nations, who moves his headquarters to Baghdad from where he launches his plot for world domination. The saviours of the human race are a plucky group of born-again Christians – the 'Tribulation Force' – who take up the fight against the devil's plans for a one-world government under the mandate of the UN.

Left Behind was crude, ridiculous, bigoted, entirely transparent in its religious and ideological obsessions, but also surprisingly entertaining in a fast-paced thriller-ish sort of way. It was also a huge bestseller which spawned a series of sixteen novels, four movies and a videogame franchise. By some calculations, the *Left Behind* series was America's bestselling fiction franchise of the decade. More than just an opportunity for trashy entertainment, however, the series offers a glimpse into the obsessions of the conspiratorial fringes of American conservatism at the end of the twentieth century – a paranoiac distrust of government, especially in its liberal, globalisation-embracing forms; a powerful desire for the clarity of a Manichean view of reality, the clear lines of us versus them, the saved versus the damned, the pure versus the impure; and a yearning for history and politics to be conducted on the grand scale of civilisational struggles, rather than the mundane, small-scale work of liberal administration. Its success was also a sign of the growing influence of the evangelical Christian right in American politics, a demographic group that would help to propel George W. Bush to the White House in 2000. His presidency would bring its own Manichean vision of good versus evil that centred on another demonic figure based in Baghdad.

↖↑↗

In his 1999 historical study of apocalyptic belief systems, *Longing for the End*, Frederic Baumgartner observes that millenarians of all stripes experience an 'intoxication with the future'. Millenarians anticipate the coming of a new world that hovers just beyond the horizon of the present moment. In their fervent wish for the final catastrophe that will bring about this new dispensation in human affairs, they express their dissatisfaction with the gradualist model of historical change that most of us take for granted.

But this intoxication with the future can take different forms; the futures that millenarians so desperately wish for have different meanings and express different desires. Christian millenarians like David Koresh and Jerry Falwell longed for the end of secular history and the advent of Christ's kingdom upon earth. At the furthest point of their fantasies was the moment of transition from the merely human time of minutes, hours, weeks and years to a state of eternal peace: they longed for a future outside of time altogether. In many ways, though, Christian millenarianism was the least interesting style of apocalyptic thinking that flourished in the decade preceding the start of the third millennium CE. Right-wing evangelicals simply grafted conservative dissatisfaction with secular modernity on to the visionary contents of the Book of Revelation. As crackpot religious schemes go, it was hardly innovative and lacked any real creative spark.

The truly inventive apocalyptic cults of the 1990s were the techno-accelerationists, groups like Heaven's Gate, the Raëlians and Aum Shinrikyo, who didn't simply wish to escape from the modern world but instead to speed it up, grasp hold of its most potent forces and break on through to the next level of human evolution. These groups combined a hodgepodge of beliefs, drawn from Christian millenarianism and other world religions, with a fetishistic worship of the most cutting-edge aspects of modern science and technology. Their intoxication was with a future whose emerging forms could already be detected in the high-tech culture of the present: cyberspace and the birth of the internet; genomics and the biosciences; military technology and laser weaponry; and, perhaps most of all, the fantastic representation of these technologies in popular sci-fi series like *Star Trek* and *The X-Files*.

Techno-accelerationist cults were in love with those aspects of modern technology that seemed most like magic, most like the eruption of some new dimension of experience into human existence. All religions begin life as cults; it is only the passage of time that renders some religious beliefs more plausible – more natural seeming – than those of more recent growth. But how much time would have to pass before the techno-accelerationist cults of the 1990s came to seem like familiar parts of the great ecosystem of human beliefs? From the perspective of the early 2020s, they still seem weird and sinister, and yet, in their worship of the magic of technology, they also seem more than ever to express the spirit of the age.

On 27 May 1993, a strange full-page advertisement appeared in *USA Today*, America's highest-selling newspaper: '"UFO" Crew From Evolutionary Level Above Human Offers LAST CHANCE TO ADVANCE BEYOND HUMAN.' The dense, text-heavy advert continued, 'Earth's present "civilization" is about to be "spaded under". Its inhabitants are refusing to evolve. The "weeds" have taken over the garden and disturbed its usefulness beyond repair.' According to Heaven's Gate, the group who placed the advert, the true pathway to the next level of human evolution lay in the furthest reaches of outer space, or what they referred to as 'headquarters'. This was a physical place on the very edges of the cosmos that existed outside of time, which was inhabited by the immortal souls that had been temporarily housed within the physical bodies of the myriad alien races that existed throughout the universe. In order to prepare for the short window of the 'harvest time' when human souls would be able to ascend to headquarters, and in order to be protected from the evil clutches of the Luciferians, an alien race equipped with warp-speed spaceships, telepathic minds and super-advanced genetic engineering technology, who had enslaved the majority of humankind by posing as the gods of traditional religions, members of the reading public should take this one-time opportunity to join Heaven's Gate and prepare for lift off.

Heaven's Gate was formed in Texas in the early 1970s by Marshall Applewhite and Bonnie Nettles, a music professor and a nurse. Their belief system was woven together from the disparate elements of the culture around them: the works of R.D. Laing and the anti-psychiatry movement, which held that madness was a social category rather than an inherent flaw within individual minds; science fiction novels by the likes of Robert Heinlein and Isaac Asimov; the popular myth of the Roswell UFO sightings and Area 51, the secret US government research institute for the study of alien technology; and key passages from the Book of Ezekiel, which state that God will communicate with mankind via a celestial vehicle, which Applewhite and Nettles took to mean a literal spaceship. From these materials, they crafted their own homemade religion with a snug place for themselves right at its centre as a pair of extraterrestrials who had taken on human form in order to spread the good news from outer space. After their early efforts to generate publicity and recruit members stalled, they went underground and did not resurface until their strange advertisement appeared in the newspaper in 1993.

In the meantime, the small group led an extremely disciplined and ascetic existence. All property was held in common. Daily routine revolved around long periods of silence and simple spiritual exercises, such as concentrating on a single tone made by a tuning fork. On 'missions' in the wider world, cult members had to check in with home base every twelve minutes via public telephone or pager. Gender differences were neutralised by the group's simple uniform of black shirts, black slacks and the same unisex haircut. Members were forbidden from drinking caffeine or alcohol. No drugs or tobacco were allowed. Sexual abstinence was mandatory. Several of the male cultists underwent voluntary castration in order to suppress their sexual urges entirely. The mania for ascetic simplicity was further expressed in the various names the Applewhites adopted in their new guise as extra-terrestrial spirit guides: Bo and Peep, Do and Ti, or just 'the UFO Two'. The simple monosyllables of their paired names mimicked the binary structure of digital information. The Heaven's Gate cult was obsessed with simplicity, devoted to reducing the chaos of the world via ritualistic sci-fi cosplay.

When it resurfaced in the early 1990s, Heaven's Gate was based at Rancho Santa Fe, a lavish San Diego mansion, from where they ran a successful web design business, aptly named Higher Source. Their escape to the next level of human evolution would be funded by building rudimentary websites for local clients such as the San Diego Polo Club and a Christian music store. They also built their own website – what today looks like a classic retro-futurist combination of brightly coloured text, black background and Heaven's Gate logo hovering over an image of the earth seen from space – which included lengthy explanations of the group's mythology, as well as personal testimony from beings of pure light by the names of Chkody, Glnody and Srrody. It was from a post on an internet message board in 1996 that the group learned about an unidentified object trailing in the wake of the Hale-Bopp comet, which was making its first perihelion transit in an estimated 4,200 years. The cultists took this object to be the spaceship mentioned in the Book of Ezekiel which had been sent from headquarters to transport the elect to the empyrean at the edges of the cosmos. The only way to get on board the ship, however, was by releasing the eternal soul from the prison house of the flesh by mass suicide.

Heaven's Gate was an example of what the philosopher Paul Virilio has called a 'cybersect', a fringe religious group that spreads its message and engages in forms of ritual or worship online. But for Heaven's Gate, the internet was not just a technical apparatus that could be used for practical purposes; instead, it was a vehicle for religious fantasy, an integral part of their utopian vision of spirit flight through the cosmos to the next level of human evolution. They took the cyber-utopianism of the early 1990s and turned it into a religion.

The appointed day for the group to leave their earthly existences behind was 26 March 1997, when Bo and thirty-seven followers took their own lives by drinking fruit juice laced with vodka and phenobarbital (Peep had died of cancer in 1985, but was said by Bo to be waiting on board the comet-spaceship ready to be reunited with her spirit mates). Two cultists stayed behind to explain their actions to the press, but they also committed suicide a month later when the media interest had died down. In addition to their black uniforms and Nike running shoes – in a TV interview, the two remaining cultists explained how they had negotiated a bulk discount on the purchase of the shoes – each member wore an armband that read 'Away Team', a reference to *Star Trek*. They also spoke in their goodbye video messages of being 'beamed up' to the spaceship in the comet's wake. Remarkably, the *Star Trek* references extended beyond the language they used to describe their mission and included the family history of one of the cult members. Thomas Nichols, who was part of the suicidal Away Team, was the brother of Nichelle Nichols, the legendary Nyota Uhura from the original *Star Trek* TV series.

Heaven's Gate weren't just obsessed with the future; they were also haunted by the past, and in particular the utopian promise of the 1960s that had failed to come to pass. Their 1993 *USA Today* advertisement asked:

> Can a society that is still dealing with bigotry and prejudices against races, religions, and sexual preference extend the *right of existence* to some who see *humanity* as a *stepping stone* toward the kingdom of God, and the desire to take that step and briefly offer it to others. Or is earth's present civilization still as primitive as it was 2000 years ago. We'll see!

They issued a challenge to human civilisation at the end of the second millennium: why have we not gone faster, progressed further? As Uhura, Nichelle Nichols was one half of the first ever interracial kiss on American television. *Star Trek* depicted a multiethnic intergalactic empire that explored the cosmos and always obeyed the 'prime directive', or the anti-colonial injunction never to interfere with indigenous cultures. Marshall Applewhite was a gay man who had lost his university teaching job in the 1970s after having an affair with a male student. The world he wanted to live in didn't exist yet, so he built a techno-accelerationist cult and had himself castrated in a deranged attempt to find that world in the outer reaches of the cosmos.

↖↑↗

Techno-accelerationist cults fed on the signs of the future that could be detected in the present. For Heaven's Gate that meant the internet and cyberspace; for the Raëlians, biotechnology and cloning. Raëlianism came into being in 1973 when Claude Vorilhon, a high school drop-out and sometime motorsports journalist who had spent most of his twenties on the fringes of the French counterculture, was visited by a 4ft-tall, grey, oily skinned extra-terrestrial being while hiking inside the rim of a volcanic crater in the Clermont-Ferrand department of central France. This messenger from the skies divulged to Vorilhon, who renamed himself Raël, or 'messenger of the Elohim', the true history of mankind's origins not in the slow ascent from the primordial sludge via natural selection, but instead through an act of genetic engineering by an alien super-race, the aforementioned Elohim, who, while only 4ft tall, were nevertheless masters of such cosmic powers as intergalactic space flight and dazzling feats of bio-technological wizardry.

Raël repeatedly insisted that the premise of his neo-religion was not simply lifted from the pages of Erich von Däniken's *Chariots of the Gods? Unsolved Mysteries of the Past*, the 1968 bestseller that claimed that the great monuments of the ancient world were the product of alien technology, rather than human ingenuity and slave labour; and yet it sounded suspiciously similar. In the years following his visitation, Raël spread the word, gathered his disciples and, in the early 1990s, relocated to Quebec, where he built UFO-Land, a UFO-themed amusement park and Raëlian world headquarters, complete with giant landing pad for an Elohim spaceship, in preparation for the return of humanity's original extra-terrestrial parents. Raël and his followers embraced the most upbeat and optimistic aspects of high-tech modern society. They preached a gospel of sexual and religious tolerance, and practised meditation and mindfulness; they extolled the importance of nanotechnology and cloning as ways to extend human longevity and create a global society free from the burdens of sickness and work. Thanks to funding from wealthy

Japanese members, they also started the Raël Racing Team, which competed on the international motor-racing circuit in the mid-1990s. In the absence of an actual Elohim spaceship, Raël piloted high-performance racecars around tracks in Japan, Europe and America. This was techno-accelerationism of a more terrestrial variety.

What really put the Raëlians in the spotlight, though, was the founding in 1997 of the bio-tech company Clonaid, and the announcement to the world's press in 2002 that they had succeeded in producing the world's first human clone, rather predictably named Eve. The 1990s saw a series of spectacular leaps forward in genetic science. In 1990, Craig Venter and his team began their work on the Human Genome Project, which aimed to sequence every line of code in the human genome by 2015. The project was completed two years ahead of schedule due to advances in computer processing speeds (thanks, Moore's Law!). In 1996, the birth of the world's first cloned mammal was announced at the Roslin Institute in Scotland. This, of course, caused the world's media to descend into a paroxysm of moral panic and bad puns. Dolly the Sheep was dubbed a 'farmyard freak'. One UK tabloid announced the news with the pun-tastic headline, 'Cloners' Ewe Turn Stuns'. In Germany, *Der Spiegel* ran a cover story about the possibility of cloning exceptional humans. Just imagine, a whole army of Hitlers, Einsteins or Marilyn Monroes! The panic quickly spread to the political establishment. France's minister of agriculture warned of a dystopian future in which six-legged chickens would be bred for the tables of the world's developing nations. Bill Clinton called for a ban on all research into cloning and related biotechnologies.

The overheated response to Dolly's birth stemmed not only from the obvious scurrility of a large portion of the media, but also from the fact that the cloning of a mammal from a single adult cell was, in reality, a very big deal. Science tends to progress by tiny increments, which are the product of many hours of often very dull work in the laboratory. Dolly the Sheep was the successful outcome of the 277th attempt at the nuclear transplantation process. Victor Frankenstein would have given up long before that. But sometimes, era-defining breakthroughs do occur; discoveries are made that redraw the map of human possibilities. In their 2001 book *The Second Creation*, Ian Wilmut and Keith Campbell, the leaders of the Roslin team, explained how Dolly completed the three-part structure of modern biotechnology – genetic engineering, genomics and cloning – and thus inaugurated the new age of 'biological control'. In the coming years, humankind will have complete control over the processes of organic life, right down to the molecular level.

'Human ambition will be bound,' mused Wilmut, 'only by the laws of physics, the rules of logic, and our descendants' own sense of right and wrong.' If that doesn't send a shiver up your spine, nothing will.

For a brief period, before Clonaid was revealed to be a sham and baby Eve a figment of the cultists' imagination, the Raëlians were right at the cutting edge of contemporary debates about bioethics and genetic engineering. In the media storm generated by the announcement, government officials and scientists were compelled to respond: some denounced the birth of baby Eve as a gross act of immorality; some called for greater restrictions on cloning and genetic engineering; many doubted the veracity of Clonaid's claims. And yet, regardless of the truth of their claims, the Raëlians had inserted themselves into the space where the future of humankind was to be determined. The wacky mythology, the UFO theme park, the motor-racing team, the sham cloning breakthrough: these were all ways of getting closer to the signs of the future that were already here in the present.

↖↑↗

With their UFO mythology and hippy-ish vibes, as well as the important fact that they never actually killed anyone in the course of their neo-religious activities, the Raëlians existed at the comedy end of the techno-accelerationist spectrum. Their polar opposite in this respect was Aum Shinrikyo, who were to the culture of techno-futurism what the Manson Family had been to the hippy counterculture – a negative image, a dark mirror, a death's head inversion.

On Monday, 20 March 1995, at exactly 8.15 a.m., right at the peak of the morning rush hour on one of the world's busiest subway systems, three trains converged on Kasumigaseki, the heart of the Japanese administrative state. As their synchronised watches ticked down to the appointed second, five Aum Shinrikyo cult members used the tips of their umbrellas to burst the bags of sarin gas that they had carried on board the trains. The gas had been synthesised in the cult's secret laboratories by their own scientific experts from ingredients purchased from criminal gangs in post-Soviet Russia. Sarin gas was first made in Nazi Germany as part of Hitler's preparations for the Second World War. It was also used in the 1980s during the Iran–Iraq War by Saddam Hussein, both against Iranian armed forces and Iraq's own Kurdish population in Halabja. Sarin is one of the deadliest poisons on earth. A drop the size of a pinhead can kill a human. As the particles spread through the train carriages and out on to the platforms, passengers and railway workers started to cough, then asphyxiate, then vomit and bleed from the nose, and then, in the worst cases, to cease to breathe altogether. It was only because the terrorists did not have a more effective way to circulate the sarin gas in the stagnant air of the subway system that casualties were not higher. As a result of the attack, twelve people died and 1,400 were injured.

The men who carried out the attack were recruited from the Japanese 'super-elite'. Ikuo Hayashi, the most senior member of the group, was a graduate of the distinguished Keio University, former head of circulatory medicine at the National Sanatorium Hospital in Tokai and an advisor to Japan's Ministry of Science and Technology. The other attackers held postgraduate degrees in physics, applied physics, engineering and artificial intelligence. All had renounced promising careers as research scientists to join the cult. Aum Shinrikyo actively targeted disaffected members of the Japanese technocracy, preying upon a desire for spiritual wisdom that so often went unfulfilled in an academic culture devoted to passing exams and mastering endless reams of technical information. At the time of the attacks, Aum Shinrikyo had 40,000 members and had amassed a vast fortune by charging members exorbitant fees for the spiritual training that would enable them to progress through the pyramid-like stages of its religious system towards the pinnacle of enlightenment.

The ultimate aim of Aum Shinrikyo was not simply personal enlightenment, but literally to take over the world. The cult was organised as a series of ministries which reflected the structure of the Japanese state. In 1990, at the same time that its candidates were failing to win a single seat in national elections, the group was also carrying out gas attacks on US naval bases and Japanese government offices in the hopes of triggering an international conflict (it turned out that the aerosolised gas they sprayed from passing trucks dispersed before it could have any effect). The attack on the Tokyo subway was meant to be the opening salvo in what would become the final battle between the forces of good and evil; the beginning of the apocalyptic end times that would pave the way for the eternal reign of Aum.

Aum Shinrikyo was founded in 1984 by Shoko Asahara, a partially sighted yoga instructor with delusions of messianic grandeur and a deep vein of sadism in his heart. The Aum belief system was woven together from the Buddhist and Hindu mysticism that Asahara picked up on a trekking holiday in the Himalayas and the apocalyptic strains of Christian millenarianism and Nostradamus's prophecies. Its central spiritual practice was yoga. Many of the cult's members seem to have been ignorant of its terrorist activities, which were conducted by an elite inner core, and were mainly devoted to the group's daily rituals of yoga and meditation. Asahara's charisma derived not only from the exceptional poise and calm of his manner, as was often remarked upon by acolytes who were granted a personal audience with their leader, but also from his claim to be the 'Final Liberated One', whose powers of levitation and prophetic foresight were derived from Aum's innovative brand of mystical discipline.

Aum's mysticism was also accompanied by an extreme form of techno-fetishism, which sought to enhance its members' spiritual powers via experimental means. In addition to synthesising sarin gas and attempting to build a portable nuclear weapon, The Ministry of Science conducted hare-brained experiments with electrode caps and psychedelic drugs in the hopes of unlocking the mind's latent capacity for extra-sensory perception. As part of their recruitment efforts, Aum published a series of magazines with titles like *Mu* and *Twilight Zone*, which included articles on astral teleportation machines and magical DNA alongside yoga instructions and mindfulness advice. Hideo Murai, the group's chief scientist, was obsessed with Isaac Asimov's *Foundation* series of science fiction novels, in which the scientist hero, Harry Selden, discovers the laws of 'Psychohistory', which enable a small cadre of enlightened technocrats to foresee the coming collapse of civilisation and prepare for life in the end times.

Over the course of the 1990s, the group's activities became increasingly violent. Recruits were subjected to gruelling initiation rites involving prolonged sensory deprivation and large doses of LSD. One former cult member told Haruki Murakami, the Japanese novelist who compiled an oral history of the Tokyo subway attacks, how he could hear these experiments taking place in the building where he worked: 'I could hear these louds screams from above, real shrieks, people yelling, "Kill me! Put me out of my misery!" – the kind of barely human voice wrung out of someone in excruciating pain.' For Aum, the extremity of the discipline seemed to go hand in hand with the techno-accelerationism. Asahara wanted enlightenment, now! Spiritual discipline had to be harder, faster and more intense; the mind had to be freed from the charnel house of the body via mystical-technological add-ons, gadgets and gizmos designed to bring about the impossible moment of transcendence, the point where the apocalyptic future arrives in the mundane present. Unlike the Raëlians, with their upbeat message of secular progress and human flourishing, Aum Shinrikyo embraced the death drive that manifested itself in hyper-modern science and technology. Hence the echoes of Hitler and Saddam Hussein in the group's use of sarin gas as their weapon of choice. The Tokyo subway attack evoked the most horrific aspects of the twentieth century's grim history of mechanised terror.

Murakami embarked on his oral history out of a desire to revise the media narrative that had been spun in the wake of the attacks – as a counterbalance to the idea that Aum Shinrikyo was a demonic aberration utterly at odds with mainstream Japanese society. By patiently listening to the testimony of victims, witnesses and cult members, Murakami enabled a more complicated picture to emerge, one in which the sterility and conformism of post-Second World War Japanese society helped to create the conditions in which the death cult could take root. But the Tokyo subway attack was not just a national event; its significance resonated well beyond the shores of Japan. This was a new style of terrorism in which a tiny cadre struck at the centre of a hyper-modern metropolis in the hopes of provoking a global conflict between good and evil. Aum were also the first ever non-state actor to mass produce a chemical weapon; their ability to mount an attack on the Japanese administrative state depended upon the miniaturisation of advanced weapons technology and the power of networks to magnify the impact of a strike. In this respect, Tokyo, 1995 foreshadowed New York, 2001.

↖↑↗

New Year's Eve 1999 was a night of celebration and bacchanalia for billions of people around the world. People feasted, danced, watched fireworks displays, attended mass gatherings in public squares, paid over-inflated ticket prices for nightclubs and concerts, got sozzled, squiffy, blitzed, hammered and wasted, all with a slightly elevated sense of the momentousness of the occasion. It felt good to party like it was 1999, or 12.19.6.15.2 in the Mayan calendar (which takes as its starting point the birth of the Mayan cosmos in our year 3114 BCE), or the twenty-fifth day of the eleventh month in the Chinese year of the rabbit, or the twelfth day of Nivaise in the French revolutionary calendar, 208 years after the zero point of 1792, when the First Republic was declared. Ultimately, all calendrical systems are arbitrary attempts to impose meaning and order on the infinite flux of time; but the advent of the year 2000 in the Gregorian calendar was still a good excuse for a party.

As the festivities unfolded on 31 December 1999, groups of administrators, computer scientists and military personnel huddled in purpose-built command centres in order to make sure the world wasn't about to end. US military generals gathered at a secret facility in the hollowed-out core of Cheyenne Mountain in Colorado, from where they scrutinised their computer screens for signs of errors in early warning radar systems which might trigger a Russian nuclear attack. Citibank and Chase Manhattan deployed teams of analysts in locations throughout the US to monitor ATM activity and credit card transactions for early signs of systemic failure. At the Bank of Canada in Ottawa, security guards watched over vaults stocked with four times the regulation amount of paper currency in case of a run on the banks.

As we all know, civilisation did not collapse at the end of 1999. Most of us woke up on the morning of 1 January 2000, perhaps with a fuzzy head from the previous night's festivities, and went about our ordinary lives. For the most part, the world's computer systems ticked from one date to the next without causing so much as a flicker in the fabric of everyday life. As a result of Y2K-related glitches, some women in the UK received false positive Down's Syndrome test results for their unborn babies. A nuclear power station in Japan was briefly taken offline. But no major cataclysm took place; no rupture in the fabric of time. It wasn't long before the sceptics and naysayers started to cast retrospective doubt on the Y2K phenomenon. The whole thing had been overhyped, they claimed, by consultants and systems analysts keen to make a buck. The scramble to ensure compliance had been driven by the threat of litigation, rather than a sober appraisal of the risks. The media had peddled overblown doomsday scenarios to a credulous public raised on Hollywood action films and still hooked at a subconscious level on a millenarian conception of history inherited from 2,000 years of Christian influence. The fear that two simple digits could wreak havoc upon high-tech modern society was a form of secular superstition and collective mania that should really be consigned to the past.

While each of these claims contained at least a grain of truth, none properly accounted for the effect of the hundreds of millions of hours of labour that went into the decades-long global effort to assess and debug trillions of lines of potentially faulty computer code. Y2K was a massive anti-climax because the computer scientists won. They were the unsung heroes who staved off the threat of civilisational collapse, or at least the threat of some rather annoying and possibly quite costly disruptions to the smooth functioning of the digital systems that were woven throughout all domains of everyday life in the affluent West at the end of the second millennium. (The cost of Y2K preparedness was negligible in large parts of the world because they didn't yet rely on computers so much.)

It was the manner of the victory that was disappointing. We live in a culture saturated with high-action spectacles in which a man in a grubby vest saves humanity from an apocalyptic threat through a mixture of physical bravery, tactical cunning and the ability to deliver pithy wisecracks while escaping from burning buildings. In the case of Y2K there was no grand finale, no giant explosions, no swelling music, no kiss in the last scene between the hero and his girl. In the end, nothing happened, which was exactly what should have happened. The catastrophe was averted by the quiet efforts of thousands of anonymous software engineers hunched over their glowing screens in the years leading up to the millennium. For all of our apocalyptic fantasies, for all of the innate human love of drama, reality is often duller than we expect it to be.

15

The Falling Man

MOST OF the time reality is less spectacular than the movies, but on a few rare occasions real life and cinema collide. The cliché about 9/11, a cliché that was uttered on the day of the attacks by witnesses all over the world, was that it looked just like a movie. The conflagration as the first and then the second planes hit the towers – the smooth gliding motion through the sky, followed by the moment of crumpling impact, followed by a billowing cloud of orange and yellow flame as jet fuel, aluminium, plastic, glass, steel, rubber and human flesh ignited in mid-air – was something we had all seen before. It was like watching *Die Hard* or *Independence Day* or *Armageddon* or whatever high-definition, big-budget, surround-sound spectacle of sublime terror and violence was playing that week. But this was a non-fiction spectacle: real death, actual trauma.

In those pre-smartphone days, witnesses recorded the attacks with handheld camcorders and disposable cameras bought from downtown drugstores. They called their loved ones on Nokia and Motorola cell phones. They sent text messages and pinged pagers. By the time the second plane hit, mobile news crews were in place to capture the event. The biggest terrorist attack in American history was broadcast live on TV. After a massive initial surge of calls, cell phone service went down throughout the wider New York area. North American airspace was shut down; incoming flights were redirected to Canada and Mexico. George W. Bush was rushed aboard Air Force One, which was escorted by fighter jets as it flew in a randomised pattern above the American continent for several hours before landing at a secure location so that the president could address the nation.

America and much of the world went into a state of shock. Billions of people stopped what they were doing and gathered around the nearest TV screen. The events of 9/11 generated an unfathomably large number of images, only a few of which were selected for the carousel of now familiar scenes that played on news channels in the subsequent days. Crowds escaping into the street as smoke billows behind them. The towers falling, their vertical lines broken, masonry collapsing into itself as a giant dust cloud fills the surrounding space. Firefighters silhouetted against broken shards of architecture. Members of the public staring into the sky in attitudes of horror and grief. And the eeriest image of them all, perhaps one of the eeriest images ever caught on camera, the falling man, one of the poor souls trapped on the floors above where the planes hit, who chose to leap from the towers rather than be consumed by the fire and smoke within. Richard Drew, the Associated Press photographer who took the photograph, later recalled, 'That picture just jumped off the screen because of its verticality and symmetry. It just had that look.'

Over the course of the day itself, as news filtered out of an attack on the Pentagon and a fourth plane crash in Pennsylvania, the footage of the planes hitting the towers was replayed again and again. The silent glide. The crumpling impact. The vivid ball of flame. And then, all of a sudden, it stopped. The American news media ceased to play the footage and instead flooded the airwaves with stories of heroism, grief and the steady drumbeat of war. As several commentators later pointed out, the TV coverage of the attacks followed the pattern of traumatic memory: the shocking event and the compulsion to repeat, followed by an unconscious repression.

The spectacular nature and instant spread of the footage was a central part of Al Qaeda's strategy. How else does a small group of religious fanatics sheltering in a remote cave system in eastern Afghanistan capture the attention of the world's most powerful nation? It was not until June 1999, after Al Qaeda attacked US embassies in Nairobi and Dar es Salaam, killing 213 and 11 people respectively, that Osama bin Laden made it on to the FBI's most wanted list. Even after Ramzi Yousef's failed attempt to blow up the World Trade Center in 1993, the American security forces were slow to adapt to the threat of Islamic terrorism. Al Qaeda were a new kind of terrorist organisation for the age of the global network. This was terrorism on the franchise model, with a central hub responsible for strategy and funding connected to semi-autonomous local cells responsible for planning and executing attacks.

Al Qaeda were engaged in a form of radically asymmetric warfare that was oriented as much towards generating publicity as to making territorial gains or even to taking American lives, which of course it did in abundance. Bin Laden once claimed that 'It is obvious that the media war in this century is one of the strongest methods. In fact, its ratio may reach 90 per cent of the total preparation for the battles.' The strategy on 9/11 was to shock America into taking Al Qaeda seriously, to grant it the dignity of attention and enmity. The attacks were a lure with which to capture eyeballs, terrify the public, solicit the support of disaffected young Muslim men, and to draw America into a war in Afghanistan, the legendary 'graveyard of empires'.

Between 1996 and 2001, roughly 20,000 young men from Pakistan, Saudi Arabia, Chechnya, Bosnia, the UK, France, Canada and elsewhere passed through Al Qaeda training camps in Afghanistan. They underwent a forty-five-day course in physical fitness, weapons maintenance, map reading, trench fortification and hand-to-hand combat. In the evenings, after dinner and prayers, the recruits relaxed by watching Hollywood action movies. Their favourites, apparently, were the works of Arnold Schwarzenegger. Those images – the silent glide; the crumpling impact; the vivid ball of flame – were a kind of reverse broadcast action movie, a blockbuster in which the terrorists win and the all-American heroes die.

Originally, bin Laden had planned to watch the attacks on satellite television from his hideout in the Tora Bora caves, but when the time came his chief communications technician couldn't get a clear enough signal. Instead, he and his men listened to the news on the BBC's Arabic radio service. Huddled in his cave in the distant mountains of Afghanistan, bin Laden was both utterly distant from and seamlessly connected to the centres of modernity in the West. He was himself the product of the rapid and highly uneven process of modernisation that had been unleashed in Saudi Arabia and the Gulf States in the second half of the twentieth century. Bin Laden's father was a building contractor who had risen to great wealth and status as a result of the Middle Eastern oil boom. Throughout the 1960s an '70s, the Saudi Binladin Group built highways, airports, office towers, telecommunications infrastructure and oil refineries, as well as the Al-Aqsa Mosque in Jerusalem and the Grand Mosque in Mecca. Osama grew up in the air-conditioned compounds of the Saudi elite but rejected the worldly power of his father and the oil sheiks he served in favour of the dogmatism of Wahabi fundamentalism. His religious fanaticism was a response to the hyper-accelerated history of the Gulf, a history which saw a semi-nomadic desert culture transformed into a collection of oil-rich, globally connected nation states in the space of little more than a couple of decades. The desire to turn the clock back to 632 CE, the year of the prophet's death and the purest form of Islam, was the perverse negation of the leap forward in history that was precipitated by the oil boom.

The image of bin Laden settling down to watch his big show on television from his cavernous lair is both grotesque and familiar. It encapsulates something of the vertiginous scale of global civilisation at the beginning of the twenty-first century. This is a world in which there are precious few dark places on the map, a world of near total connectivity in which the depths of the Tora Bora caves can be linked up to the tip of Manhattan and the anti-modern ideology of violent jihad is pursued via the hyper-modern tools of the jetliner and satellite TV.

The imagery of the cave and the skyscrapers thrums with mythic significance. Bin Laden hid out in the dark recesses of the earth, the involuted feminine space inside the land's body, a mystical retreat from which to conjure a new reality. The targets were symbols of American wealth and power. The Capitol and the Pentagon are the centres of the American imperial state. The Twin Towers, gleaming phalluses that probed the sky of southern Manhattan, were the tallest buildings in the world between 1971 and 1973. They were monuments to American technological and financial power that had attracted the attention of worshippers and iconoclasts for decades. Long before 9/11, the Twin Towers were looming presences in countless films, television shows and music videos, the backdrop to the exploits of Biggie Smalls, Homer Simpson and Spiderman. They were also an irresistible challenge, a giant existential come-on, to Philippe Petit, whose famous tightrope walk between the towers in 1974 was documented in the 2008 film *Man on Wire*. The cave and the towers, the female and the male, the ancient and the modern – 9/11 was a moment in history that seemed to have too much meaning, too potent a symbolic force.

It is possible for me to say these things now without giving too much offence. But in the immediate aftermath, the symbolism and aesthetic power of the attacks were taboo subjects. At a press conference for an upcoming performance of his *Licht* opera cycle in Hamburg on 17 September 2001, the German classical composer Karlheinz Stockhausen remarked that the attacks were 'the greatest work of art that is possible in the whole cosmos' and, with an almost heroic lack of judgement, expressed his own sense of envy: 'I couldn't do that. In comparison with that, we're nothing as composers.' Unsurprisingly, Stockhausen was pilloried in the press for his bad taste and narcissistic self-regard. His upcoming concerts were cancelled; his daughter, a concert pianist in her own right, chose to perform under a pseudonym. And yet, for all of his bluster, Stockhausen had a point. When Don DeLillo had expressed a similar idea in his 1991 novel, *Mao II* – 'I used to think it was possible for an artist to alter the inner life of the culture. Now bombmakers and gunmen have taken that territory'; 'In societies reduced to blur and glut, terror is the only meaningful act' – he was cast as an edgy prophet, rather than a tasteless crank.

As the mood of shock and grief descended upon America and much of the world, public speculation about the relationship between terrorism and art became offensive. What was once ironic and playful became insensitive and even traitorous. The observation that American foreign policy in the Middle East might be one of the causes of the attacks was deemed distasteful. The idea that Islamic jihad was itself a product of social and historical forces and not an unconditioned source of pure evil was discounted as academic cavilling. The notion that the attacks could be both a moral outrage and a sublime spectacle was deemed beyond the bounds of public taste.

In the days following the attacks, President Bush made several public appearances during which he made a series of statements, some scripted, some impromptu. He praised the first responders and members of the public who were providing heroic assistance at the scene of the atrocity. He offered prayers and condolences for the bereaved. He highlighted the numerous expressions of support for America in its time of crisis from governments around the world. He stressed that terrorist jihad was a perversion of the true message of the Qur'an and the peace-loving Muslim faith. He praised Congress for its cross-party unity and singleness of purpose in its determination to capture those responsible for the attacks. He announced the formation of the Office of Homeland Security, a new federal agency that would amalgamate several existing government departments and extend America's capacity to fight terrorism at home and abroad. He compared Al Qaeda both to the Mafia and the Nazis. And he prepared the nation for war.

During an unguarded moment at a hectic press conference on 17 September, he also said, 'This crusade, this war on terrorism, is going to take a while … I want justice. And there's an old poster out West, I recall, that says, "Wanted. Dead or Alive".' In the confusion and grief that followed the attacks, a great many people wanted clarity of meaning and purpose. Of all the official statements that Bush made, it was the language of frontier justice that cut through loudest to a large section of the population; the narrative of retribution and vengeance, Us versus Them, Good versus Evil. Twenty years after the fact, it is no longer considered treacherous, but merely a matter of common sense, to point out that this was precisely the narrative that bin Laden wanted.

↖↑↗

To many at the time, 9/11 seemed to represent a turning point in history, the inauguration of a new epoch in world affairs. The US, the UK and their allies embarked on a 'Global War on Terror', which funnelled vast amounts of energy and resources into a militarised campaign against the vaguely defined threat of 'terror'. Infamously, in his 2002 State of the Union address, President Bush identified an 'Axis of Evil' that comprised Iraq, Iran and North Korea, against whom it was the moral duty of all freedom-loving democracies to fight. Other leaders were more circumspect in their language. In his speech to Parliament before it voted to authorise the Iraq War, Tony Blair spoke of UN Security

Council resolution 1441, of weapons-inspection regimes, of the enforcement of international law, of the threat posed by 'rogue states' and 'extreme terrorists' to the stability of the global liberal order. Nevertheless, in spite of their rhetorical differences, both Bush and Blair relied on a dubious connection between Al Qaeda's brand of global jihad and Saddam Hussein's regional despotism. As we later came to learn, they also relied on falsified intelligence.

Beyond the justification for the wars in Afghanistan and Iraq, the Global War on Terror fed into a new narrative about world history in the twenty-first century. In his 1996 book *The Clash of Civilizations*, Samuel Huntington argued against the dominant realist account of geopolitics, which placed the competing interests of nation states at the centre of world affairs, and for a new model based on the competition between large-scale civilisational blocs and the myriad local cultures of which they are composed. According to Huntington, the twenty-first century would be defined by the struggle between the West and the six or seven other great world civilisations: Sinic, Japanese, Hindu, Islamic, Orthodox, Latin American and African (although he had his doubts as to whether Africa counted as a single civilisational bloc). Nation states were still important and the homogenising effects of globalisation were undeniable, but these were ultimately superficial trends in comparison with the deep-rooted civilisational histories that were stirring back into life. In this new multipolar and multicivilisational world, global politics was taking a cultural turn. Battles over symbols such as flags, crosses and headscarves were moving to the centre of political discourse. With a renewed focus on ethnicity and identity, new sources of enmity were being discovered.

Regardless of its accuracy as a diagnosis of global politics, Huntington's thesis had a grandeur and sweep that appealed to many. It was a riposte to Fukuyama's glib universalism, 'an end to the end of history'. For readers in the West, it was both chastening and aggrandising. On the one hand, it rejected the universality of Western civilisational ideals, casting liberal democracy and Enlightenment reason as local traditions that emerged in a particular time and place; but on the other hand, it invited readers to identify more closely, perhaps even more fiercely, with that tradition. Huntington's book was both a carefully argued analysis of geopolitics and a call to arms. It invited readers in the West to recognise and defend what made their civilisation different from – and potentially in conflict with – others.

The appeal of this vision of the world cut across many of the old polarities. Osama bin Laden approvingly cited Huntington's thesis in his video messages from his hideout in Tora Bora. He had enmity aplenty, and Huntington was a convenient prop in his propaganda war. Conservative politicians in the West would increasingly talk in grandiose terms of Judaeo-Christian heritage and Enlightenment values. The language of civilisational complaint wasn't just the preserve of fringe figures like Pat Buchanan and Jean-Marie Le Pen, with their ethno-nationalisms and paranoid fears of an encroaching Muslim 'umma', but also academic historians like Niall Ferguson, who in a series of books and TV programmes in the early 2000s offered a defence of American empire and paeans to the 'killer apps' of competition, science, property, medicine, consumption and work that made the West better than 'the Rest'. Many members of the post-1968 generation of former radicals would also find something appealing in the clash of civilisations. A certain kind of ageing Marxist would rally to the fight against 'Islamofascism', as though the ideological polarities of the mid-twentieth century were still in place. Christopher Hitchens, one of the great heroes of the mid-Atlantic left, famously turned apostate over the War on Terror. In an interview with *Frontpage Magazine*, a right-wing political website, he reported feeling a sense of 'exhilaration' after 9/11. 'Here we are then, I was thinking, in a war to the finish between everything I love and everything I hate. Fine. We will win and they will lose.'

But did 9/11 really inaugurate a new historical era? Were these really the fault lines that would define the twenty-first century? To be sure, the Global War on Terror left a turbulent slipstream for many years to come. Everybody knows the story of what happened next. The new security fever. The faked intelligence dossiers. The mass surveillance of American citizens by the NSA. 'Enhanced interrogation procedures.' Waterboarding. Guantanamo Bay. Abu Ghraib. Belmarsh Prison. Al Qaeda attacks in Tunisia, Bali, Mombasa, Riyadh, Casablanca, Jakarta, Istanbul, Madrid, London, Baghdad, Islamabad, Paris. The polarisation. The hyper-nationalism. The 'with us or against us' rhetoric. The Islamophobia. The mosque burnings. The racial profiling at airports. The beheading videos. The cartoons of the prophet. Kiefer Sutherland's Jack Bauer torturing suspects to extract information in the ticking-clock anti-terror drama *24*. The vast anti-war demonstrations. The 'freedom fries' and 'cheese-eating surrender monkeys'. *Team America: World Police*. Extraordinary rendition. CIA black sites. The drone strikes. And, underneath all of this, working at a slower, more insidious pace, the erosion of some of the core principles of liberal democracy: *habeas corpus*, the right to privacy, the illegality of torture, international law.

But for all of the terror of 9/11 and the evil of Al Qaeda, the Global War on Terror was systematically oversold. What might have been a worldwide policing operation was converted into a titanic struggle between good and evil, a grandiose vision of civilisational conflict. In 2004, Karl Rove, George W. Bush's chief political strategist, addressed his critics, saying they exist 'in what we call the reality-based community. That's not how the world works any more. We're an empire now, and when we act, we create our own reality.' Rove was at the cutting edge of post-truth politics. In the newly globalised and digitised world, power was becoming detached from traditional notions of expertise and judgement. On the geopolitical stage, reality was up for grabs, defined as much by one's power to engage in disruptive action and control the digital misinformation campaign, as by one's adherence to the principles of international co-operation and evidence-based policymaking. Rove's statement could just as easily describe the mindset of Putin's Russia or Trump's America.

The first world leader to speak with George W. Bush to offer support after 9/11 was in fact Vladimir Putin. In the early noughties, Putin was seen by many in the West as a modernising figure who would steer Russia towards further integration with the world economy and greater democratic transparency. At a press conference earlier that year, Bush claimed that he had looked Putin in the eye and got a 'sense of his soul' as a trustworthy counterpart. But, as we now know, Putin was playing an old game with new tactics. For Putin, the former KGB agent and judo blackbelt, the deregulated global marketplace would become a new arena for the imperialist struggle against the West. The Soviet era disruption campaign would now be waged via the new means of compromised oligarchs, the soft power of football, troll farms and social media disinformation campaigns, alongside the great tides of Russian oil and gas wealth sloshing through dark money networks in Cyprus, Jersey and Panama as well as the London stock exchange and property markets. Underneath the twenty-first-century dirty tricks there lurked the atavistic drive to reconstitute the territorial integrity of the Russian homeland. The seeds of future wars were being sown.

If we look around the world of 2001, there are several alternative candidates for the most consequential events and trends of that year. In 2001 China joined the WTO, which inaugurated a new phase in one of the greatest experiments in social engineering ever conducted. According to the World Bank, since 1981 China has lifted more than 800 million of its citizens out of poverty and triggered one of the largest ever migrations from the countryside to the cities. In the space of half a century, China has catapulted itself from the famine and desperation of Mao's 'Great Leap Forward' to one of the few genuine challengers to American hegemony in the twenty-first century. In doing so, it has thrown into question what once seemed to be the necessary historical connections between modernisation and Westernisation, and between market capitalism and liberal democracy. Perhaps future historians will look back on 2001 as the first year of the Chinese century, the beginning of the age of post-liberal, post-Western, AI-enabled market socialism.

In 2001, the Kyoto Protocol, which had been thrashed out at the global climate summit in Japan in 1997, was in the process of being ratified by its 192 signatories. The agreement would come into force from 2005. At the start of the new millennium, climate change remained for most people a future threat. In Kyoto the nations of the world signed up to limits on CO_2 emissions that were designed to ward off a potential catastrophe by keeping future temperature rises within an acceptable range. That was before the wildfires, hurricanes, floods, droughts and ice storms really started to bite, before 'global warming', as we called it back then, become immediately apparent in the here and now – the 'climate crisis'. Climate change is another large-scale threat that signals the possible end of 'the end of history'. What is climate change, after all, if not the return of the past in the form of CO_2 deposits built up in the atmosphere as the by-product of centuries of industrial capitalism? What is climate change if not the unintended consequences of liberal capitalism coming home to roost?

In September 2001, the NASDAQ stock exchange was nearing the bottom of its post-crash low. In spite of the losses, pundits were eagerly anticipating the arrival of 'web 2.0', the next phase of the great internet experiment. Dial-up connections were giving way to high-speed broadband and mobile Wi-Fi. The age of streaming and social media and seemingly infinite connectivity was just around the corner. The new technology was already unleashing a tidal wave of disruption in the worlds of journalism, publishing, finance, commerce, education and much else besides. Google, which very nearly went bust in the crash, was in the process of expanding its small advertising department in order to secure a durable revenue stream for the medium and long term. A new internet business model was being born: the product, whether it was a search engine or a social media platform, would be free for users, but the users themselves would be packaged up as streams of data and sold to companies who wished to predict and influence their behaviour. The age of digital surveillance capitalism was dawning.

It is no manner of hyperbole to refer to the 1990s as the start of the 'digital revolution'. The invention of the printing press in fifteenth-century

Germany was one of the great engines of modernity, which helped to spark the Protestant Reformation and the Scientific Revolution. That the networked digital computer will help to precipitate similarly tumultuous upheavals is clear. But what form those upheavals will take and what consequences they will have remain opaque. As Zhou Enlai, the chairman of the Chinese Communist Party, famously remarked to Richard Nixon in 1972 when asked for his opinion of the consequences of the French Revolution: 'It is too early to tell.'

↖↑↗

Looking back from today, the world on 10 September 2001, let alone the world on any day in 1999 or 1995 or 1991, seems to exist on the other side of a historical boundary. Some of the most characteristic features of 1990s culture – the post-Cold War optimism, the 'end of history' smugness, the third-way politics, the digital utopianism – seem like relics from a lost age. Even 9/11 now seems like an event from a prior era. Its distance can be gauged by the way in which people found out about what was happening on that day: via relatively scarce mobile phones, ubiquitous landlines and cable TV. There was no immediate social media commentary, no livestreaming of the attack by the terrorists on Facebook. While the event unfolded principally on television, the conspiracy theories that emerged in its wake – it was the American secret services staging a 'false flag' attack to justify war in the Middle East; it was a secretive Jewish cabal that runs the world economy; it was the aliens whose super-advanced space ships are stored by the US government at Area 51 in New Mexico – spread via the social media platforms that came online in subsequent years.

But rather than viewing the 1990s as a distinct era in its own right – the arbitrary decade-slicing approach to history – perhaps it makes more sense to zoom out and take a longer view. From this wider perspective, the 1990s can be seen as a mere blip in the long history of modernity, in which everyday life is relentlessly and unceasingly uprooted by humankind's drive to invent new forms of science and technology, new modes of commerce, new ways of being in the world. The anthropologist Marc Augé would call the 1990s an example of 'super-modernity' – not a break with the grand narratives of the past, but an intensification of their characteristic features, an *acceleration* of their major trends to the point at which it becomes almost impossible to recognise the continuity between eras. But while social acceleration can be thrilling, it can also be fearful; it can lend meaning and shape to existence, or it can blur our perception of reality, distort our vision of the world as it races by. For the sociologist Hartmut Rosa, the last thirty years have been a period of 'frenetic standstill', in which the accelerated pace of change in the post-Cold War, multipolar, globalised, digitised world has produced a paradoxical sense of stasis, of movement without progress. We have experienced a great leap forward, but without a new vision of where we're going and what it's all for.

For those of us who lived through the 1990s – especially for those of us whose dubious status as members of Generation X or the X-ennials make the 1990s *our* decade – there is a strong temptation to look back with nostalgia. We yearn for the heady days of our youth, the lost silver age of rave, or grunge, or hip hop, or whatever it was that we felt defined our relationship to the present moment and gave us the sense of being on the cusp of something new. We are nostalgic for the old ways of keeping up with the times, for a time in which the sense of acceleration seemed thrilling rather than vertiginous. Ironically, we are nostalgic for a time that was itself riddled with nostalgia, steeped in retro culture and revivalist aesthetics, a time plagued by its own phantasms of lost golden ages and simpler times. We are nostalgic for a time that was already out of joint, just as all times are.

Nostalgia is a trap; but memory, nostalgia's older sibling, is the pre-condition for knowledge and the source, at least potentially, of wisdom. The exercise of historical memory faces new challenges in the twenty-first century. Drowning as we are in digital information, it is harder than ever for us to sift signal from noise. There are so many voices and channels and platforms and pundits and perspectives on offer, so many different ways of apprehending the unceasing sequence of events, that the exercise of historical memory seems almost impossible. It often feels as though we have too much zeitgeist. It's hard to tell what really matters, what will last, what is worth remembering. After all, the zeitgeist is precisely that, the *spirit* of the age, the ghost of the times; it is fleeting, insubstantial, only half real. But we should at least try to remember; we should at least try to achieve knowledge and wisdom. In the words of that great icon of 1990s popular culture, Keanu Reeves, who in the cyberpunk thriller *Johnny Mnemonic* played a man whose childhood memories have been surgically removed in order to smuggle stolen information in a silicon chip implanted in his brain, 'I want a full restoration. I want it all back.'

Notes

Chapter 2: Surfing at the End of History

21 'overlit bathroom mirror': David Forster Wallace, 'E Unibus Pluram: Television and U.S. Fiction', *Review of Contemporary Fiction*, 13.2 (1993), p.152.

23 'one of the best in European history': Timothy Garton Ash, '1989!', *New York Review of Books*, 5 November 2009 (www.nybooks.com/articles/2009/11/05/1989/).

31 'so beautiful, so absolutely beyond bureaucracy': quoted in Brett Martin, 'Extreme Oxford Sports', *Vanity Fair*, 5 August 2013 (www.vanityfair.com/style/2004/02/oxford-university-dangerous-sports-club).

31 'Because it's there': George Mallory, quoted in Wade Davis, *Into the Silence: The Great War, Mallory, and the Conquest of Everest* (Vintage, 2012), p.465.

36 'In the nineties … yes, we were ecstatic': Svetlana Alexievich, *Secondhand Time: The Last of the Soviets* (Random House, 2016), p.10.

Chapter 3: Desert Spectacular

40 'the spectre of Vietnam has been buried forever in the desert sands of the Arabian Peninsula': quoted in William Schneider, 'The Vietnam Syndrome Mutates,' *The Atlantic*, April 2006 (www.theatlantic.com/magazine/archive/2006/04/the-vietnam-syndrome-mutates/304891/).

43 'revolutionary in the history of warfare': Fred Frostic, 'Air Campaign Against the Iraqi Army in the Kuwaiti Theatre of Operations', RAND Corporation, 1994 (www.rand.org/content/dam/rand/pubs/monograph_reports/2006/MR357.pdf).

45 'Prince of the Global Village': *Time Magazine*, 6 January 1992 (http://content.time.com/time/subscriber/article/0,33009,974617,00.html).

45 'News is evil. It makes people feel bad': quoted in Patrick Parsons, *Blue Skies: A History of Cable Television* (Temple University Press, 2008), p.453.

46 'I learn more from CNN than I do from the CIA': quoted in Frank Stech, 'Winning CNN Wars', *Parameters: Journal of the U.S. Army War College*, Fall 1994 (24.3), p.38.

51 'The idea of a clean war, like that of a clean bomb': Jean Baudrillard, *The Gulf War Did Not Take Place*, translated and with an introduction by Paul Patton (Indiana University Press, 1995), p.43.

54 'We may come from a fragmented, MTV, rap-video culture, but they do not': *Rising Sun*, directed by Philip Kaufman, 20th Century Fox, 1993.

54 'it is [homosexuals'] deliberate, disgusting, revolting conduct that is responsible for the disease': quoted in 'Helms Puts the Brakes to a Bill Financing AIDS Treatment', *New York Times*, 5 July 1995, p.12.

Chapter 4: Middle of the Road

59 'Trickle-down economics has failed': Clinton's speech is widely available online and can be viewed at www.c-span.org/video/?27166-1/bill-clinton-1992-acceptance-speech

64 'there is no one more powerful than a member of a focus group': Richard Carr, *March of the Moderates* (I.B. Tauris, 2019), p.44.

66 'dance, prole, dance': Owen Hatherley, *Uncommon: An Essay on Pulp* (Zero, 2011), p.48.

66 'proletarian chic is all the rage': Tina Brown, *The Vanity Fair Diaries: Power, Wealth, Celebrity, and Dreams – My Years at the Magazine that Defined a Decade* (Henry Holt, 2017), p.376.

74 'product-improved fascism': Edward Luttwak, 'Why Fascism is the Wave of the Future', *London Review of Books*, 7 April 1994 (www.lrb.co.uk/the-paper/v16/n07/edward-luttwak/why-fascism-is-the-wave-of-the-future).

75 'We must not trade in our sovereignty': quoted in Jeff Greenfield, 'Trump is Pat Buchanan with Better Timing', *Politico Magazine*, September/October 2016 (www.politico.com/magazine/story/2016/09/donald-trump-pat-buchanan-republican-america-first-nativist-214221/).

75 'sounded better in the original German': Molly Ivins, *Nothin' But Good Times Ahead* (Knopf, 2010), p.136.

Chapter 5: Generation X, Y, Z

79 'common location within the social and historical process': Karl Mannheim, 'The Problem of Generations', in Paul Kecskmeti (ed.), *Karl Mannheim: Essays* (Routledge, 1952, republished 1972), p.291.

79 'the inescapable fate of living': quoted in Mannheim, 'The Problem of Generations', p.282.

81 'If I could have it thus': Douglas Coupland, *Generation X: Tales for an Accelerated Culture* (St. Martin's Press, 1991), p.130.

85 'Each new generation is a new people': Alexis de Tocqueville, *Democracy in America: Part the Second, the Social Influence of Democracy* (J & H.G. Langley, 1840), p.58.

87 'how you and your peers fit': Neill Howe and William Strauss, *Generations: The History of America's Future, 1584–2069* (Quill, 1992), p.8.

88 'rock 'n' roll is not just an important part of our culture': quoted in John Harris, *BritPop: Cool Britannia and the Spectacular Demise of English Rock* (Da Capo, 2004), p.191.

92 'The most exciting time for a band': Michael Azerrad, *Come as You Are: The Story of Nirvana* (Doubleday, 1993), p.187.

Chapter 6: You Take Me Higher and Higher

101 'the street finds its own uses for things': William Gibson, *Burning Chrome* (Harper Collins, 2014), p.180.

105 'There is no such thing as society': Interview for *Woman's Own Magazine*, 23 September 1987, www.margaretthatcher.org/document/106689.

107 'You could take any human being, of any sort': quoted in John Harris, 'If we must look to the past, let's make it 1989 – a year of transformation', *The Guardian*, 1 January 2019 (www.theguardian.com/commentisfree/2019/jan/01/1989-eastern-europe-britain-optimism).

107 'the distinct feeling that we were changing the world': Felix Denk and Sven von Thülen, *Der Klang Der Familie: Berlin, Techno and the Fall of the Wall* (Longform, 2014), p.138.

109 'getting up in the morning and having a cup of tea': *The Independent*, 30 January 1997 (www.independent.co.uk/news/drugs-are-cup-tea-says-noel-1285833.html).

113 'New age travellers? Not in this age. Not in any age': Leader's Speech, Tory Party Conference, Brighton, 1992 (http://britishpoliticalspeech.org/speech-archive.htm?speech=138).

Chapter 7: Moore's Law

119 'Integrated circuits will lead to such wonders as personal computers': Gordon E. Moore, 'Cramming more components onto integrated circuits' in *Electronics*, 38.8, 19 April 1965.

122 'anything potentially connected with anything': Tim Berners-Lee with Mark Fischetti, *Weaving the Web: The Original Design and Ultimate Destiny of the World Wide Web by its Inventor* (Harper Collins, 1999), pp.1–2.

125 'It was ground zero': Michael Woolf, *Burn Rate: How I Survived the Gold Rush Years on the Internet* (Touchstone, 1999), p.26.

127 'The truth is that no online database will replace your daily newspaper': Clifford Stoll, 'Why the Web Won't Be Nirvana', *Newsweek*, 26 February 1995 (www.newsweek.com/clifford-stoll-why-web-wont-be-nirvana-185306).

128 'Even in this very primitive form, the kids who were playing them were so physically involved': 'William Gibson, The Art of Fiction No. 211', *The Paris Review*, 197, Summer 2011 (www.theparisreview.org/interviews/6089/the-art-of-fiction-no-211-william-gibson).

130 'Governments of the Industrial World': John Perry Barlow, 'A Declaration of the Independence of Cyberspace' (www.eff.org/cyberspace-independence).

132 'Mondo 2000 is here to cover the leading edge in hyperculture': quoted in Vivian Sobchak, 'New Age Mutant Ninja Hackers: Reading Mondo 2000', in Mark Derry (ed.), *Flame Wars: The Discourse of Cyber-Culture* (Duke University Press, 1994), p.14.

132 'a hardboiled hacker with anarchist inclinations': 'R. U. A Cyberpunk?', *Mondo 2000*, 1993, p.30.

Chapter 8: Into the Void

151 'lateral thinking with withered technology': quoted in Richard Stanton, *A Brief History of Videogames* (Robinson, 2015), p.113.

154 'The spirit, the state of mind of a kid when he enters a cave alone': quoted in Stanton, *A Brief History of Videogames*, p.124.

155 'It's going to be like fucking *Doom*': quoted in David Kushner, *Masters of Doom: How Two Guys Created an Empire and Transformed Pop Culture* (Random House, 2003), p.262.

157 'there have always been, and there always will be': Senate Hearing 106-1144 'Marketing Violence to Children', 13 September 2000 (www.govinfo.gov/content/pkg/CHRG-106shrg85009/html/CHRG-106shrg85009.htm).

Chapter 9: Shock, Horror!

164 'what is pornography to one man is the laughter of genius to another': D.H. Lawrence, *Pornography and Obscenity* (Faber, 1929).

164 'I went through moral conflict': quoted in Robert Rosenblum, *The Jeff Koons Handbook* (Rizzoli, 1992), p.130.

164 'I'm interested in love, I'm interested in reunion': quoted in Kirsten Strom, 'Made in Heaven: Politics, Art and Pornography', *Iowa Journal of Cultural Studies*, 1998 (17), p.59.

166 'I will not even acknowledge that it is art': Allan Parachini, 'Serrano Answers Congressional Critics', *Los Angeles Times*, 2 August 1989 (www.latimes.com/archives/la-xpm-1989-08-02-ca-488-story.html).

166 'deplorable, despicable display of vulgarity': Elizabeth Kastor, 'Funding Art that Offends', *Washington Post*, 7 June 1989 (www.washingtonpost.com/archive/lifestyle/1989/06/07/funding-art-that-offends/a8b0755f-fab9-4f7f-a8ef-2ccad7048fe2/).

170 'part of the politically correct, left-wing ideology of New York City': Tyler Foggatt, 'Giuliani vs. The Virgin,' *The New Yorker*, 28 May 2018 (www.newyorker.com/magazine/2018/05/28/giuliani-vs-the-virgin).

173 'the sheer fact of women talking, being paradoxical': Chris Kraus, *I Love Dick* (Semiotexte, 2016), p.210.
177 'Where there is dirt there is system': Mary Douglas, *Purity and Danger: An Analysis of the Concepts of Pollution and Taboo* (Routledge, 2001), p.36.

Chapter 10: Lonely Planet

187 'the economic equivalent of a force of nature': 'Remarks at Vietnam National University, Hanoi, Nov 17 2000,' *Public Papers of the Presidents of the United States, William J. Clinton*, Book 3.
196 'because its proposal is to cease being an army': 'The Punch Card and the Hour Glass – Interview with Subcamandante Marcos by Gabriel Garcia Marquez and Roberto Pombo,' *New Left Review*, May/June 2001 (https://newleftreview.org/issues/ii9/articles/subcomandante-marcos-the-punch-card-and-the-hourglass).
197 'Marcos is gay in San Francisco, black in South Africa': quoted in Ziga Vodovnik (ed.), *Ya Basta! Ten Years of the Zapatista Uprising* (AK Press, 2004), p.16.

Chapter 11: Crash

205 'the stuff of which fairy tales are made': quoted in Andrew Morton, *Diana: Her True Story – In Her Own Words* (Simon and Schuster, 2017), p.199.
209 'dabbling their fingers': quoted in Morton, *Diana*, p.30.
216 'conjugal and maternal love': Hilary Mantel, 'The Princess Myth,' *The Guardian*, 26 August 2017 (www.theguardian.com/books/2017/aug/26/the-princess-myth-hilary-mantel-on-diana).
217 'One-party state' and 'floral fascism': Jonathan Freedland, 'A Moment of Madness,' *The Guardian*, 13 August 2007 (www.theguardian.com/uk/2007/aug/13/britishidentity.monarchy).

Chapter 12: Prizes for All

221 'some weird bunch of anti-rebels': David Forster Wallace, 'E Unibus Pluram: Television and U.S. Fiction,' *Review of Contemporary Fiction*, 13.2 (Summer 1993), p.192.
224 'never had it been harder to avoid aesthetic experience': Eric Hobsbawm, *Age of Extremes: The Short Twentieth Century*, 1914–1991 (Abacus Books, 1994), p.520.
225 'If I were a little less snobbish': Brian Eno, *A Year With Swollen Appendices* (Faber, 1996), p.67.
228 'It's like shagging wi a durex oan': Irvine Welsh, *Trainspotting* (Norton, 1996), p.42.

230 'The only thing I rely on is the truth': quoted in Will Ashon, *Chamber Music: Wu-Tang and America (in 36 Pieces)* (Faber, 2019), p.1.
231 'We are shown how to fashion masks': David Foster Wallace, *Infinite Jest* (Little, Brown, 1996), p.694.
232 'He's so modern': quoted in D.T. Max, *Every Love Story is a Ghost Story: A Life of David Foster Wallace* (Penguin, 2012), p.xi.
233 'InterLace TelEntertainment, 932/1664 R.I.S.C.': Wallace, *Infinite Jest*, p.620.
234 'privately theorizes that what passes for hip cynical transcendence': Wallace, *Infinite Jest*, p.694.
236 'mimic the information-flood and data-triage': Max, *Every Love Story is a Ghost Story*, p.195.
237 'couldn't feel my ass in the chair': Max, *Every Love Story is a Ghost Story*, p.49.

Chapter 13: Irrational Exuberance

245 'We're facing twenty-five years of prosperity': Peter Schwarz and Peter Leyden, 'The Long Boom: A History of the Future, 1980-2020', *Wired*, 1 July 1997 (www.wired.com/1997/07/longboom/).
245 'there has been a profound and fundamental alteration': 'Remarks by Chairman Alan Greenspan at the Haas Annual Business Faculty Research Dialogoue, University of California, Berkeley, 4 September 1998 (www.federalreserve.gov/boarddocs/speeches/1998/19980904.htm).
253 'No recession, no inflation, no voodoo': *Fortune Magazine*, 18 March 1996 (https://money.cnn.com/magazines/fortune/fortune_archive/1996/03/18/210627/index.htm).

Chapter 14: False Apocalypse

267 'I turn back to your ancient prophets': quoted in Frederic J. Baumgartner, *Longing for the End: A History of Millennialism in Western Civilization* (St. Martin's Press, 1999), p.239.
277 'Human ambition will be bound': Ian Wilmut, Keith Campbell and Colin Tudge, *The Second Creation: Dolly and the Age of Biological Control* (Farrar, Straus and Giroux, 2000), p.5.
279 'I could hear these louds screams from above': quoted in Haruki Murakami, *Underground: the Tokyo Gas Attack and the Japanese Psyche* (Vintage International, 2001), p.298.

Chapter 15: The Falling Man

286 'That picture just jumped off the screen': quoted in Tom Junod, 'The Falling Man,' *Esquire*, September 2003.

286 'It is obvious that the media war': quoted in Stephen Marche, 'Al Qaeda Won', *Foreign Policy*, 10 September 2018 (https://foreignpolicy.com/2018/09/10/al-qaeda-won/).
288 'the greatest work of art that is possible': quoted in Frank Lentricchia and Jodie McAuliffe, *Crimes of Art + Terror* (Chicago University Press, 2003), p.7.
288 'I used to think it was possible for an artist': Don DeLillo, *Mao II* (Penguin, 1992), p.41.
288 'In societies reduced to blur and glut': DeLillo, *Mao II*, p.157.
291 'Here we are then, I was thinking': interview with Christopher Hitchens by Jamie Glazov, http://hnn.us/articles/1881.html.
292 'in what we call the reality-based community': quoted in Ron Suskind, 'Faith, Certainty, and the Presidency of George W. Bush,' in *The New York Times Magazine*, 17 October 2004 (www.nytimes.com/2004/10/17/magazine/faith-certainty-and-the-presidency-of-george-w-bush.html).

Select Bibliography

Aburish, Said K. *Saddam Hussein: The Politics of Revenge* (Bloomsbury, 2000)

Alexievich, Svetlana. *Secondhand Time: The Last of the Soviets* (Random House, 2016)

Ashon, Will. *Chamber Music: Wu-Tang and America (in 36 Pieces)* (Faber, 2019)

Augé, Marc. *Non-Places: An Introduction to Super-Modernity* (Verso, 2nd ed., 2009)

Azerrad, Michael. *Come as You Are: The Story of Nirvana* (Doubleday, 1993)

Baudrillard, Jean. *The Gulf War Did Not Take Place*, trans. and with an introduction by Paul Patton (Indiana University Press, 1995)

----, *Simulacra and Simulation*, trans. Sheila Faria Glaser (University of Michigan Press; 14th ed., 1994)

Baumgartner, Frederic J. *Longing for the End: A History of Millennialism in Western Civilization* (St. Martin's Press, 1999)

Berners-Lee, Tim, with Mark Fischetti. *Weaving the Web: The Original Design and Ultimate Destiny of the World Wide Web by its Inventor* (HarperCollins, 1999)

Birkerts, Sven. *The Gutenberg Elegies: The Fate of Reading in an Electronic Age* (Faber, 1994)

Bracewell, Michael. *The Nineties: When Surface was Depth* (Flamingo, 2002)

Bronson, Po. *Nudist on the Late Shift* (Broadway Books, 1999)

Brooks, David. *Bobos in Paradise: The New Upper Class and How They Got There* (Simon and Schuster, 2000)

Brown, Tina. *The Vanity Fair Diaries: Power, Wealth, Celebrity, and Dreams – My Years at the Magazine that Defined a Decade* (Henry Holt, 2017)

Campbell, W. Joseph. *1995: The Year the Future Began* (University of California Press, 2015)

Carr, Richard. *March of the Moderates: Bill Clinton, Tony Blair, and the Rebirth of Progressive Politics* (I.B. Tauris, 2019)

Collin, Matthew. *Altered States: The Story of Ecstasy Culture and Acid House* (London: Serpent's Tail, 2009)

Coupland, Douglas. *Generation X: Tales for an Accelerated Culture* (St. Martin's Press, 1991)

Cusset, Francois. *Une Histoire (Critique) Des Annees 1990* (Centre Pompidou Metz, 2015)

Davis, Mike. *Planet of Slums* (Verso, 2017)
DeLillo, Don. *Mao II* (Penguin, 1992)
Denk, Felix, and Sven von Thülen. *Der Klang Der Familie: Berlin, Techno and the Fall of the Wall* (Longform, 2014)
Derry, Mark (ed.). *Flame Wars: The Discourse of Cyber-Culture* (Duke University Press, 1994)
Evans, Jules. *The Art of Losing Control: A Philosopher's Search for Ecstatic Experience* (Canongate, 2017)
Fukuyama, Francis. *The End of History and the Last Man* (Avon Books, 1992)
Galbraith, John Kenneth. *A Short History of Financial Euphoria* (Penguin, 1994)
Garcia, Tristan. *The Life Intense: A Modern Obsession*, trans. Abigail and Christopher Ray Alexander (Edinburgh University Press, 2018)
Garland, Alex. *The Beach* (Riverhead Books, 1997)
Garton Ash, Timothy. *History of the Present: Essays, Sketches, and Dispatches from Europe in the 1990s* (Vintage, 2001)
Giddens, Anthony. *The Third Way* (Polity, 1998)
Greenspan, Alan. *The Age of Turbulence: Adventures in a New World* (Penguin, 2007)
Harris, John. *BritPop: Cool Britannia and the Spectacular Demise of English Rock* (Da Capo, 2004)
Hatherley, Owen. *Uncommon: An Essay on Pulp* (Zero, 2011)
Hitchens, Christopher. *No One Left to Lie To: The Triangulations of William Jefferson Clinton* (Twelve, 2012)
Hobsbawm, Eric. *Age of Extremes: The Short Twentieth Century, 1914–1991* (Abacus Books, 1994)
Howe, Neill, and William Strauss. *Generations: The History of America's Future, 1584–2069* (Quill, 1992)
Huntington, Samuel P. *The Clash of Civilizations and the Remaking of the World Order* (Simon and Schuster, 2003)
Isaacson, Walter. *The Innovators: How a Group of Hackers, Geniuses and Geeks Created the Digital Revolution* (Simon and Schuster, 2014)
Jameson, Fredric. *Postmodernism, Or, The Cultural Logic of Late Capitalism* (Duke University Press, 1992)
Jenkins, Henry. *Convergence Culture: Where Old and New Media Collide* (New York University Press, 2008)
Kelly, Kevin. *Out of Control: The New Biology of Machines, Social Systems, and the Economic World* (Basic Books, 1995)
Kraus, Chris. *I Love Dick* (Semiotexte, 2016)
Kruse, Kevin M., and Julian E. Zelizer. *Fault Lines: A History of the United States Since 1974* (Norton, 2019)
Kushner, David. *Masters of Doom: How Two Guys Created an Empire and Transformed Pop Culture* (Random House, 2003)
LaHaye, Tim, and Jerry B. Jenkins. *Left Behind: A Novel of the Earth's Last Days* (Tyndale House Publishing, 1995)
Lawrence, D.H. *Pornography and Obscenity* (Faber, 1929)
Lentricchia, Frank, and Jodie McAuliffe. *Crimes of Art + Terror* (Chicago University Press, 2003)

Liu, Alan. *The Laws of Cool: Knowledge Work and the Culture of Information* (University of Chicago Press, 2004)
Lyotard, Jean-François. *The Postmodern Condition: A Report on Knowledge* (University of Minnesota Press, 1994)
Marcus, Sharon. *The Drama of Celebrity* (Princeton University Press, 2019)
Max, D.T. *Every Love Story is a Ghost Story: A Life of David Foster Wallace* (Penguin, 2012)
Morton, Andrew. *Diana: Her True Story – In Her Own Words* (Simon and Schuster, 2017)
Murakami, Haruki. *Underground: the Tokyo Gas Attack and the Japanese Psyche* (Vintage International, 2001)
Murray, Jerome and Marilyn. *Computers in Crisis: How to Avert the Coming Worldwide Computer Systems Collapse* (Petrocelli Books, 1984)
Nagle, Angela. *Kill All Normies: Online Culture Wars from 4Chan and Tumblr to Trump and the Alt-Right* (Zero, 2017)
Negroponte, Nicholas. *Being Digital* (Vintage, 1996)
O'Neill, William L. *A Bubble in Time: America During the Interwar years, 1989–2001* (Ivan R. Dee, 2009)
Parsons, Patrick. *Blue Skies: A History of Cable Television* (Temple University Press, 2008)
Pimlott, Ben. *The Queen: Elizabeth II and the Monarchy* (2012)
Pleshakov, Constantine. *There is No Bread without Freedom! 1989 and the Civil War that Brought Down Communism* (Farrar, Strauss and Giroux, 2009)
Reynolds, Simon. *Energy Flash: A Journey Through Rave Music and Dance Culture* (Softskull, 2012)
Rosa, Hartmut. *Social Acceleration: A New Theory of Modernity* (Columbia University Press, 2013)
Rosenblum, Robert. *The Jeff Koons Handbook* (Rizzoli, 1992)
Sassen, Saskia. *The Global City: New York, London, Tokyo* (Princeton University Press, 1991)
Stallabrass, Julian. *High Art Lite: The Rise and Fall of Young British Art* (Verso, 2nd ed., 2006)
Stanton, Richard. *A Brief History of Videogames* (Robinson, 2015)
Stiglitz, Joseph. *The Roaring Nineties: A New History of the World's Most Prosperous Decade* (Norton, 2003)
Swofford, Anthony. *Jarhead* (Scribner, 2003)
Troy, Gil. *The Age of Clinton: America in the 1990s* (Thomas Dunne, 2015)
Turner, Alwyn W. *A Classless Society: Britain in the 1990s* (Aurum Press, 2013)
Turner, Fred. *From Counterculture to Cyberculture: Stewart Brand, the Whole Earth Network, and the Rise of Digital Utopianism* (University of Chicago Press, 2006)
Venturi, Robert, Denise Scott Brown and Steven Izenour. *Learning from Las Vegas* (MIT Press, 1972)
Vodovnik, Ziga. *Ya Basta! Ten Years of the Zapatista Uprising* (AK Press, 2004)
Wallace, David Foster. 'E Unibus Pluram: Television and U.S. Fiction', *Review of Contemporary Fiction*, 13.2 (Summer 1993)
----, *Infinite Jest* (Little, Brown, 1996)

Welsh, Irvine. *Trainspotting* (Norton, 1996)
Wiener, Norbert. *Cybernetics: Control and Communication in the Animal and the Machine* (MIT Press, 2nd ed., 1965)
Wilmut, Ian, Keith Campbell and Colin Tudge. *The Second Creation: Dolly and the Age of Biological Control* (Farrar, Straus and Giroux, 2000)
Woolf, Michael. *Burn Rate: How I Survived the Gold Rush Years on the Internet* (Touchstone, 1999)
Wright, Lawrence. *The Looming Tower: Al Qaeda and the Road to 9/11* (Knopf, 2006)
Zuboff, Shoshana. *The Age of Surveillance Capitalism: The Fight for a Human Future at the New Frontier of Power* (Public Affairs, 2019)

Select Filmography

21 Grams, dir. Alejandro González Iñárritu, Focus Features, 2003
2046, dir. Wong Kar-Wai, Mai Ah Entertainment/Océan Film, 2004
A Better Tomorrow, dir. John Woo, Cinema City Company, 1986
Amores perros, dir. Alejandro González Iñárritu, Nu Vision, 2000
American History X, dir. Tony Kaye, New Line Cinema, 1998
Basic Instinct, dir. Paul Verhoeven, TriStar Pictures, 1992
Bend It Like Beckham, dir. Gurinder Chadha, Redbus Film Distribution, 2002
Billy Elliot, dir. Stephen Daldry, Universal Pictures, 2000
Brassed Off, dir. Mark Herman, FilmFour Distribution, 1996
Broken Arrow, dir. John Woo, 20th Century Fox, 1996
Chungking Express, dir. Wong Kar-Wai, Ocean Shores Video, 1994
City of God, dir. Fernando Meirelles and Kátia Lund, Miramax Films, 2002
Crash, dir. David Cronenberg, Alliance Communications, 1996
Crash, dir. Paul Haggis, Lions Gate Films, 2004
Crouching Tiger, Hidden Dragon, dir. Ang Lee, Sony Pictures, 2000
East is East, dir. Damien O'Donnell, Channel Four Films, 1999
eXistenZ, dir. David Cronenberg, Alliance Atlantis, 1999
Eyes Wide Shut, dir. Stanley Kubrick, Warner Bros, 1999
Face/Off, dir. John Woo, Paramount Pictures, 1997
Falling Down, dir. Joel Schumacher, Warner Bros, 1993
Fight Club, dir. David Fincher, 20th Century Fox, 1999
Hackers, dir. Iain Softley, distributed by MGM, 1995
Happy Together, dir. Wong Kar-Wai, Golden Harvest Company, 1997
Heat, dir. Michael Mann, Warner Bros, 1995
In the Mood for Love, dir. Wong Kar-Wai, Block 2 Pictures/Océan Films, 2000
Irma Vep, dir. Olivier Assayas, Dacia Films, 1996
Johnny Mnemonic, dir. Robert Longo, distributed by TriStar Pictures/Alliance Atlantis/MDP Worldwide, 1995
Lost in Translation, dir. Sofia Coppola, Focus Features, 2003
Mississippi Masala, dir. Mira Nair, Cinecom Pictures/Samuel Goldwyn Co, 1991
My Beautiful Laundrette, dir. Stephen Frears, Mainline Pictures, 1985
Natural Born Killers, dir. Oliver Stone, Warner Bros, 1994
Point Break, dir. Katherine Bigelow, 20th Century Fox, 1991

Pulp Fiction, dir. Quentin Tarantino, Miramax Films, 1994
Reality Bites, dir. Ben Stiller, Universal Pictures, 1994
Requiem for a Dream, dir. Darren Aronofsky, Artisan Entertainment, 2000
Reservoir Dogs, dir. Quentin Tarantino, Miramax Films, 1992
Rising Sun, dir. Philip Kaufman, 20th Century Fox, 1993
Showgirls, dir. Paul Verhoeven, MGM Distribution, 1995
Slacker, dir. Richard Linklater, Orion Classics, 1990
Strange Days, dir. Kathryn Bigelow, 20th Century Fox, 1995
The Big Lebowski, dir. Joel and Ethan Coen, Gramercy Pictures/PolyGram Filmed Entertainment, 1998
The Full Monty, dir. Peter Cattaneo, Fox Searchlight Pictures, 1997
The Lawnmower Man, dir. Brett Leonard, New Line Cinema, 1992
The Matrix, dir. the Wachowskis, Warner Bros, 1999
The Net, dir. Irwin Winkler, Sony Pictures, 1995
The Rock, dir. Michael Bay, Buena Vista Pictures, 1996
The Silence of the Lambs, dir. Jonathan Demme, Orion Pictures, 1991
The Truman Show, dir. Peter Weir, Paramount Pictures, 1998
Three Kings, dir. David O. Russell, Warner Bros, 1999
Traffic, dir. Steven Soderbergh, USA Films, 2000
Trainspotting, dir. Danny Boyle, PolyGram/Miramax Films, 1996
True Romance, dir. Tony Scott, Warner Bros, 1993
You've Got Mail, dir. Nora Ephron, Warner Bros, 1998

List of Illustrations

Index

Note: *italicised* page references indicate illustrations